THE MAGIC KINGDOM

My Experience in Riyadh

Nicola M Stewart

*To Alan, Calum and Andrew with fond memories of our time
in the land of sand.*

CONTENTS

INTRODUCTION

If you don't take opportunities when they arise, you'll always be left wondering 'what if?' I joined my husband to live as an expat in Riyadh, Saudi Arabia between August 2005 and June 2007. During that time I kept a journal which has formed the basis for this book.

Since my return to Scotland friends, acquaintances and family members asked me what it was really like. I found it impossible to sum up life in Riyadh, which was a world away from life at home in so many ways, and on so many levels. Life there was full of contradictions, the bizarre and the unexpected, causing me to ponder over many things I had never even thought about or taken for granted as a Western woman.

This book is an attempt to provide an insight into my time and experiences whilst in the Magic Kingdom (the expatriate name for the Kingdom of Saudi Arabia), but it only scratches the surface of expat life in Saudi as seen through my eyes. I lived in Riyadh for just under two years and do not profess to be an expert in the culture and traditions of the Kingdom. I have tried to portray things as accurately as possible, apart from changing some names for privacy, however, if there are any discrepancies along the way they are not intentional.

CHAPTER 1

No Going Back (August 2005)

What on earth had I done? There was no going back now!

As the plane took off, I was trying to calm down my youngest son of nearly two, who was having a major tantrum while my insides were churning faster than they had ever done before. Goodbye to Glasgow Airport, to friends, to family and hello to new experiences and a new life in Riyadh, Saudi Arabia. The piercing noise was escalating, and I had tried every distraction I could think of to stop my son's screaming. Perhaps he could sense the turmoil that was going on inside me. I was aware that the passengers in our section of the plane were becoming uncomfortable, concerned at the prospect of sharing a long Emirates flight with us to Dubai.

With my eldest son Calum on one side of me constantly asking questions, excited about being on a plane for the first time at five and a half, and Andrew's screams directly penetrating my other eardrum, it took all my willpower to contain my mixed emotions on my first business class flight, courtesy of the company my husband was working for. Eventually the bursar took pity on the other passengers before they started to complain, cradled Andrew in her arms and took him through to the economy section where she carried him up and down the aisles in an attempt to pacify him. Having shown Calum how to operate the in-flight entertainment system on the screen in front of him, he at least was happily settled watching cartoons. I was exhausted, both physically and mentally, as

I had only slept for a couple of hours the night before in the midst of frantic packing and the chaos of getting everything in order prior to leaving.

Basking in the luxury of some rare time to myself, the realisation that we would not be home in Scotland again until Christmas for a short holiday struck me hard. Christmas was nearly five months away.

I had been given briefing paperwork from my husband's company in terms of personal effects to avoid bringing out with us, due to the sensitivities of Saudi Arabia's customs and immigration rules. The list was an education in itself. Whilst some of the items would not be allowed through any airport or customs control worldwide, others were an eye-opener. Specific items highlighted as unacceptable included all foodstuffs, Christmas trees and decorations (as Christmas is not officially celebrated in Saudi, being a strictly Islamic country), dried flower arrangements (in case they contained poppy seeds), communications equipment and high frequency radios (presumably to stop you receiving or broadcasting information), statues or ornaments (as these are seen as idolatry), binoculars and telescopic equipment (surveillance is not permitted), stuffed animals, any kind of medicine (many of the contents of our everyday medicines are not allowed), military uniforms, weapons or firearms, alcoholic beverages (including kits or books relating to the manufacture of alcohol as alcohol is banned), any religious items (unless Islamic), and finally pornographic literature or any materials which contain sexual references (This included magazines or newspapers showing women wearing underwear or swimsuits, exposed arms or legs, or clothing which was too revealing or tightly fitting by Saudi standards).

I was advised explicitly that if any of these items were found in my hand luggage or baggage it would severely delay customs clearance, subject the goods to confiscation, and I would be subject to severe fines or penalties. In addition, records, video tapes, exposed film, CDs, DVDs and all kinds of printed material including books and magazines were also subject to censorship by customs officials if they were considered to be offensive or contrary to Islamic teachings.

My husband Alan had advised me not to bring out any CDs, as when he had first brought out some of his music collection he had to sit and wait for hours while they were all scanned through a machine. The very thought of sitting and waiting for any length of time at the end of a long plane journey was not worth contemplating with my two young children present, so my CDs had remained in Scotland. I had also been forewarned that passengers arriving in Saudi Arabia could be refused entry if their dress or behaviour was considered inappropriate by Saudi standards, or if they appeared to be intoxicated in any way.

Sitting on the plane making the most of the peace and quiet, I had the chance to reflect on the enormity of what I was doing.

Alan had started working in Saudi Arabia in December 2002, over two and a half years previously. The opportunity had come up through a colleague he used to work with, and after much discussion following his redundancy, he felt it would be a good career move. Whatever the circumstances, redundancy is taken personally and it had taken Alan off guard. When an interesting new opportunity came up to more than double his previous salary and for the wage to be tax free when there was nothing else on the horizon, it had made sense for him to take the job.

At that time I was aware there had been some car bombings in Saudi because of the news coverage over William Sampson and Sandy Mitchells' confessions. Also in 2002, a Brit, Simon Veness and a German; Max Graf had been killed in separate car bombs in Riyadh, but there was no information available as to who had been responsible.

Alan came home for ten days for Christmas and New Year, before leaving for Riyadh on 2 January 2003. He planned to come home every two or three months for a couple of weeks at the most. On the rare occasions when he was in the UK on business, he arranged his meetings at the beginning or end of the UK working week allowing him to fly up to see us for the occasional night or weekend. He came home for the birth of our second son in September, but only had a couple of weeks with us after his birth, which was hard and trying. Once he was away I was fully occupied with the two children and frequently got cross when I received texts from him informing me that he was lying in the sun when I hadn't had enough sleep or a minute to myself.

I had found it hard juggling being at home on my own and working full time with a young family, so our circumstances enabled me to take a career break and join him in 2005 to spend quality family time together. Life had been somewhat restrictive at home in Scotland coping with two young children myself, and although Saudi was a strict country by Western standards, I was convinced I would not find life quite so confined in some ways, living in Riyadh as a family. It had to be an improvement on living more than three thousand miles apart.

Going through a pregnancy and working whilst Alan had been living abroad had been hard and trying, as had being solely responsible for our two children. My husband always found it hard when he saw how the boys had grown since he had seen them last, and it was hard for him to gauge how they had developed educationally and behaviourally when he hadn't been there.

Although we had spoken frequently, it was impossible to keep Alan informed of absolutely everything within short phone calls. He didn't just miss birthdays, anniversaries and special dates together, but important milestones of development in the children's lives and general day-to-day life. He would sometimes give me a hard time over little things I hadn't related to him while he was away, which would become apparent when he was back home with us. Our eldest son would deliberately attempt to play one of us off against the other, as he was only too aware that if he approached his Dad for something I would not allow, there was a chance Alan would agree to his request as he liked spoiling them when he came home. As anyone with children knows only too well, boundaries and rules are always changing, so it was no wonder Alan didn't have a clue as the boys attempted to exploit the situations that arose whenever they could. Alan would get annoyed when the boys would ask my permission to do things and not him, as it was me who was constantly there. After he had more or less caught up with what was and wasn't permitted and when, it was time for him to leave, and by the time he was home next things had moved on.

A long distance relationship is difficult, particularly when every telephone conversation is interrupted by young children's noise, demands, or mischief. Our youngest son had a habit of always wanting my attention whenever I was on the phone or making such a noise it was difficult to have a proper conversation. Both boys would talk to my husband, which would usually centre round a quick good night, as they had little interest in talking into the handset. Time differences of two or three hours between us at different times of the year, together with an unbelievably early rise for Alan to get to work, made it tricky at times to actually find a time to suit both of us that coincided. Whenever there was something important to discuss, it was impossible to get through or the line was so bad you couldn't hear what the other person was saying, or one or other of the boys were playing up, so any important dialogue ended up being through e-mails. I was looking forward to living together and spending quality time together properly as a family, in the same place and in the same time zone.

Al Qaeda terrorism seemed to have originated at the end of the Cold War and the situation in post-Soviet Afghanistan. Around this time Saudi froze the assets of Osama bin Laden and rescinded his citizenship in 1994. After the bombing of the USS Cole in Yemen in 2000 and after the attacks of September 2001, Saudi increased its efforts to find those responsible for supporting terrorism and extremism.

Terrorist insurgency targeted expats in Saudi Arabia from November

2000 with car bombing attacks. The Authorities blamed the first incidents on a group of Western expats, who they accused of being involved in a turf war over illegal alcohol distribution. Confessions were obtained and the men sentenced to death. A few months after Alan went out to Riyadh, a Britain was shot at lights in the Granada district in February 2003. In the same month, there was an explosion in the Al Jazira district of Riyadh. A Saudi had blown himself up when manufacturing a bomb at a private villa. Explosives, weapons and false documents were found. Travel warnings were issued and it was only then reported that Westerners were potential terrorist targets. In May 2003, the US State Department made it public knowledge that terrorists were in the final stages of planning attacks in Saudi Arabia and issued warnings. The Saudi government did the same, publicising an alert for nineteen men who they believed were involved who had escaped from a shootout in the Al Jazira district. Following this, a large stock-pile of arms and explosives were discovered nearby in another villa.

British Airways flights were cancelled as there had been intelligence to suggest an attack was being planned at Riyadh's main airport. In January '05 BA axed services to Saudi Arabia, as the war in the Middle East had deterred business and leisure travel to the region. By the end of March BA stopped all flights to and from the Kingdom, stating the routes were no longer commercially profitable due to a decline in passengers. Whilst it cannot be argued that there was a decrease in passenger numbers, this was as a direct result of terrorism, even if that was not the official line at the time. Another airline saw its opportunity and eventually BMI flew the same routes that BA had done previously, no doubt doing rather well out of it in the process.

It is believed that Al Qaeda was provoked by Saudi's stance on terrorism and what was going on in Iraq, as many Muslims were upset that US forces had remained in Saudi after the Gulf War in 1991 when Saddam Hussein invaded Kuwait. Al Qaeda commenced its attacks in the Kingdom, targeting Westerners with car bombs and kidnappings before things escalated to compound bombings.

In August 2003, the two Western expats who had been given a death sentence were released in a deal to release detainees from Guantanamo Bay. They claimed their innocence, citing that their confessions had been obtained under torture. They took the matter to the High Court in the UK, but the court supported Saudi's defence under the State Immunity Act 1978, as they claimed that the attacks had been carried out on the instructions of MI6, the British Secret Intelligence Service.

Although Saudi had made a great deal of progress in terms of capturing terrorists, Al Qaeda's campaign continued, and a compound housing Saudis was hit, a building that used to house police was bombed and a number of Westerners were shot and killed in 2004. It was believed that many Saudi militants fled to Afghanistan or Iraq to take up the cause there after the compound bombings in May 2003 and some had been responsible for the 2004 attacks on their return. A severe clampdown anti-terrorist operation was underway resulting in huge successes in killing and capturing many insurgents and terrorist cells.

Despite the relatively recent events in Saudi, Alan had persuaded me that life in Riyadh no longer posed an extremely high risk terrorism threat and although there was still a perceived threat, we should consider coming out to live with him in Riyadh. Whilst I was yet to be convinced, he provided me with sufficient information which addressed my immediate concerns, so I eventually agreed to go out for a holiday at the last minute in March 2005.

The boys and I flew out and joined Alan for our Easter holidays, to enable us to make an informed choice as to whether we thought we could live in Saudi. We spent a week in Riyadh based in a rented villa on a compound where we could choose to live if we decided to go out, and as well as having some time to relax by the pool, we visited the school and the nursery where the boys could enrol. Alan drove us out and about in the city several times during the week so we could get a feel for the place. I had the opportunity to meet as many Western families as I could, and to glean as much information as possible first-hand. I was lucky to spend time in Riyadh on holiday, as most people make that decision without ever having set foot in the country first. It gave me the chance to briefly visit and see what life on a Western compound would be like, but with hindsight, experiencing life in Riyadh for a week could not possibly have prepared me for the realities of living there as an expat. My husband then flew with us to Dubai, where we had an amazing few days on holiday before we went our separate ways, Alan back to Saudi to work, and the boys and I back to our lives in Scotland.

The decision to take my children and join my husband in Saudi Arabia was not taken lightly and was taken jointly. We had spent a long time deliberating over the pros and cons. Despite this, for the whole flight from Glasgow to Dubai my brain kept conjuring up terrible images of some of the news stories that had bombarded our living room over the last few years - the dreadful events of 11 September 2001 and how the majority of the pilots were Saudis or Saudi-born; February 2003 when Robert Dent was shot at traffic lights in Riyadh; May 2003 when three expat compounds in Riyadh were attacked killing more than thirty and injuring hundreds (thankfully when this happened my husband was home on leave with us in the UK); May 2004 when six foreign nationals and one Saudi were killed at Yanbu and there were also four attacks in Al Khobar targeting oil companies and compounds in which twenty-two were killed and twenty-five injured; June '04, the kidnapping and subsequent beheading of Paul Johnson, a BBC cameraman, Simon Cumbers shot dead and a reporter Frank Gardner injured; September '04, Tony Christopher shot dead; January 2005, British Airways axed flights to and from Saudi Arabia due to intelligence warnings of perceived threats from groups linked to Al Qaeda and later suspended all flights a couple of months later; July 2005, terrorism attacks in the UK - in London - four simultaneous explosions, three in tube trains and one in a bus killing fifty-two and injuring seven hundred.

To top it all, the popular monarch, King Fahd, had just passed away a couple of weeks before. He had been ill for some time after suffering a series of strokes, and his half-brother Crown Prince Abdullah had effectively been running the country for several years during his illness. However, given the history of the rulers of Saudi Arabia, there was the story of the possibility of an internal uprising for the throne now circulating in the media.

I had been on the Foreign Office website frequently over the last month checking travel advice to Saudi Arabia which had only just changed from essential travel only. I never have managed to establish a definitive explanation of exactly what that term meant.

What on earth was I doing uprooting the children and taking them to live in Saudi Arabia in the midst of such uncertain risky times?

At the start of the flight the pilot had described the route we would be taking, and at specific times throughout the flight, had provided us with snippets of information relative to our location. He let us know when we were flying over the Alps, which were spectacular, especially when the mountain peaks permeated through white, candy floss textured, fluffy clouds. Checking our progress on the flight path from the flight information channel, it was interesting to note that our plane took us directly over Iraq and Iran, although the pilot omitted to mention this to his passengers. The flight itself took around seven hours and thankfully there had not been too much turbulence. It was great to be able to watch events as they unfolded through the plane's cameras, switching them manually between downward facing to front facing, staring down on the moving traffic and flat rooftops of Dubai as we drew closer. We watched the lit-up arrows and lights directing the plane to our designated runway in the dark, as we finally touched down safely at Dubai Airport.

As the plane taxied along the tarmac for what seemed like ages, several of the Arabs, clad in their white *thobes* (a traditional ankle length robe with long sleeves which is the traditional dress for male Arabs) and headgear got out of their seats and opened the overhead lockers next to them before the illuminated fastened seatbelt signs had even been switched off, or the plane had come to a halt. Despite the vocal attempts of the cabin crew to stop them from doing so, they paid little attention and carried on retrieving their hand baggage. Once we had successfully made our way out of our seats and joined the line of crammed passengers and their baggage, we then had to keep our wits about us and our eyes open. Bags and cases, holdalls, laptops, and parcels were swung down from above with apparent careless abandon. Ensuring nothing was going to land on the boys' heads (or mine for that matter) took every ounce of my concentration whilst we stood in the aisle. I made a mental note, then and there, that on future flights in this part of the world, when travelling with the children I would remain seated for as long as I possibly could, unless we were in a hurry. Eventually the exit doors were opened, the queue dissipated and we swapped the comfort of an air conditioned plane for instant humidity as soon as or feet touched the external steps which led us to the waiting crowded airport shuttle bus.

Stepping up onto the bus as it pulled away, we listened carefully to the repeated announcements, as there was more than one drop-off point. I found it exceedingly clammy and unbearably hot, even though it was late at night, standing on the packed bus full of sweaty passengers, holding on to the nearest available grab-rail above my head. Andrew was tired and sleepy and felt hotter than a hot water-bottle. He was settled in my arms, clinging tightly to me with his arms round my neck and I couldn't budge him. He seemed to be becoming stickier and heavier the longer I held him, and was so close his body melted into a natural extension of mine.

My rucksack was on the floor wedged firmly between my trainer-clad feet which were getting hotter by the minute. The bus stopped and started, rocking its passengers in all directions unpredictably, as it weaved its way jerkily along the tarmac past rows and rows of aeroplanes. Calum took in the differing graphics on the planes' tails, identifying aeroplanes from different countries, airline companies, logos and colours. Getting off the bus, we had to hurry to find our way to the departure gate for our connecting flight as time was against us, but we managed it with enough time for a short sit-down and quick visit to the toilets before being herded into the departure lounge (where there were no facilities).

By the time we were seated on the Saudia plane ready for take-off to Riyadh, I had only just managed to gather my jumbled emotions together and put them into some kind of perspective. After all, if things didn't work out, then we could always come home, couldn't we?

Sitting on the plane listening to numerous announcements advising us that we were waiting for several Arabs who had still to board the plane, it became obvious from the behaviour of the passengers and cabin crew that this was nothing unusual. However, when we were advised that we would be further delayed as an item of baggage had been checked onto the plane without its owner, I found that information alarming. There were no complaints on the flight about the additional delay whilst the baggage in question was located and removed from the plane. Clearly everyone's safety was paramount, and given the times we were living in, it was reassuring to know that precautions and procedures were being followed, in spite of the disruption and inconvenience that arose as a result. It did make me question why baggage had been automatically checked through onto connecting flights, when this posed a security risk in the event that a passenger failed to board a connecting flight. Although this saved time, I couldn't help questioning our safety on the plane while unaccompanied baggage was somewhere in the hold, directly under our seats.

As the plane finally moved slowly along the runway at Dubai, on the final leg of our plane journey, the announcements were made in Arabic as well as English. I felt ready for a new life and new experiences. Looking around at the occupants of the plane, noticing many of them clutching prayer beads anxiously, I felt strangely comforted by the unfamiliar Arabic prayers that were said over the in-flight Tannoy system before take-off, and again after landing safely in Riyadh, an hour or so later.

Putting on my *abaya*, a black, shapeless, long cloak that all women are required to wear over their clothes in public in Riyadh, and wrapping my headscarf round my neck (just in case I needed to cover my hair), I woke up the boys (both of whom had finally fallen asleep half an hour before landing). We gathered together our belongings before disembarking the plane into what can only be described as an oven - when the hot, dry air hit us.

CHAPTER 2

First Impressions

   Hot, sweaty and jetlagged (having had no sleep on the journey), I felt too tired to take much in after we finally made our way through the passport immigration queues at King Khalid International Airport. We had been ushered to a family queue, but even so, the queue we joined still involved a long wait. By the time we got through, our baggage was circling round the carousel waiting for us to pick it up. Choosing one of the uniform clad porters who had started to follow us, our porter found a trolley, collected our baggage and put it through the X-ray machine for a few Saudi riyals. I will never forget walking through the bustling concourse, which was crammed full of foreign colourful male faces, filled with mostly Arab men in traditional white *thobes* to their ankles wearing plain white or chequered white and red Arabian headgear, and Asian men in T-shirts and jeans waiting for friends, relatives, business colleagues or hotel guests to arrive. The only women appeared to be those who had been on the plane with us, and were all accompanied or met by their husbands at the airport. I was aware of many eyes fixated on me which made me feel particularly self-conscious as I made my way past the throngs of waiting men in the concourse on the other side of the barrier, doing my best to avoid tripping over the trailing hem of my *abaya*. I distinctly remember a no smoking sign, directly above an enormous sculptural geometric feature ashtray. I looked away, my brain not quite able to register what I had just seen. I glanced back again, only to confirm my mind was still intact and I was not imagining things after lack of sleep and a long journey. There were now three Arabs puffing away on the stubs of their cigarettes under the no smoking sign. They took turns to extinguish their cigarettes in the biggest, most elaborate ashtray I had ever seen as they moved on their way.

Once outside, we bundled ourselves into one of the waiting white taxis and were driven along what is known as airport road, which had palm trees on either-side, and plants along the central reservation. We passed through a huge archway with geometric Arabic patterns, built to commemorate the centenary of Saudi Arabia. We glimpsed the Islamic University through an immensely decorated geometric Islamic archway at the side of the road, where I was to learn later the Muttawa (religious police) undertake their studies and training. After this point, the traffic was incredibly busy and how we eventually reached our compound without being involved in an accident I have no idea.

Once the boys were settled, I was glad to clamber into bed in the villa that was to be our home away from home in the land of oil, sand, camels and magic carpets. As I drifted off to sleep, with only one light freshly laundered cotton sheet over me, I could just make out the local imam singing the call to prayer from the nearest mosque above the drone of the air conditioning.

The next three weeks were extremely trying. I had decided to come out in August to allow ourselves time to get the villa organised and the boys settled before they started school and nursery. Alan had done remarkably well getting the lease in place for the villa, and then equipping it sufficiently for us to stay in. Within a week, he had bought bed-linen, towels, plates, glasses, mugs and had stocked the fridge from the shop on the compound (which stocked limited food supplies) with bread and milk, jam and cereal ready for us. As women are not permitted to drive and are generally accompanied when they go out in Saudi, I was unable to pop out to get what I needed during the day when the supermarkets were open, while Alan was at work. From what I had seen of the driving at that stage, I would not have considered risking taking the children in a taxi anywhere. In any case, until we all had our photos taken for our *iquama* (an identity document/residence permit which I was required to carry with me at all times) and our company identity card, I had to make do with trips outside the compound with my husband late in the evenings with the boys in tow, to fit round prayer-times when everything shut down and when Alan wasn't too tired after a day's work.

The temperature was unbearable, rising to the early fifties by the middle of the day and it was too hot for the boys to be outside, apart from very early in the morning. I would get them up and take them to the shaded play park and the pool with water bottles, sun block and sunhats before the sun became too strong. I have vivid memories of trying to get the villa sorted, making endless lists of things needing done or to be purchased, and doing my best to occupy them indoors with only a few books, coloured pencils and paper to hand. It was an extremely frustrating time… I was unable to do things for myself, and most things I made an attempt at starting, I found I didn't have what I needed to complete the simplest of tasks. Cleaning, ironing and cooking all needed household items to be purchased, and it surprised me to realise how many things are necessary when putting a home together from scratch.

It was impossible to get the boys into a routine, as they were up late in the evening and wouldn't sleep during the hottest part of the day, not being accustomed to siestas. We were all jetlagged and incredibly tired, and took what seemed like weeks to adapt to the extreme dry heat and the time difference. We had no internet provision initially, which I found I missed more than I thought I would. There were no other families with young children on the compound, as they were all wisely on holidays to cooler climates at the hottest time of year, before school and nursery started back.

Hanging the washing to dry in the back yard, I soon learned to bring it back in within half an hour or it would be too dry to iron if left outside for any longer. We had a water container in the kitchen dispensing chilled water from a large water container, as the water from the taps wasn't suitable for drinking. Very often the tap water would be sandy or brown and gritty when one of the water pipes on the compound burst. It was amazing how quickly we would go through a large water container and it was important that we always had plenty of water available - I made sure that at least one spare water container was on standby at all times. It was far too hot and we were all far too thirsty to run out of drinking water, which I quickly became aware was a major priority. Even going for a walk round the compound, I always ensured I had a chilled bottle of water with me, as I would need it in the heat. Being used to turning a tap, it gave me an instant appreciation of tap-water and an awareness of how much water was required for drinking and cooking on a daily basis.

Ridiculous things like preparing meals became an effort at times, as I would start making something, only to realise too late that I didn't have the ovenware, ingredients or utensils required. The cooker was a cooker unlike any other I had ever used. Not only did it frequently refuse to work, but the grill was in an incredibly useless location; under the oven only a couple of inches above floor level. There was no way I was going to lie on the floor to cook, or bend down to retrieve a laden hot grill pan at floor level, so subsequently all meals required to be baked, boiled, fried or poached at a more convenient cooking height. Given that a large percentage of my cooking had been grilled until then, this presented me with a challenge, and I needed to adapt and extend my cooking repertoire rapidly around the ingredients I could get hold of, the limited cooking utensils Alan had initially bought me, and the villa cooker's cooking capabilities. This was no easy task.

Weekends in Saudi were Thursdays and Fridays, which was confusing as it threw me completely with the days of the week. We decided to go and get a traditional takeaway breakfast the first Thursday after we arrived, and Alan drove us and parked outside our local bread and foul shop in one of the streets not far away from our compound. Alan and the boys went into the shop to watch the circular flat un-leavened bread being made over the oven, and I had to stay in our 4x4 as I would not have been allowed to venture into the shop which was full of men, as society is segregated. The windows to the rear passenger seats of the car had been fitted with tinted solar film for privacy and to keep the car cool, but I remained seated in the front. Although I had my sunglasses on and was cloaked in my *abaya*, within minutes a group of men congregated in front of the car staring at me. It was extremely unnerving because they just stared blankly into my face, without stopping. It took me a minute to comprehend that showing my face in the local neighbourhood was perhaps not such a good idea and I was becoming increasingly uncomfortable to find myself the focus of unwanted attention.

Thankfully I had brought my scarf out with me. I unravelled it from around my neck, and hastily bundled it round my hair, leaving my face exposed but my sunglasses still firmly on. I am sure the men watching my every move had never seen a headscarf thrown over a woman's head in such a haphazard way before, but it stopped their stares and they soon dispersed. I stayed underneath the scarf until I saw Alan and the boys exiting the shop. By the time they opened the car doors my scarf was back round my neck. While Alan drove us back to the compound, I sat in the front passenger seat wondering what I would have said to the boys to explain my strange head attire if they had made it back to the car before I had taken it off. The bread and foul was worth the excursion as it was so tasty, but that was the first and last time I sat in the car on my own in the local streets in the area round our compound. Both boys delighted in filling me in on their bread and foul excursion on the way home. They described how the men made the bread with their hands and how it was cooked over an open oven, which was a new experience for them. It seemed bizarre to listen to them describe somewhere they had just been to me, knowing that it was an experience that I had been unable to share with them, as it was off-limits to me as a woman.

I rapidly felt incredibly isolated, hemmed in, homesick, and completely out of my comfort zone. I hated asking my husband to drive and accompany me anywhere I needed to go outside the compound once he was back in from work, and to explain why we needed whatever it was that was required and having to ask for money to pay for it as I was no longer earning a salary. Life back home, together with my independence, felt like a million miles away.

I started buying the *Arab News*, a daily newspaper in English providing the latest local and international news coverage stories, which was to intrigue and inspire me to read and find out as much as I could about the country I was living in.

The first article I read in the Islamic perspective section was unforgettable - a long feature on how women should dress, walk and behave in order that they do not seek to attract mans' natural behavioural instincts. I had to read it several times to take it all in - if I had been reading what was printed in a newspaper back in Scotland I would have thought it was some kind of wind-up. However, this article on women's expected behaviour in Saudi grabbed my attention. If I didn't want to cause offence or to bring attention to myself in one of the strictest, most religious, segregated countries in the world, according to what was written, I would clearly have to keep my eyes lowered, avoid looking directly into men's eyes, walk slowly without swinging my hips, only converse with males if they were close male family (my husband and sons) whilst out and about, and the list continued. There was no way I was walking several paces behind Alan - even he had to concede I had to draw the line somewhere, although he often joked about it when we were out, particularly if, as was often the case, I dared to walk in front of him. Whilst the article clearly stipulated a woman's expected behaviour, it did not specify whether these rules were for all women, or Muslim women only. Given that all women were required to wear an *abaya*, I decided to err on the side of caution for the most part when out and about outside the compound until I was more familiar with what was acceptable behaviour for Western women.

The *Arab News* was always a good read, providing good up to date coverage of local news and main international stories, together with classifieds, leisure, letters to the editor and sports. The letters to the editor page was always topical and I found the paper provided a window into life here from many differing perspectives. On a Thursday there was a review section on food and health, fashion and interiors, books, travel, movies and a children's page. The first time I read this, I found myself re-reading it, finding it somewhat perplexing that in a country with no cinemas, the paper had a section which was devoted to reviewing newly released films.

On a Friday there is a page called 'Islam in Perspective' with an article on a specific part of the Quran, a section on prayers, or how every Muslim should live his or her life in accordance with the Islamic teachings of the Quran, and a question and answer section within this, relative to everyday life situations. The leisure page would have a crossword, a Sudoku, a quiz or word puzzle and cartoons. I laughed when I recognised Dilbert and Dennis the Menace amongst them.

The classifieds cover jobs, tuition, items for sale, announcements, miscellaneous and matrimonial. I found this part of the paper to be quite revealing. The tuition advertisements were predominantly for language tuition, mostly English or Arabic. The matrimonial advertisements seemed to be placed by parents stipulating ideal requirements for a good match for their son or daughter, with the minimal stipulations listing of good family, of fair complexion, religious requirements and often of graduate calibre. Announcements and miscellaneous covered change of name, missing passports, missing workers, missing people, runaway maids, and study opportunities. I was somewhat taken aback that so many of the job adverts within the paper requested that Saudi applicants only need apply.

Both boys reacted differently to the change in their environment - Andrew went through a spell of extremely bad behaviour for a few weeks, clamouring for the wrong kind of attention - during which time he wrecked Alan's mobile by picking it up and placing it in a glass of water, flooded the kitchen with the water dispenser, reprogrammed the television so the few channels we did have didn't work and he drew on the walls. Calum, on the other hand was unbelievably quiet and seemed to withdraw into his own imaginary world, so much so that I began to think he had a hearing problem as he didn't seem to hear a thing I said to him. He was unable to follow any simple instruction without me repeating myself at least three times. He was also lethargic and it took an enormous amount of effort to get him interested in doing anything at all, let alone getting him to do it. He was required to sit an entrance examination test for school and I couldn't believe it when I found out afterwards that he had deliberately made a bad attempt at it, as if he thought that if he did badly, then he wouldn't get a place and we could all go back to Scotland.

Expatriate education in Saudi Arabia is private and very expensive. There were several schools to choose from, and my husband's company paid for schooling as part of his job package. Most expat employers offer either an education allowance or funded school fees here for a stipulated number of children, but as with anyone who has had experience of private schools, fees are not the only costs which require to be met. We chose the British International School as its curriculum was the closest that seemed to be on offer to the Scottish curriculum.

Our compound was made up of around a hundred villas, housing employees and their families from the same company. Guarded by a private security firm and by the Saudi Royal Air Force Guards, security was highly visible with vehicular and personnel checkpoints, roaming machine guns, tanks behind camouflage positions and armed guards. The compound itself was double walled, with barbed wire and security lighting and cameras along the top of the boundary walls, with only one way in and out, flanked on all sides by other compounds, work quarters and vacant, sandy and stony ground. Given the relatively recent attacks on residential compounds housing Westerners, a couple of years previously, although the security took a lot of getting used to, it was there for our benefit and gave some peace of mind. It was the un-armed security guards at the front gate that were the most vulnerable - I didn't envy them their jobs one bit.

There were things that never failed to amuse me - some of the guards' antics frequently took me aback... you would see them fully kitted out in their body armour and helmet, carrying a loaded gun, sitting down in the heat, wearing flip-flops with their boots cast to one side, or see two guards walking hand in hand, which was not uncommon. The images I have conjured up just don't fit the whole picture as you would expect to see it, but then that is the nature of life in Riyadh.

Because of the heightened security and the fact that we required to show our numerous identity cards whenever we went anywhere, both boys picked up on this. Calum made himself an ID badge, with my help printing off the correct size of photograph from the computer. He managed to persuade his Dad to give him a holder for his ID, (a spare one from his work), and he promptly set himself up an ID as a manager of an airport and hotel group. On one occasion, we were coming back after having been out, and as usual were having to show our IDs in order to be granted access into the compound, when Calum decided to present his homemade ID at the same time. (We hadn't even realised until that moment that he had smuggled it out of the compound in his pocket). We had to tell him to put it away very quickly and extremely forcefully when the guard on duty at the front gate started to look at the IDs or we could have all ended up in a lot of trouble. The homemade ID cards were only allowed if they stayed inside the villa from that day on.

There were several reasons why we chose the compound that we did to live on. We had a choice of compounds available to us, and all had a pool and good amenities for the residents. Some had amazing modern furnished accommodation within large villas with fantastic room layouts. The compound we chose had a nursery, a covered play-park, a large number of residents with young children, was child-friendly and had a nice feel to the place.

In addition the compound had lots of greenery, flowers, plants and trees which softened the hard lines of the concrete villas and streetscape. There were fig trees, stem-less palm trees and date trees throughout the compound and in gardens, and a couple of areas with only trees. There was also a grassed area with goalposts for football. Some areas had been planted with shrubs and flowers, and most gardens had flowering magenta pink shrubs creeping up a wall or fence which looked amazing, due to the vibrancy of the flowers in direct contrast with the pale surroundings. There were lots of cactus-like plants, with hairy or spiky leaves and fern-like plants, straggly plants and bushy shrubs with woody stems. Outside the children's nursery was a series of tall, green, long leaved stemmed plants with lots of large yellow flower heads that brightened the place up. Many of the villas had flowering or spiky plants in containers or tubs outside their front doors.

The villas themselves were certainly large enough and generously proportioned - they were all three bedroom semi-detached properties, of predominantly concrete construction with prefabricated panels with simple Islamic patterns cast into the exterior. However, the furnishings and the state of repair, whilst adequate, were somewhat dated, having many of the original furniture and fittings from when they had originally been built, which I reckoned was in the 1970s.

The furnishings generally weren't to our taste, so I was relieved to learn that there was an *IKEA* in Riyadh, which I planned to visit as soon as Alan had the time to drive us. I wasn't intending on buying large items of furniture, but kitchenware, picture frames, accessories, cushions and throws, which would be enough to personalise the spaces and make the villa seem a bit more like home. The built-in wardrobes and storage cupboards in the bedrooms in particular left a lot to be desired, but they fulfilled their purpose. The kitchen was adequate and even had room for a small table and chairs in it. It also had a dishwasher, which was more than we had at home although the huge fridge-freezer and our water cooler and dispenser dominated the kitchen space out of necessity. Because of the age of the children, it was more important to us to live on a compound that had a strong community with young families, than to live in a beautiful modern villa on a compound that didn't appear to be quite so family-orientated.

All aspects of daily life here were affected by prayer-time (Saalat, pronounced saala) for everyone in Saudi Arabia, whether Muslims or not. On our compound, as there were several mosques nearby, it was common to hear the call to prayer from the loudspeakers of each mosque's minaret at once, with slight differences in timing so they reverberated and echoed in your ears. At times, and depending on the imam, the chant was a joy to listen to, but at others (I seem to recall Fridays in particular, which is the

Islamic holy day), the tone was monotonous and seemed to go on and on. I couldn't help but wonder whether some of what was being said was comparable with a minister's sermon back home. It definitely wasn't my imagination, but parts of it appeared to be in the same tone, even though what was being said was totally incomprehensible to me.

Mosques are everywhere and anywhere - on every street block, mosques inside shopping centres and malls, supermarkets, petrol stations, airports and offices. Prayers are held five times a day, each with a call to prayer first and day to day life revolves around prayer-time, with times differing slightly every day based on the location of the sun and moon. Times vary from city to city and region to region. I learned that in every mosque there is a black and a white sheet of linen in an area with no artificial light. The official dawn prayer commences when the eye can see the difference between the two sheets of linen and this time coincides exactly with dawn showing on the horizon.

For me, there was something magical about listening to the dawn call to prayer in particular - before it everything was asleep, still, dark and silent, and when the prayer starts everything gradually wakes up and becomes alive at the same time as daylight emerges - the birds, the dogs, the traffic and general sounds of life. It was worth deliberately getting up to listen to, as the experience was memorable. It was however also particularly unforgettable to wake up to, if you had been up late the night before. I never found the need to set an alarm clock in Riyadh.

The moon was always amazing. It was larger, clearer and more beautiful, appearing and disappearing much more quickly than in the UK. The full moon sometimes had the appearance of being a giant golf ball in the sky - it seemed to hover closer to the earth and to be more colourful than I had seen it before, with an almost luminous quality. A crescent moon looked very different, and it took me a while to figure out why, as it wasn't immediately apparent. Viewing the moon from the opposite side of the world meant that the crescent was the opposite way round from how I was accustomed to seeing it. Crescent moons and star finials could be seen at the top of some mosque's domes on the skyline.

When I was out and about, I couldn't get over the fact that all houses and compounds, no matter how big or small, were behind high boundary walls. In some instances great lengths had been taken to ensure any glazed areas on view above the height of the wall could not be visible from outside. Arabs are very private people and clearly privacy is paramount. There were glimpses of amazing villas behind elaborate gates, and glistening, meringue-topped palaces behind decorated walls with simple, Arabic geometric patterns. Particularly affluent properties would house a drinking fountain or water taps within their outer walls together with some shrubs or small trees. What was incredible to me though, was that all over the city, directly outside the walls of the houses and in the areas next to them and vacant areas between them were piles of rubble and rubbish, amongst which you would see stray cats and dogs rifling for scraps.

Around one Western compound, the Arabic villas that surrounded the main entrance gate were particularly grand, but the glazed windows that could be glimpsed over the high external walls had been completely obscured with newspaper from the inside. This was likely to have been undertaken to stop views into the villa being available, (which was highly unlikely, as these windows were so high), but equally it would have resulted in a view of newspaper articles and filtered daylight for those inside. For the occupants of such beautiful villas to resort to this was beyond my comprehension when they could have had window film applied or glazing fitted which would have done the same job. Maybe the newspaper articles were of special interest worthy of putting up on the windows, but from the hap-hazard way they could be viewed from the outside that wasn't my impression. Throughout the time we spent in Riyadh, these villa's windows remained unchanged in their appearance.

The first notable building to grab my attention was Sabic, Riyadh's Arc de Triomphe, forming a rectangular archway which towered above the buildings nearby. SABIC stands for Saudi Basic Industries Corporation, and its seventeen storey headquarters in the Tadawul area of Riyadh forms a recognisable landmark. It is the largest public company in the Kingdom, and the largest company in the Middle East. The Saudi government owns seventy percent of shares in the company that manufactures chemicals, fertilisers, plastics and metals.

As a priority, my husband required to attend to our multiple exit-re-entry visa, which I had insisted on him getting, in case unpredictable circumstances necessitated that we required to exit the country in a hurry. Once issued, it would be valid for six months. In the midst of Alan attending to this, I learned that his company had our passports. I wasn't comfortable with this, and thought it rather odd, so I pressed him for more information. I found it incredulous when I established that your sponsor (who is your employer) is legally responsible for you and your family, and that whilst in the Kingdom they required to have possession of your passports and that is just the way things are done in Saudi with no exceptions.

Thankfully this did not cause us any problems, but for many expats working for unscrupulous employers, they could find themselves exploited and unable to get out of the country, stuck in a job or a situation they were unable to escape from. Numerous articles appeared in the press on this issue on a regular basis, and there was always a section requesting information on the whereabouts of certain individuals who had gone missing.

I recall once when Alan was home on leave, a few days before he was due to return, gathering together his passport and flight tickets, only to realise that his exit/re-exit stamp on his passport had expired while he was in the UK. He had to rapidly make numerous phone calls and get his company to undertake the necessary arrangements which would enable him to fly and return to Riyadh as scheduled. Given that his company was responsible for his passport, visa and tickets, it was a huge kerfuffle. It was just as well he noticed when he did, and subsequently it was something we always remembered to double check ourselves.

Supermarket shopping especially, as all shopping in Riyadh, was an experience - the smells at the frozen meat and the fresh fish sections were so vile I always hurried past as quickly as possible without stopping. When you saw something, if you wanted to purchase it, you had to buy it then and there, as it was unlikely to be there the next time. The fruit and vegetable sections were always interesting… I made a point of purchasing items I hadn't tried before, and very often I wouldn't even know the name of whatever it was I had purchased, let alone how to peel, cook or eat it. Through trial and error, and sometimes with the help of the internet or women on the compound I got to know some of the fruit and vegetables' names and how to prepare, peel, cut, cook or eat them at their best.

Generally speaking there was a good selection of supermarkets to choose from, although I was unable to find everything I was looking for, and I had to get used to buying some local equivalents and making do without some foods altogether. Some supermarkets lend themselves to Western tastes more than others, but at an additional cost to your pocket. There are no pork products and no alcohol, although the aisles and aisles and rows upon rows of different fruit juices to try are truly thirst-quenching. I had never seen so many different types of fruit juice and fruit juice combinations before. The mango juices were always so thick they would need to be diluted. Fruit juice and sparkling mineral water were always on my shopping list. My personal favourite juice, which I haven't managed to find back home, was grapefruit and cranberry that, with the sweet and sour flavours together, was particularly refreshing and thirst-quenching to drink in the heat.

Timing everything around prayer-times became a way of life very quickly - on numerous trips with the boys, when having finished loading up the trolley with our food, and having stood in the queue at the checkout, prayer-time would rapidly descend on us. An announcement would come over the Tannoy system in Arabic and shortly afterwards the cashiers would just get up and leave the tills then and there, and the shutters would go down. Some supermarkets would give you a short reminder that it was nearly prayer-time and there would be a mad clamour for the checkouts. If you weren't first in the queue it was more than likely that you and your shopping would be unable to leave the supermarket before the shutters came down.

We got to know of some supermarkets where you could do your shopping during prayer-time if you timed it well (although you would be locked in during salaat which prompted me to have concerns in terms of what would happen if there was a fire) and then pay for your goods once prayers had finished. Otherwise it was a choice of abandoning your trolley and leaving empty-handed in the knowledge that you would have to do the shop again later in the day, or alternatively trailing round with a fully laden trolley for anything between fifteen and thirty minutes listening to salaat. Walking round a supermarket pushing a laden trolley gazing at the goods in the aisles to keep you occupied when you have already put all the items you need in your trolley is not an experience anyone would choose to repeat. Absolutely everyone gets caught out from time to time and this has to be one of the most annoying experiences ever, especially if you have young children with you.

On one memorable occasion, we were standing in a long queue at the tills as it was nearly prayer time when our youngest son Andrew decided to throw an absolute wobbler of a tantrum - luckily one of the supermarket workers took pity on us and opened another checkout and hurried us through. It made a pleasant change not to be cross or frustrated at our son's behaviour in public, as we were so relieved to have finished our food shop before the shutters came down. That has to be the only occasion I can think of, when Andrew threw a tantrum and as a direct result he got his way, we didn't tell him off and we all benefitted from it at the same time.

The main thing I couldn't help noticing, apart from the rotten meat and fish smells, was that most Arabian women shop with their husbands - as women are legally not allowed to drive here and women are generally accompanied outside the home, then most men obviously go with them and pay for the shopping. (Only a small percentage of women worked in Riyadh when we were there). All the cashiers and supermarket workers were male. It took a bit of getting used to, having your bags packed for you by an Indian/Sri Lankan/Filipino/Pakistani and then him wanting to push the trolley for you to the car, hoping for a tip, while you or your husband were perfectly capable of pushing the trolley yourself. The number of plastic bags and cellophane wrapped goods were extreme, and I couldn't help but find it somewhat bizarre that the only paper bags I had seen were from designer clothes shops.

The first few times I entered the supermarket, I was approached by staff as I was carrying bags containing items from other shops, which I had to deposit at the supermarket lockers on my way in as they were not allowed in the store. I learned quickly that if intending on doing a supermarket shop, I required to purchase small items that I could conceal in my oversized handbag, which I could carry round the store with me, otherwise I would have to queue to deposit any larger purchases in the lockers, for which I would receive a locker key, with a ridiculously oversized square number fob that would only just fit inside my handbag. Given the temperatures, you would return to the car and straight home after undertaking a food shop, even if it was just a few odds and ends, so we learned to do other shopping on a separate trip.

Traditional clothing for Saudi men is a white cotton *thobe*, a loose, long-sleeved, ankle-length garment, buttoned at the neck and wrist. Sometimes in the winter months, darker woollen ones are worn. The *ghutra*, a white cotton scarf or the red and white checked *sham'agh* head covering is worn folded across the head, with a *tagiyah*, a white knitted skull-cap underneath and the *agal*, a thick doubled black cord worn on top of the ghutra to hold it in place. In sandstorms, the end of the scarf can be draped across the face and the scarf used to protect the face and neck from the strong sun. Open toed sandals worn with bare feet complete the look. Most Saudi men dress traditionally. Prayer beads, sometimes referred to as worry beads or *sibha*, made from wood, plastic, metal, precious or semi-precious stones are often passed through the fingers to pass the time, with each bead representing the greatness of Allah.

Women and girls from the age of puberty wear an *abaya*, a long black cloak made of silk or synthetic fabric, loosely worn over clothes in public. Islam requires women to dress modestly to hide their shape from anyone who is not close family. Until I went out to Saudi, my husband thought all *abayas* were the same, and couldn't quite understand why there seemed to be so many differing outlets selling them. There are a huge selection of *abayas* varying from extremely plain with no decoration or embroidery to *abayas* with colourful exquisite embroidery and sequins around the hemline, cuffs, and borders of the material, sometimes more. Some supermarkets sell *abayas*, but there are also *abaya* shops and more tailored designer *abaya* shops, where the wearer can make a fashion statement with her choice.

Saudi women wear differing veils - some cover their faces and eyes completely with sheer black material, which allow a certain degree of visibility, others wear a *boshiya*, a black veil worn across the lower part of the face, with a black gauze headscarf, a *tarha*, to cover the hair. There seems to be numerous styles of veils and headscarves and many ways of wearing them. In some areas in Saudi leather masks replace the veil, and in others women partially veil their faces with a decorated *burqua*, leaving the forehead bare, with openings for the eyes.

Traditionally women wear an embroidered *thobe*, a loose, colourful, ankle-length dress, under the *abaya*, embroidered and decorated at the front, or cotton or silk traditional trousers. Some women wear gloves and cover up their feet completely, although in the heat this must be uncomfortable at times. Many Saudi women wear Western style clothes and designer sandals or jeans and trainers underneath their *abayas*. Designer sunglasses or beautifully made up kohl-lined eyes, waxed eyebrows and the most glitzy, sparkly sandals and manicured polished toenails together with a designer handbag make for the finished look if the occasion arises.

I find Saudi women incredibly beautiful - when all you can see of someone is their dark kohl-lined eyes that have so many expressions that when the rest of the face is veiled, they truly are a view into the soul. I couldn't help but look into the eyes of veiled women, and their dark eyes all smiled back at my blue eyes when we acknowledged each other's presence, sometimes curiously or hesitatingly uncertain at first, but always happily and accepting of my interest in making a connection, even if it was only no more than a glance in passing.

Although in public Saudi women wear black *abayas*, there is a large market for designer fashion and haute couture in Riyadh, with mall after mall of designer clothes stores and shopping malls. The Middle East accounts for forty percent of the haute couture clientele. It was quickly apparent to me that Arabic women love designer shoes and footwear, handbags and sunglasses - I had never seen so many impractical high-heeled, delicate, sparkly shoes and shoe-shops, but then a quick flash of a jewelled foot (maybe even an ankle if you are looking very closely) under an *abaya* has to be the ultimate fashion statement when that is what is visible.

Saudi women love jewellery, especially the Bedouin, as it indicates status and can provide cash in times of need. Bedouin jewellery is known for its hanging elements that make a jingling noise, allowing men the time to disappear before women approach. Traditionally Bedouin jewellery is made of rustic silver. When a woman dies, her jewellery is melted down and not passed on, as second hand jewellery is frowned upon.

The advice from the foreign office on dress-code for expatriates in Riyadh was to dress conservatively and as expected in public in deference to religious requirement and Saudi society. For women this would mean wearing an *abaya* and covering hair with a scarf to avoid confrontation with the Muttawa (religious police) who patrol the souqs and shopping centres. Some of the Muttawa insist that all women cover their hair, especially during prayer-time, out of respect, whilst others approach women (their husbands first, if present), at any time, requesting that the hair be covered up. For men, long legged trousers should be worn together with short or long-sleeved shirts or T-shirts as the wearing of shorts or exposing the shoulders in public is not acceptable. When wearing a shirt in public, if a tie is not worn, then the shirt should not be open below the collar-bone.

Riyadh during the day was mostly a blend of sandy colours everywhere, and viewed through strong sun and sunglasses the colours were very much subdued. However, Riyadh comes into its own at night with multi-coloured neon lights, lit-up buildings, facades, strobe lights shining into the sky, lights that change colour and create contrasts of light and dark colours and shadow, making the place look like another city entirely from during the day. A few stores had laser lights outside, beaming up into the sky - you would have no trouble locating the store that way I suppose, but I did wonder what the pilots thought when they flew planes overhead. I particularly liked how any road works were cordoned off with cones and concrete bollards, but how the cones would always be draped in bright and sparkling fairy lights, usually flashing. It was almost as though each set of road-works was trying to outdo the other in terms of its decoration.

Trips to the shops in the evening were unforgettable - I would push my youngest son round in his buggy and at that time he had curly, fair hair. In just about every shop we would enter into, both he and his brother would be made a fuss of by the staff and they would be given presents, even if we hadn't bought anything. Saudi society is completely centred round the family and the children and we found it extremely child-friendly. Saudis love children and see them as a special gift from God.

Although slightly alarming at first, I soon got used to Arab men and women giving my children attention, reaching down to touch my youngest son's hair or pat him on the head wherever we were, or shaking hands with my older son and saying hello and asking them where we came from. Due to the segregation laws and customs, a male would not approach a female, let alone try to start up a conversation, so the men would ask my husband or address the children directly. I understood the situation, so I did not find it rude, but it did take a bit of getting used to. On numerous occasions women would follow me round subtlety, and sing to Andrew gently under their breath as I pushed him round in his buggy, their eyes smiling back at mine when I acknowledged them. I couldn't help but notice that this would only happen when Alan wasn't right next to me, when I had wandered off to look at something whilst pushing Andrew in his buggy. It is considered good luck to touch a child with fair hair and thankfully, he seemed to enjoy being the centre of so much attention. He accepted without question the fact that he could only see the eyes of the women who were lavishing so much attention on him. Calum, however, was full of endless questions and theories about why they covered their faces, and would somehow always end up coming out with the most inappropriate questions or commentary for the situation we found ourselves in at the time. Very often, he had to be told to be quiet or that his questions would be answered later, once we returned to the car or the villa.

Children are named when they are around a week old and boys are traditionally circumcised. Most Saudi children spend time with their close female relations until around eight, when boys then spend more time with their father. Children are brought up to respect their elders and not to interrupt or contradict them. They often look after their brothers and sisters from a very early age.

Saudis are judged by their backgrounds, history, family's reputation and family ties. Saudi history is tribal and a Saudi's responsibilities and loyalties are to the family and tribe. The main pressure on a Saudi is to avoid dishonouring the family. In the city, there is more financial independence and smaller families generally, whereas in more rural areas several generations may live under one roof. The head of the family is the eldest male, who is responsible for the family's finances and wellbeing. The eldest woman tends to be in charge of domestic matters. Saudi families can be large, as a man can have up to four wives, as long as they are all treated equally.

Having eventually discovered *Toys-R-Us*, *Jarir's Bookstore*, and the *Early Learning Centre*, the purchase of a few board games, a football, a basketball and some children's books and crafts made a huge difference to life on the compound for the boys. It had definitely been worth going out late with them in the evenings, as they had more things to do inside during the hottest part of the day which made life so much more bearable.

The first of our numerous trips to *IKEA* was unforgettable. We made it inside the building before it shut for prayer, locking the shoppers inside to find the lights dimming. I was pushing Andrew round in a trolley, while my husband and Calum had wandered off, looking at something else. The call to prayer started up on the loudspeakers, and I was absolutely horrified when, at the top of his voice, Andrew joined in, so much so that he was drowning out the imam's voice leading the prayer.

Unfortunately telling him he was too loud and he needed to be quiet this instant had the opposite effect and his noise level increased. I didn't know where to put myself and could feel numerous Arabs' eyes on me. Many of them looked a bit fierce from the quick glances I was able to glean without looking them in the eye when they turned round, but I am sure my imagination wasn't getting the better of me when a few of them turned back round again rather quickly trying not to laugh when they realised that the noise was coming from such a small boy who was just trying to join in.

Scouring the kitchenware area in *IKEA*, it became obvious where Alan had bought many of the things I had found in the villa when we came out. He told me that for all of the guys out in Riyadh on single status, it was a standing joke amongst them that their apartments all contained the same *IKEA* starter packs of white plates, bowls and mugs, cutlery, a tin opener, a frying pan, a pan and a wooden spoon. Apparently only male expats with girlfriends or wives in Riyadh had kitchens with other plates and bowls. We made do with the bowls and plates Alan had already purchased. As far as I was concerned, although they may not have been what I would have chosen, they were fit for purpose.

Thankfully a few days before school and nursery were due to start back, families started arriving back on the compound. Until then the place had seemed eerily quiet apart from the air conditioning, the birds, the calls to prayer and my children. The only other adult I had had any conversation with during the day while Alan was at work had been the Indian shopkeeper on the compound. I always said hello to the gardeners and maintenance men when I saw them out of common courtesy, but given my limited understanding of social etiquette on the compound, I wasn't sure if that was the right thing to do, as although they smiled and nodded or moved their heads from side to side back at me, they always seemed embarrassed when I did so. I always made a point of acknowledging them, as to me it would have been rude to ignore them, and whilst I wasn't interrupting their work, I felt it only right to give them a brief exchange in passing.

CHAPTER 3

Settling In

Things improved dramatically once school and nursery started, and I got to know some of the other women through the children. The compound's occupants were all employed by one company, or one of its main subcontractors and were British or English speaking, mostly with young families. The majority of families employed Filipino nannies to look after their children, and I found myself being constantly asked if my boys needed a nanny. Given that I was no longer working and had decided I wanted to spend quality time with our boys while we were in Riyadh, I politely declined the continuous offers from nannies and workmen working on our compound who had friends or relatives looking for a position.

Everyone on the compound had gone through what it was like experiencing life in Riyadh for the first time, and because it was a small compound it was relatively easy to get to know people quickly and make friends. There was a village atmosphere about the place and frequent activities and events organised by the residents with lots of things laid on for the children. Bikes, go-carts and toys were left abandoned all over the compound and most children played and roamed around outside most days in the late afternoon once the sun's rays were not too fierce. It felt incredibly safe, but then ironically at the same time I was only too aware of the immense security that was surrounding us. The facilities were great - a small library, a pool, football area, tennis court, squash courts, a gym, a nursery, a children's shaded play area, a snack bar and a central clubhouse with a hall, a stage and a bar area. The children's externally shaded play area on the compound was fantastic, and I was most impressed to learn that many of the Dads on the compound had got together and built it. The play area kept many children occupied for hours, including ours and was one of the best I've seen, with a variety of activities to suit different ages.

We were assigned a house-boy to undertake domestic duties six mornings a week by the company my husband worked for. Everyone on the compound had a house-boy and I suppose from the company's viewpoint it meant that the properties remained clean and tidy whilst they were being lived in, eliminating any last minute problems requiring additional work between one family moving out and another moving in. It felt very strange having someone else in the house doing the cleaning, washing and ironing and I felt very spoilt. However, I continued to do some of the work as I didn't want to get too used to the idea of having someone else to do it all for me. My house-boy's ironing skills far surpassed my own and I established that some of the marks on clothes I had previously ironed were down to me using tap-water without thinking, because of the particles of sand in the water. Bottled water was the secret ingredient in steam ironing, which took a bit of getting used to, as I repeatedly kept filling the water container for the iron straight from the tap out of habit. Due to the climate, far more housework was required due to the sandy environment and dusty conditions, which meant that constant dusting, sweeping and mopping was necessary, as dust and sand would build up very quickly and get into absolutely everything.

Most Saudi families have maids who undertake the cleaning or cooking or any other domestic work needing done. In some households there are many maids, who all have separate duties. Calum would frequently tell me stories of Saudi children at school and the different maids they employed in their villas. One boy's family apparently employed eight, and Calum took great delight in explaining each of their roles to me. I had initially thought he was having me on, but with the level of detail he had gone into it was clear that wasn't the case.

Our house-boy was Sri Lankan and we were extremely lucky to have been assigned him, as he became part of the family while we were there. He very quickly undertook the tasks I asked of him and I don't think I have ever lived in such a clean house. He found it amusing that the boys would follow him round to try and help with the cleaning when he was there, as of course that is what they would do when I was cleaning at home, but from his reaction I don't think that was the norm for most expat Western families.

I always felt a bit uneasy with the term 'house-boy', as the house-boys on our compound were all men and therefore I felt the term was misleading, as well as being somewhat derogatory. George was only a few years younger than I was, and was definitely not a young boy. He was also extremely intelligent, but could earn a far better salary for himself in Riyadh and support his family back home working as a house-boy and driver than any job in Sri Lanka. All of the house-boys had recognisably English names, some of which were their real names, but in many cases they adopted names for their job that could be more easily pronounced and remembered by the families they worked for.

In some ways, life felt somewhat colonial at times which made me uncomfortable. I was aghast at some of the behaviour I came across... I had heard there was one woman who had a bell which she would ring when she wanted her house-boy to undertake some task or other for her, which she particularly delighted in doing when she had guests and wanted him to make some drinks. I saw this first-hand when I was one of several women invited to attend a talk on Persian and Arabic rugs and carpets in one of the villas on our compound, which sounded fascinating. Our hostess and her husband had lived in Saudi for many years, and I only knew her to say a quick hello to on passing, so I felt it was nice of her to ask me. I was looking forward to finding out a bit about rugs and carpets from this part of the world. I was sure I was in for an interesting evening and I was hopeful that perhaps those present would pass on some useful information on living in Riyadh with me. However, I felt increasingly uncomfortable whilst in her company, as although she was a different generation from myself, it became apparent that she had a memsaab mentality. I considered making a joke about a butler, but thought better of it. There was no doubt that her houseboy was treated extremely well and seemed perfectly happy, but the whole set-up just didn't sit easily with me. I felt as though I had been transported back in time to the times of the Raj. The local trader and several of his assistants spent the evening in her villa with around twenty women, and I left shortly after the talk had finished as, although it was educational, unlike the majority of the other women present, I had not gone along to part with a huge amount of money or spend my whole evening haggling over rugs and carpets.

I was absolutely appalled at how another woman treated her house-boy. I had noticed him standing in the full midday sun one day when walking to the compound shop. He was still there and didn't even have a bottle of water with him when I walked back so I asked him if everything was ok, as I didn't understand why he was standing in the heat. He assured me he was fine, but I could tell something wasn't quite right. I found out later that this was not the first time he had been sent out to stand in the sun, but that this was a frequent punishment when his cleaning failed to meet the standard expected of him. On this particular occasion, he had failed to remove a hair from the bath. A little power can clearly be abused by some, or perhaps too much sun had gone to the woman's head. Thankfully, the couple he worked for moved away shortly afterwards, and the house-boy was assigned to another family where I am certain he was treated with the respect he deserved.

There was a camaraderie amongst the expat community which existed on all kinds of levels. Women with young families would help each other out as they were away from extended family at home and did not have a support network around them. For other women it was all about being in the know as to what social events were going on and where, which supermarkets were best for different foods or where and when the best clothes sales could be found. For men it centred round sussing things out in a foreign country where they were responsible for just about everything - where to go to buy fake Rolexes, where to get the best deals on anything from four wheel drives to takeaways, how to make the most out of the various company work expenses and allowances, the best directions and roads to take, where to go for a night out, tips on home brewing techniques etc.

There was a Scottish network of expats who stuck together who were known as the 'McMafia' - not for any sinister reason, but because they didn't moan about things. When there was a problem they would just get to the bottom of it, sort things out and get whatever was needed done without fuss. The Scots were also known for taking everything and everyone at face value, getting along with the Saudis and not putting up with nonsense. Many of those within the expat community were experts at moaning about things, and the same conversations would go on for weeks without those who were actually being so vocal about their gripes doing a single thing about them. Although there were some things they were clearly most unhappy about, they seemed to take great pleasure in going on and on about them, which would drive Alan and I to distraction, especially if we had volunteered suggestions on what they could do to improve a situation and they were still moaning about it weeks later, having done absolutely nothing themselves.

Many of the compound's occupants had shaded parking outside their villas. It didn't take long before Alan decided to pay the maintenance men to put up a shaded canvas tented canopy to shade our car outside too. It had been so hot that getting into it was unbearable, and even with the car's air conditioning it would take ages to bring the temperature down. We very often got small electric shocks when we touched the door-handles to open them. The majority of car parking in Riyadh was shaded under tensile roof canopies for good reason. Small electric shocks when touching metal objects in Riyadh was a frequent occurrence because of the heat, but I always got a fright whenever it happened.

On one of our shopping trips to Carrefour (a French hypermarket) in the Granada Shopping Centre I purchased a mobile phone. This was essential as if I was going to be out and about outside the compound. My new phone details required to be registered with my husband's company's security service, which would then automatically send me security alerts via text message. In addition, it was vital that I could be contactable at all times, that I would be able to request help or assistance if I needed it and that I could be notified of areas to avoid or incidents that I required to be aware of. Although I had a mobile in the UK, I tended to use it for work and emergencies only. I did not always carry one with me back in Scotland then, but out of necessity I soon got used to making sure it was always charged and that I had it on me at all times whilst in Saudi Arabia.

I enjoyed browsing through the Arabic ring tones and being able to establish prayer-times in advance, which was to prove extremely useful. Mobile phones are extremely popular and I saw a large number of Arab drivers talking on their mobiles whilst driving erratically at the same time. (If they weren't on their phones when driving, most of them flicked or fiddled about adjusting their headgear if they were wearing it).

Many mobiles on sale in Riyadh had an integral camera, which I was surprised at, as taking pictures whilst out and about is frowned on for security reasons, and photographs are seen as a form of idolatry which is unacceptable. Many Westerners have got themselves into trouble innocently photographing government buildings or men or women without asking the man's permission first (a strict no-no). Having said that I have seen many Arabs taking pictures on their mobiles, but then that is a typical example of one of the many double standards that seem to apply here.

Looking through the DVDs, CDs, newspapers and magazines was an experience… a censor with a black marker pen had been there first, obliterating any naked flesh, arms or legs of women, and in some cases even hiding their figures and faces. Advertisements for underwear were completely blacked out and occasionally whole pages were ripped out. However, I couldn't help finding it amusing that one of the DVDs I had purchased had black pen all over the cellophane wrapper, but that I discovered the DVD itself to be unmarked when I removed the packaging later.

A routine made life so much easier with the children, but it did take a while to get used to such an early rise. Alan would get up for work and leave around six in the morning or even earlier in order to start his working day at seven at the latest. We would get up shortly after he had gone, as the bus left from the compound for an early school start. Pupils in the junior school finished at lunch-time and older pupils finished an hour or so later. This meant that homework could be done in the afternoon and there was time to lounge round at the pool later in the afternoon when the sun wasn't too strong. It was great because in theory Alan would get back (when he wasn't putting in additional hours) with time to spend with the boys after work. Although it didn't happen as frequently as we had hoped, it made a real change to have some quality family time together during the week at the pool on the compound.

The first time Alan joined us at the pool after work, the boys distracted him and he ended up going straight into the pool with his company mobile still in his trunks pocket. He had to go two weeks with a temporary phone while his was being fixed and I never let him live that down. I would always ask him where his mobile was before he got into the pool after that, but as it was always in his pocket, it was just as well I asked.

As we were all up so early during the week, by early evening we were tired, so trips out after our evening meal did not happen frequently, as prayer-time would inevitably make it a rather late night by the time we would venture out and return back again. Alan worked a five day week, although many companies had a standard six day working week.

Now the schools and nurseries were back during the weekdays (Saturday to Wednesday) I made the most of having a few hours to myself in the morning while my youngest son was at nursery. I thoroughly appreciated my new-found freedom with relatively few domestic chores and being able to go to the pool to swim or lie in the sun, read, go to the gym or venture out to the shops. There was also a hairdresser who came to the compound and a beauty clinic at certain times, but I never booked, as they didn't fit around my limited child-free time.

I had extremely mixed, highly charged emotional feelings when I established in the first week of term that the school that we were sending our eldest son to was on one of the compounds that had previously been damaged in the compound bombings in May 2003. The security to the compound and the school was incredibly tight, as it was everywhere, but at the same time it heightened my awareness of where we were and I did find it hard at first, sending him off on the school bus in a foreign country where there was still such a perceived terrorist threat against Westerners. I think most Mums felt the same, but in all honesty the children were safer going to school on the bus than being driven to school by individual drivers in private cars or taxis. We soon became used to the school bus pick-up routine, although I did feel for the Mums of the youngest children who were going to the school's nursery for their pre-school year. As the working day starts so early, it was out of the question for Dads to drive their children to school regularly, even though school started far earlier than it did back home. The terrorism threat was real and I found out later that very often undercover security cars would shadow the bus on its route to or from school. I was always pleased and relieved to meet my son when he stepped off the bus at the end of his school day in more ways than I had ever thought possible when he had finished his school day the previous year in Scotland. Coming to terms with the fact that my eldest son was going to school on a compound that had previously been attacked was hard to get my head round, but the security that was in place was extremely impressive.

I can still remember when we found out about the compound attacks - Alan was at home on leave, having come back for a holiday that coincided with our Easter break in 2003. He arrived in Scotland amidst news and travel warnings that Westerners were terrorist targets, as there was intelligence at the time to suggest that terrorist attacks were being planned. We had all gone away for some family time together in the Lake District in May. Our son was three years old then, and I was pregnant with our second. Alan had a company mobile phone and despite the fact that he was on holiday, had taken it with him much to my disgust. By doing so this would mean he would inevitably end up working at some point while we were away. I was in the living room of our holiday accommodation when he received a text message. Reading it, his facial expressions instantly changed from being relaxed to being terribly concerned and all colour drained instantly from his face. I asked him what had happened, but it was evident he didn't want to talk. He gave me a mumbled excuse about how he had to go outside to make some important calls immediately and promptly disappeared.

About half an hour later, he returned and told me that terrorists had bombed several compounds in Riyadh. He had phoned his best friend and work colleague in Riyadh to see if he was ok, and to attempt to find out exactly what had happened. Thankfully he got through straight away to Andy, who was fine and was able to provide Alan with a bit of information on the situation. They were both extremely worried about friends and colleagues that had not yet been accounted for, people they knew on the compounds that had been attacked and the occupants of the compounds. It wasn't until later in the day that news reports made their way to our television screens, but the information given out was less than Alan had established from Andy earlier.

Alan spent much of the rest of his holiday finding out the details of what had happened and accounting for colleagues and people he knew. He was due to return to Riyadh a couple of weeks after it had happened and wanted to get as much first had information as possible as to what he would be going back to, as the information available to us in the UK was sketchy. By the end of the following week Alan had established that on Thursday 12 May terrorist attacks had been mounted on three compounds in Riyadh more or less simultaneously, leaving many dead and wounded. Having spoken at length to colleagues and his manager, he reassured me that he was happy with the tightened security measures that his company had already implemented as a result, and that he would be returning to Riyadh to work as originally planned.

Leaving family behind is never easy, but to return to work in Saudi so shortly after the bombings must have been a hard decision for him to take. Although I did think about it, I wouldn't have stood in his way and asked him not to go back out, as it was him that was living out there and therefore he was more informed than I was. I hate goodbyes, but in the midst of such troubled times my mind kept questioning the risks he was putting himself under, whether we would see each other again, and more to the point if he would be there for our eldest child and our unborn child. I was very much aware that the feelings I was experiencing were probably not unlike those of many families whose husbands, sons, brothers or uncles in the armed forces when they are sent away on foreign missions to do their bit for their country. Despite having tried to convince myself that the reality of the situation was that those who work in the armed forces have a far riskier job, it didn't make parting any easier. I had put his passport in the wash by mistake when he had got back, as he had left it in his jeans pocket, but despite being in a far more fragile state than it had been in previously, it was still legible. Part of me wondered whether this was a sign that he should not go back out, although I am generally not superstitious, and I secretly hoped that his return would be delayed for a bit longer and he would be told to obtain a new passport when he turned up at the airport, but that didn't happen.

One of the things Alan omitted to tell me until I was writing this book was that when he returned to Riyadh, he discovered that the British Embassy and many other embassies had just shut down. It was thought that even larger attacks were planned, and many Western expats and their families were getting ready to leave the country, if they hadn't already done so and a mass exodus was underway. It was only once he had returned to Riyadh that I was able to comprehend the full extent of what had happened.

On Thursday 12 May at 11.15 p.m. a car attempted to enter the back gate to Jadawel compound in Riyadh, which housed mostly American expats working for defence companies. Guards at the main gate shut off the power to the gate when they noticed a car on their security cameras attempting to enter through the back entrance. When the security guards approached the vehicle, one of them was shot, together with a Saudi policeman. The terrorists wounded two unarmed guards, one of whom managed to secure the inner gates of the compound before escaping. In a last attempt to get into the compound, the terrorists detonated their explosive packed vehicle, killing themselves and a Filipino worker in the process. Several villas on the compound were damaged as a result, but miraculously there were no losses of life to the residents on the compound.

At around the same time a car carrying a bomb and terrorists drove through the gate at Vinnell compound, which housed civilian expat men employed by the Saudi National Guard in four storey dormitory accommodation. The bomb was detonated next to one of the housing blocks resulting in this compound and its residents being the worst affected. Surrounding compounds suffered blast damage. Alan's friend Andy, who was in Riyadh at the time in the same housing block where Alan lived, said that all his windows rattled in the blast, which happened over a mile away.

Simultaneously at Al Hamra Oasis Village, terrorists followed a resident's car into the compound, once it was checked through security. Guards tried to stop the first terrorist car but were shot as the car forced its way through the gate, closely followed by a second vehicle. Both cars headed towards the pool area where a resident's party was underway, firing indiscriminately, and the second car was then detonated, leaving a crater where it had previously been. The blast was so intense residents reported that the car flew up into the air before landing in the pool. All the terrorists were killed by the force of the blast and around twenty villas and a dozen apartment blocks were destroyed or seriously damaged. The school on the compound was also damaged. However, incredibly, not one British teacher living on the compound was killed, although many suffered minor injuries.

Final figures reported thirty-five dead and over one hundred and sixty wounded, not counting the suicide bombers. Those killed included Americans, Saudis, Egyptians, Filipinos, Jordanians, Brits, Australians, Irish, Lebanese and Swiss nationals.

After these attacks, Saudi Arabia recognised Al Qaeda as a threat to their country and they began a serious crackdown on insurgency. The Saudi security forces did not appear to consider human rights or legalities and terrorists were considered guilty until proven innocent. When a militant was caught, members of that man's family and friends were also arrested. There was a huge amount of anger, sorrow and grief amongst all levels of the population over what had happened, and an acknowledgment that Saudi required to work together with the West to tackle terrorism both inside and out-with its borders.

In November 2003, a residential compound in Riyadh was attacked which housed Muslims, killing seventeen workers and injuring more than one hundred people. This second attack on the Saudis themselves turned many Saudi nationals against Al Qaeda, which meant that intelligence on suspicious activity within the local community increased. As Saudi society is family orientated and tribal, the population do not move about in the same way as they do in the UK. A group of men moving into a villa or apartment or having regular meetings would not be normal behaviour amongst established communities, where families and extended families live together. Newcomers would stand out and be noticed and questions asked. After these attacks there were reports that over six hundred terror suspects had been arrested, together with seizures of bomb making equipment, materials and thousands of weapons.

One day after having met Calum off the school bus at the bus stop on the compound, on our way back to the villa we noticed that one of the boys from one of the neighbouring villas was playing with something at the kerb-side. Stopping to talk to him as we walked past, we were stunned to see the biggest, fattest caterpillar we had ever seen - it was about two inches long. The boy had found a large leaf and a twig, and had coaxed it onto the leaf. When we spoke to him he was trying to figure out if he had anything that was suitable to keep the caterpillar in, as he wanted to take it home. I established later that it would turn into a lime butterfly, a common species in Riyadh.

There was a shopping bus laid on for the women from the compound, which would drop off at the souqs (traditional open air markets/bazaars) and modern air-conditioned malls in Riyadh. It made a huge difference just to have the opportunity to get out of the compound for a couple of hours, even if it was just to explore the shops with some of the other women and have an iced coffee out. The shopping experiences available in Riyadh are absolutely amazing and I must admit I can understand why shopping has become a serious pastime for many expats' wives out here. (And that is from someone who used to make a list of what I needed from the shops and go straight in and out... somehow during my time in Riyadh I have to admit that that is not what happened). However, if shopping for clothes, there are no changing rooms, so you have to buy first and try at home, making sure you keep the receipt. (There is one exception to this where in Ladies Kingdom some shops do have changing facilities).

Going on the shopping bus was always a bit hairy due to the frequent speeding up and slowing down, braking and weaving in and out of the city traffic so I always made sure I was wearing my seatbelt. The blackened-out windows meant that we had privacy while en-route, but it was always interesting to look out of the window at the streetscape, buildings and surroundings along the varied routes taken and to see another couple of compounds where women were dropped off and picked up on the way there and back.

With Thursdays and Fridays being the weekend it took a long time to get used to knowing what day it was, as it was incredibly confusing. A simple change to the working week days when you have always known them differently was unbelievably difficult to adjust to. I constantly had the days of the week mixed up for the whole time I was in Riyadh. Talking with the other women when waving my eldest off to school at the beginning of the week, I would always discuss what we had done on Saturday night or ask them what they had done then, which would always raise a laugh, as it was Saturday morning when we were at the bus stop, the beginning of the week in Saudi. There was a saying amongst the expat community that once an expat started referring to Thursday and Friday as the weekend it was a result of having been in Saudi too long.

Because of the weekday differences, Saudi was out of sync with most of the world, resulting in a three-day week when the Saudis can do business with most other countries and vice versa. This prompted a continuous debate on the subject with the proposition to change the weekend to a Friday and Saturday. The two day weekend only started in the eighties and before then a six-day week was the normality, with the holy day of Friday off. The arguments put forward against it included Saudi society not accepting the start of the weekend being their religious day, Sunday being the first day of the week, and Saturday being the last would be unacceptable to the majority on religious grounds. In addition, as Jewish people have a Saturday off there were even concerns that it could be interpreted as Arabs/ Muslims celebrating a Jewish day. However the argument for changing the weekend would increase the working week by a day economically, in terms of being able to do business with most countries in the rest of the world.

One weekend I bought myself new sunglasses from Debenhams, as the sunglasses I had taken out with me to Saudi had a small framed rim and I felt that I needed a more substantial pair that would provide me with better ultra-violet protection from the sun. When I wore them to drop my oldest son off at the bus-stop one morning for school several of the other women noticed and I received quite a few compliments on them. However, another woman who was also dropping off her children for school couldn't help but get involved in the chit-chat. It turned out that she had recently purchased a new pair of sunglasses too. She had obviously spent more money on hers than I had, and took great delight in making it common knowledge that her husband had not been happy with their last credit card statement, as her new designer sunglasses were itemised on it. Elaborating further, it turned out that she had seen the sunglasses and decided to buy them, without first calculating their equivalent value in pounds sterling, as it was far too complicated for her to work out. I initially couldn't decide whether she was trying to make me aware of her husband's status within the company, as she felt she didn't need to be aware of how much items cost (although clearly her husband did), whether mental maths was just not one of her strong points, or whether she was just making conversation.

The currency in Saudi Arabia is the Saudi Riyal, which is available in one, five, ten, fifty, one hundred, two hundred and five hundred Riyal banknotes, which all bear the face of the King. One Riyal is sub-divided into one hundred halalas, but most items are rounded to the nearest Riyal. While we were out, I divided the cost by seven to give me a rough idea of the equivalent price in pounds sterling although the exchange rate at the time was seven point something. Any halalas change we accumulated were saved in a jar and handed over to the workmen on the compound at Christmas-time.

The Saudi Arabian Monetary Agency, or SAMA, is the Kingdom's central bank, and there is a currency museum within SAMA's head office. The museum displays coins and currencies and there are displays on how they are made and minted, together with information on their security feature. Visits are required to be booked in advance over the phone with the museum's director.

Alan paid a subscription for satellite channels on the television, providing us with access to selected British, American and Middle Eastern channels. It was bizarre to find that newspapers, magazines and even books are subject to the black marker pen or censorship, but that you are able to sit and watch movies on the satellite channels that have not been subject to the stringent controls of the PPV (Public Protection of Vice). I couldn't help imagining rooms full of men in their *thobes* holding black marker pens going through un-censored material and wondering whether their jobs were secretly coveted by the rest of the male population. I also wondered what their official job title was, and whether they told their wives, sisters and mothers the full extent of what they did for a living.

We subscribed to the local internet provider (there being no choice here at the time, just the one company) and eventually after numerous appointments when the workmen failed to turn up when agreed, we finally had our internet up and running. Unfortunately the connection was not reliable, but at least we had some internet access, enough to keep in touch with friends and family back home through e-mail which made a huge difference. I had enrolled on an online professional distance learning course, planning to further my qualifications and education while I was out, but found myself having to withdraw from the course due to the poor internet connection. In addition to being a huge disappointment, I found this infuriating as this was something productive I had wanted to do with my time whilst in Riyadh, in addition to having quality time with the family.

Saudi Arabia has a national firewall, which restricts access to adult or non-Muslim religious information internet sites. Of course for those who are IT buffs or know someone who knows how to get round this, this can be overcome.

I registered us with the British Embassy in Riyadh, and re-read the information online about the dos and don'ts about living in Riyadh, Saudi Arabia which made an informative if contradictory read. Reading it whilst in Riyadh, it made far more sense than when I had read it previously in the UK.

I had familiarised myself with some of the differences between UK and Saudi-law before going out to Riyadh, as it was important we adhered to the laws of the country we were in, given that Saudi laws and morals are very different to what we are used to - considerably stricter than those at home, particularly relating to dress, drink or moral behaviour, as what is not a crime in Britain can be a crime in Saudi Arabia. The Saudi legal System is based on the Muslim holy book, the Quran, and is often referred to as Sharia Law. By British standards, punishments for some offences are particularly harsh.

The death penalty is enforced for murder and sexual immorality (adultery or homosexual acts), apostasy (renunciation of the Muslim faith), and drug smuggling. For serious offences, the sentence has to go through the high courts and then receive the final approval of the King before being carried out. Beheading is usual for the death penalty, which is carried out in public. Women are shot twice - once in the heart and once in the head, or could be stoned to death if they are found guilty of adultery. Alcohol offences for consumption, smuggling, manufacturing or distribution can involve lashings, fines and imprisonment. Stiff penalties are also handed out to anyone in possession of alcohol-making equipment. Serious or persistent theft is punished by cutting off the right hand of the thief. Punishments are undertaken after midday prayers on a Friday in front of a crowd of onlookers. I heard that any Westerners present are made to move to the front for an uninterrupted view.

Non-payment of debt under Sharia Law is a crime, punishable by imprisonment, but the debt still requires to be settled so for expats working or living in Saudi, it is vitally important to avoid personal debt of any kind. Meticulous accounts need to be kept of any employer's funds or items you are paying for on credit. If you are the sole company representative in Saudi, then you can be held personally accountable for the payment of company debts. Any form of debt would be sufficient for officials to stop you from leaving the country until paid, even if you were planning a short trip away.

Prisons in Saudi Arabia are renowned for being uncomfortable and harsh. They are overcrowded and hot, with little chance for exercise or rehabilitation. Visits, though permitted, can be under difficult conditions. It did concern me to learn whilst in Saudi that suspects can be held without charge, and that it is common practice for victims and witnesses to find their family members and friends routinely rounded up and detained in some instances.

Although no society is crime-free, unsurprisingly, crime levels in Saudi Arabia are dramatically lower than in the United Kingdom, as the punishments act as a huge deterrent, together with the potential shame you could bring upon your family and tribe.

Under Islamic law, two women are equal to one man when acting as witnesses, which allows corroboration between the women. Saudi women have control of their inheritance, marriage dowry and private property. However, a man inherits twice as much as a woman as male family members support the women.

The public practice of any religion other than Islam is banned, as are attempts at conversion of Muslims to Christianity. Imprisonment and deportation would result if anyone was caught doing so and the matter brought to the attention of the authorities.

I re-read the guidelines on living in Saudi Arabia which we had been given. We were given general advice on personal security, checking a vehicle, travelling in a vehicle, what to do if you are followed or threatened, advice on parking safely and going out and about and general security issues. From time to time we would be asked to attend security briefings in the clubhouse. My husband's company employed ex-paratroopers and SAS personnel, whose remit was the security of the company's employees, their families and the compounds. One of them lived on our compound, and it was interesting to talk to him and ask questions to establish the extent of security that existed around us, as although the majority of it was extremely visible, there was far more to it than what we could see and were aware of. He was very good at responding to questions without actually providing direct answers and was even better at deliberately skirting round the more difficult ones without giving much away. It would only be when you were walking away or had left that it would dawn on you that he hadn't fully answered your question.

Although there had been car bombings and attacks against Westerners before Alan went out in 2002, things escalated considerably as soon as he started living in Riyadh. He had spoken to me briefly on the subject, but had never given me sufficient information to give me cause for concern for his safety at the time. It was only when I was out in Riyadh that I was able to ascertain precisely how difficult things had actually been then. He was given regular security training and briefings which included security updates, suggested ways of reducing risk, recommended behaviours and actions and action plans, how to observe people, describe people and undertake defensive driving techniques amongst other things. The training and talks reinforced the fact that he was in a hostile alien situation, and together with the things that were going on at the time the men felt under threat, on edge and as if they were being watched every time they left the compound. They were given tips on how to avoid stopping at traffic lights, which was considered too risky after several Westerners had been shot in their vehicles at red lights, how to drive and leave room round the vehicle, to be wary of people approaching or hanging round a vehicle and how to get out of a potentially threatening situation straight away.

Alan had a friend over one evening with whom he had spent a lot of time previously when he was on bachelor status and it was only when we were all talking that I was given a glimmer into the extent of how things had been for them. One day when they went into work they were briefed that intelligence sources had discovered that there was a perceived threat of a rocket propelled grenade attack on the company's headquarters. Desks and office furniture were moved away from windows and film was applied to the glass. For around a month they had snipers and spotters on their roof while they worked below, as the company believed the intelligence to be from a reliable source and the threat credible. The company was not in a position to consider telling employees not to come into work, as this would imply that they felt the Saudi Security Forces were not capable of providing appropriate protection and managing the threat. Continuing to work in as normal a way as possible in such circumstances and conditions must have been extremely difficult.

Following some of the bombings and shootings, some of the compounds would go into lockdown and the guys were kept from going outside their compounds or into work for a few days, after which they were advised to vary their routines in terms of the times and routes they took to and from the workplace, together with any specific security briefing information which was deemed to be relevant at that point in time. Most Westerners were peeved that there was a marked increase in absenteeism of the Saudi national employees during these periods, when they had no choice but to go into work as normal. For the Western men, a considerable part of their conversations became extremely dark and sinister. Discussions, theories and plans would centre round what they would do in the event that terrorists came over the compound wall or attacked their compounds. Not surprisingly a great deal of thought and consideration was put into their individual action plans and strategies when the trouble was at its most extreme, and lengthy debates would go on into the early hours to determine the best courses of action and see things from every possible angle.

I remembered continually watching news reports in 2004 from the safety of my living room in Scotland, when there seemed to be so much going on in Riyadh, and whenever I raised things with Alan over the phone he would play things down, telling me that these things had happened in areas he did not frequent at the time. (Of course I now know differently, being in Riyadh I was only too aware of where many of these attacks had taken place). Al Qaeda had targeted locals again in April 2004 when a car bomb was set off next to a building which had been used by the police, killing five and injuring over one hundred. Between May and August Westerners were targeted - a German chef was shot outside a supermarket, an Irish BBC cameraman, Simon Cumbers, was shot and killed while Frank Gardner, a BBC reporter, was injured but left paralysed in the same incident, an American Robert Sands was shot in his Riyadh villa, another American Kenneth Scroggs was shot outside his villa in Riyadh. Another American, Paul Marshall Johnson was kidnapped at a fake police checkpoint in the city and later beheaded, and an Irishman Anthony Higgins was shot and killed at the construction company where he worked. In September, Brit Edward Muirhead Smith was gunned down in his car outside a Riyadh supermarket. It must have been an incredibly scary time for expats in Riyadh and Alan had been there throughout. On 29 December when Alan was home, two suicide car bombs were detonated by suicide bombers in Riyadh, one outside the Saudi Interior Ministry and one outside the Special Emergency Force Training Centre, killing one and wounding several others, but although he must have received security alerts on his phone he never told me, as if the incident made the news here, I didn't see it. I only found out about these incidents after Alan had once again returned to Saudi.

Alan told me that when things were at their worst, the Saudi King relaxed the law to enable expats to own firearms. This created a huge stir amongst the expat community and my husband's company took the decision that although the law had been relaxed they would not permit their employees to own or carry firearms. Alan agreed with this, although this was not a popular opinion at the time. He felt that it would be far riskier to be exposed to mad expats with guns in the country who lived on compounds than the few terrorists who lived outside Western compounds. I was certain that Alan would not have voluntarily told me any of this if one of his friends hadn't brought it up in conversation while I was present. Alan must have had a word with him as whenever any of his friends came round after that the conversation was of a lighter nature when I was within earshot.

Some expats bought prayer beads and an Arabic head-dress, which they would permanently leave in their cars, as they believed it would make their vehicles less susceptible to terrorist attacks when parked. Alan and I did not believe this to be the case, thinking instead that being seen driving around in a vehicle displaying Arabic items would draw attention to ourselves, and although we did purchase prayer beads and Arabic clothing we did not leave them on public display in the car.

When we were out and about, on returning to the car we always followed the guidelines we had been briefed on, being particularly careful to be on the lookout for any litter under or near to the car, or anything on the car. Calum watched the precautionary mirrored search that took place under the car whenever we went through security to get into the compounds and became aware of car bomb threats. We didn't tell him, but he worked it out for himself, even though he was only five and a half. What a thing to think about at that age. Thankfully it didn't seem to pray on his mind - we had told him that the security was there to keep us all safe and he seemed to accept that. He was always interested to watch the men in the inspection pit or to see if he could get a glimpse of the views that were reflected of the underside of the vehicle in the mirrors that were used during the security checks. He could be quite a thoughtful boy, and I noticed he would never join in with any games other boys played on the compound that involved guns or bombs or play-fighting. I asked him about this and he told me that these things were too serious as they were real and were not a game and became quite vocal in his opinions.

Another thing we had to be mindful of was to make sure we did not have a set routine when we were going out and about, as this would make us easy targets. We had to vary our times, our routes and our destinations accordingly in order to reduce risks, because we were constantly being reminded that as Westerners in Saudi we were targets for terrorists.

We carried a security awareness aide memoire in the car, and I stored one in my handbag just in case. Given that it also had Arabic numbers and vehicle characters, in the event of a road traffic accident, I thought it might prove handy, as I had already seen so many accidents on the roads here in the short time we had been out. One of the realities of living in Saudi Arabia was that you were far more likely to be involved and injured or killed in a road traffic accident than a terrorist incident.

Phone-calls from the UK to Saudi were expensive and we purchased pre-paid cards for close relatives to use, but long code numbers needed to be input and then once you had been put through to the compound, getting the operator to understand which villa number to put you through to and getting it right could take several attempts. I knew this from bitter experience when trying to get hold of Alan before we moved out, so phone calls from back home were not a frequent occurrence. We were living in Riyadh in the days before Skype and Face-Time.

The compound had a company security channel which repeated itself on the television and was updated regularly. Adjacent to the inner gates of the compound was a security alert board which remained at amber (high security risk), for the whole time we were there, apart from once when it was on red.

Saudi Arabia is bounded by the Red Sea to the West, Yemen and Oman to the south, the Persian Gulf, Qatar and Kuwait on the east and Jordan and Iraq to the north. The empty quarter in the south-east of the country is a vast and impenetrable desert. There are three major areas of population - Jeddah in the West, the previous capital city, which is the gateway to Mecca and Medina, Dhahran to the east, the heart of Saudi's oil production, with Dammam nearby, and the capital city of Riyadh in the centre of the country, a man-made oasis, where much of the new city was created in the 1980s. Riyadh, as it is now known, or to be more correct, Arr'iyyadh comes from the Arabic word *rawdah*, meaning a place of gardens and trees. Until the sixteenth century, it was known as Hajr. Riyadh was formed on top of a rocky escarpment which had a number of wadis running through it, most of which are now dry. Riyadh was the birthplace of the Al-Saud family, which is why it became the capital of Saudi Arabia.

Riyadh developed rapidly from a small city built in adobe construction inside fortified adobe walls, gateways and towers to the capital city that it is today of nearly five million people within a couple of generations. Saudi's population is rapidly increasing, and Riyadh is one of the fastest growing most prosperous cities in the world. Geologists reckon that millions of years ago most of Saudi had a mild and humid climate, with much of it covered by a shallow continental sea. When the plants, animals and fish died, they were covered in soil, debris and plankton, which over a considerable time decayed into oil.

Riyadh is one of the largest cities in the Middle East, with its rapid growth attributable to the oil industry. The Kingdom has at least a quarter of the world's total oil reserves, and has the world's fourth largest gas reserves. Saudi's oil is close to the surface, allowing it to be pumped out of the ground relatively inexpensively, and as a result Saudi has the power to adjust the supply, meeting any shortages by increasing capacity as required. The Kingdom has a vital strategic role to play within the world's current and future energy requirements. However, the oil industry is vulnerable to terrorism because of the gas and oil separating plants and the pipelines in the desert which are difficult to guard and patrol. There are two industrial cities, Yenbu in the West and Jubail in the east.

It is reckoned that the population in Saudi is made up of approximately sixty percent Saudis and forty percent foreigners or expatriates, who have come to the country to work, with many Asian workers undertaking manual jobs that the Saudis do not wish to undertake themselves. Saudi's overall majority is Sunni Muslim, apart from in Dammam, where the majority there is Shi-ite Muslim.

There are vast areas of sand deserts in the country - Rub AlKhali or the Empty Quarter in the south and Great Nafud to the north with Dhaka, another large strip of desert between the two. The coastal belt near the Arabian Gulf is made up of flat marshland and salt-flats. North of the Nafud Desert are hard gravel and rock plains, and the limestone escarpments of Tuwaiq and Armah lie between the Great Nafud and Riyadh. A low mountain range from the north to the red sea coast borders North and South Yemen.

Towards the end of September, disrespectful and insensitive cartoons were printed by a Danish newspaper depicting the prophet Mohammed as a terrorist, which sparked months of violent protests and unrest in many Islamic countries.

We had arranged a birthday party for Andrew at this time and hired the clubhouse hall on the compound. Although it ended up being a huge party, and was nothing like anything we had ever done before, we figured that it was a good opportunity to meet all the children and families on the compound that had children of the same age. The highlight of the party for the children was playing with balloons and dancing but there were a handful of youngsters who spent their time attempting to pull off the costume from one of the party organisers.

I ended up with agonisingly sore heels due to the dry heat and the fact that I was wearing sandals all the time. Thankfully I found some cream in the supermarket specifically for cracked heels, something I had never suffered from before. Talking to some of the other women on the compound, I learned that it was very common for newcomers to suffer from this condition. It took a while for them to heal (no pun intended), as some of the cracks had deepened down to the skin underneath, but the cream did the trick, and I had to think about moisturising my feet on a regular basis from then on, which was something I had never done before. Given that previously they were stuffed inside boots or trainers for most of the year in Scotland, my feet had been somewhat neglected for years.

On one of my walks round the compound when I was by myself, I came across a memorial for a British man who had lived on the compound and had been shot dead several years previously - with a shudder I looked at the date and was able to recall the very day it happened - I was at work in Scotland in an open-plan office, and the radio was on. It was reported that a British man who worked for the same company as my husband had been shot at traffic lights in Riyadh. I remember calmly but hastily gathering my things together, leaving work early without saying a word to anyone, collecting Calum on my way home from the child-minders, uttering as few words as possible when I did so. When I got home I phoned and texted Alan in Saudi, but didn't receive a reply.

The next hour seemed to last forever and I recalled pacing round the house clasping my hands over my pregnant stomach, praying, convincing myself that if something really awful had happened then I would know instinctively. Eventually the phone rang. Although I was desperate to answer it, I let it ring out before I picked it up, in an attempt to pull myself together, preparing for a phone call that I hoped was the call I wanted to receive, but also not wanting to acknowledge that equally this call could go the other way. I had never been so relieved to hear my husband's voice but at the same time I felt bad, empathising with what another family were going through and how it could so easily have been us. I don't think I said much to Alan when he called me back, as I hadn't wanted him to think I was worried about him, but I told him that I'd heard the news on the radio and wanted to make sure he was ok. It was a brief phone call.

Although I was aware that it was a dangerous and difficult time for Westerners in Saudi, Alan hadn't divulged to me quite how perilous the situation was, as he hadn't wanted to worry me, especially given that I was pregnant. I made a point of keeping up to date with the news stories that made their way over to the UK from Saudi and as a result clearly had concerns. Alan brushed them off when I raised them, reassuring me that he was more than happy with the level of security that his company provided. He didn't speak to me until many years later in any great detail about the full impact of the terrorist threats and bombings on him and other Westerners who were living in Riyadh at that time.

Looking at the memorial again, the reality of the situation and where I was struck me hard, and I felt physically sick.

CHAPTER 4

Ramadan-a-Ding-Dong (October '05)

Saudis take their faith very seriously, and being an exclusively Islamic Kingdom, religion governs all aspects of life. The public practice of any other religion is prohibited. Over a billion Muslims throughout the world face Mecca to pray five times a day. It is a major expression of faith for each Muslim to make the Haj pilgrimage to the Ka'aba shrine and other religious sites at Mecca in Saudi Arabia at least once in their lives. Entry to Mecca and Medina, the two holiest cities of Islam is forbidden to all non-Muslims.

Muslims follow a twelve month lunar calendar which is ten or eleven days shorter than our Gregorian solar one. Their calendar dates from AD 622 when their Prophet Mohammed fled from Mecca to Medina. The year we went out to Riyadh was 1427 in Saudi and 2005 as we knew it. This was continually confusing for us as Saudi religious festivals and celebrations change their dates on our yearly calendar. The ninth month of the Muslim year is Ramadan when no Muslim is to eat or drink between sunrise and sunset. In Saudi Arabia, during Ramadan no-one should eat, drink or smoke in public during the fasting hours. Everyone has to adhere to this, be they Muslim or non-Muslim. Failure to adhere to this can result in strict penalties, including deportation, if caught.

I read an article in the local paper which advised that there were exceptions to this rule for the elderly, young children and babies, the sick and menstruating women. In practice I did not see anyone eat or drink a single thing during this time in public, regardless of how old, young or ill they were. Our gardener and the maintenance men on the compound were mostly Muslims, and when they were doing any work for us during this time we did not offer them water to drink as we usually would, or eat or drink in front of them out of courtesy.

As Ramadan can fall during any time of the year due to the lunar calendar, it coincided with hot months of the year when we were out, and as a direct result many things seemed to be somewhat crazier than normal. Most expats do their utmost to escape Saudi during Ramadan if possible - it has been nicknamed 'Ramadan - a - ding - dong' here, or 'the silly season'. There are many reasons for this, the major one being that after a day of no eating or drinking, then driving standards slip and frustration and tempers become even more exaggerated than normal at the wheel.

Just as the sun goes down, the roads are deserted when the whole Kingdom is settling into a feast. Our guards on the compound would break the fast and set rugs out, taking shifts at getting stuck into mounds of food. During Ramadan some of the supermarkets are open round the clock and turnover is dramatically increased. Muslims' working hours are reduced at this time, and if they are able to do so, many of them change their sleeping patterns so they sleep during the day. Many Muslim schoolchildren are tired due to so many very late nights and it is not unusual for them to fall asleep in class.

Not being able to eat, drink or smoke all day can result in short temper, and nerves that become easily frazzled. I saw some people keel over, or faint with absolutely no warning, just going about their daily lives, with no warning whatsoever. Although strictly no food is to be consumed during Ramadan, I noticed that many men chewed on a curly, woody, root-like stick at this time, called a *miswak*. The miswak comes from the root of the arak tree and is used during Ramadan to freshen the mouth. Tooth-brushing during daylight at this time is not considered to be acceptable due to the risk that water may be swallowed.

A bizarre thing about Ramadan is that some supermarkets and takeaways are open during the day, when no food is to be consumed. I took ill with a particularly nasty flu and fever and wasn't able to cook for us at all one day during Ramadan. Alan told me that he'd rustle something up, which was somewhat unusual for him. He popped out to our local Kudu to get us all something to eat, and true to his word, arrived back with takeaway food while it was still daylight. It appeared to be perfectly legal to buy food or takeaways, provided you don't eat them in public before sunset.

The two major public holidays of the year are Eid al-Fitr, which lasts for around two weeks and celebrates the end of Ramadan and Eid al-Adha, around two months later lasting about ten days celebrating the sacrifice during the pilgrimage to Mecca. At the end of Ramadan there is a three day period of feasting, sometimes abbreviated to Eid. At this time, prayers are recited, new clothes worn, presents given, sweets and delicacies eaten and relatives visit each other. The mosques appeared to have louder prayers and a great deal more preaching, giving the impression that each was trying to outdo the other. The first time I heard it, I wondered whether someone had gained unauthorised access to the loud speaker and was ranting and raving about something at the top of his voice. Alan said he thought I was mistaken and what we could hear was the commentary from a camel race, but there were no racetracks anywhere near our compound as far as I was aware.

At the end of the fasting day, the Ramadan fast is broken with a few sips of water, a few dates and an apricot puree drink, *qamar* ad-din. Zamzam water may also be drunk which is from the well revealed to Hagar by the angel Gabriel. A large meal or feast is eaten around one and a half hours after dusk after the fifth prayer, Isha. Starters could be a thick soup of wheat, lamb and tomato, flavoured with cinnamon, cardamom and shaybah leaf, foul-beans cooked with tomato, onion, oil and *sambusak*, triangular, wafer thin pastries stuffed with ground meat, onion and coriander, or cheese and spinach, or *shakshukah*, eggs cooked on an onion, green pepper and tomato base. One or two main dishes would be served - chicken, lamb or fish *kabsah*, the traditionally cooked Saudi dish with rice spiced with black peppercorns, cardamom, saffron, cinnamon, lime, bay leaves and nutmeg, in which pine nuts, almonds, raisins and onions are also sometimes added, *aysh abu laham*, leavened dough flavoured with fennel and caraway seeds filled with mutton and spring onion, topped with *tahinah*, sesame seed puree. Other local fish recipes as part of the meal could include perch seasoned with garlic, lemon or cumin, or *samak humar*, baked with a sweet and sour sauce or hamur with onion, tomato, garlic, hot pepper and cumin served with lemons or pickled lemons with turmeric. Methods of cooking include *mandi* - where meat is barbequed in a covered hole in the ground, *mathbi* - where meat is grilled over flat stones placed on burning embers or *madghut*, cooked in a pressure cooker.

To round off the celebratory meal there may be *mahallibiyah*, a pudding of ground rice and milk, flavoured with orange blossom or rose water and decorated with almonds and pistachios, or *sagudanah*, tapioca, or sago pudding, similarly flavoured and scented. For special guests more sweets are served, with some being specially made for Ramadan. *Luqmal al qadi* is a light dough spiced with cardamom and saffron, fried and dipped in syrup, pancakes stuffed with cheese or nuts and fried and covered in syrup, *basbusah*, semolina cooked with sugar syrup, baked in squares and sometimes served with *qustah* (cream), *kunafah*, pastries that look like shredded wheat, that have a middle layer of white goats cheese, butter and pine nuts, and covered in a rosewater sugar syrup.

I suffered a severe bout of what I called compound fever as a result of being unable to get out of the compound during the day, as the shopping buses were off for the duration of Ramadan. Being confined within the walls of the compound every day was restrictive and whilst it was hardly a prison sentence it was incredibly oppressive. I think it was the fact that we only went out in the evening if we absolutely had to, as the roads were crazy and driving through the traffic was the last thing my husband wanted to do after already having battled his way back from work through the traffic. Going from living somewhere where I would decide what to do or where to go and just do it to being somewhere I was unable to do so was a situation which I found incredibly difficult and was unable to adjust to. I found myself with little to do that was purposeful or meaningful and although I was always able to find myself menial things to keep me occupied I was bored. At the opposite extreme, Alan found himself under pressure with most things resting on his shoulders, from driving to paperwork, supporting his family, traffic, bureaucracy, dealing with people to get anything done, and being fully responsible for the family in ways he had never had to before, and finding himself with far more requests for things that he needed to do from me as I was unable to do them. Compound life as a family was not easy for us to adjust to.

One supermarket trip during Ramadan, we found ourselves at the sweets, spices and nuts section. We would normally buy the boys some dried fruit as a treat, and as usual we indicated what we wanted. On this occasion, the assistant serving us wanted us to taste it first, but we all felt rather guilty straight afterwards when we immediately realised we had done so without thinking, given that it was Ramadan. The looks on our faces must have been entertaining in themselves. Even though it was quiet where we were in the supermarket, I wanted to give the assistant the benefit of the doubt in that I was sure his actions were out of habit, but at the same time I found myself wondering whether he really wanted to get us all caught and deported.

In the mornings, once I had put Andrew in his buggy, we would accompany Calum to the bus-stop where he would get on the school bus. After we had waved him off, I would usually walk round the compound a couple of times pushing the buggy, sometimes on our own and sometimes with friends who also wanted a quick walk with some company. One morning, the gardeners were all in one of the garden areas, clearing it of debris, and using brushes to sweep the area clean, making quite a bit of noise as they did so. I was walking past at the time, and was astounded to see a very pale coloured thin snake quickly squiggle right in front of the buggy wheels across the path. It was the same colour as much of the dead woody stick-like part of the hedge we had been walking past, but our garden was on the other side. I had never left the boys on their own outside, as I had read up on the insects, spiders, snakes and scorpions that inhabited this part of the world. After having come across the snake that morning I ensured that I kept an eye on where we were putting our feet.

The gardeners had disturbed it, and having been frightened by the noise it was scurrying away when we fleetingly came across it. Snakes usually stay clear of people and only lash out when they feel threatened. Nonetheless I decided that as soon as Calum returned home from school that day, we would have a talk about snakes, reptiles and spiders. As soon as I had deposited Andrew at the nursery I scoured the internet, (which thankfully was working for a change) and established that it was a saw scale viper.

When Calum arrived back at the villa, I told him about our encounter with the snake on the compound. He took great delight in informing me that one of the first lessons he had had at school was identifying venomous or threatening creatures that could be harmful to humans in Riyadh. He amazed me by being able to identify the snakes and spiders I had printed off the computer and talk a bit about each. It made sense that the school covered this topic, so children knew what animals to stay away from, or in the event of something happening, being able to describe it.

I accompanied my husband to a vocational education and training evening at the British Embassy. With a large number of colleges and vocational institutions being planned in Saudi Arabia, it was informative to walk round the stands that had been set up by colleges, universities, qualifications authorities and work-based learning schemes. There were two Scotsmen who worked for the Scottish Qualifications Authority in attendance, and we had a long chat. We were also introduced to Sir Cowper-Coles, Britain's Ambassador in Saudi Arabia, whose ambassadorship had been particularly challenging from the moment he took up his post throughout the Al Qaeda campaign which had been launched against the Kingdom. (Since then he has also been Britain's Ambassador in Kabul, Afghanistan and a special representative of the UK Foreign Secretary to Afghanistan and Pakistan).

With it being Ramadan I decided to learn a bit about the Islamic faith and what being a Muslim entails, so thought I would start with the five pillars of wisdom, a Muslim's five religious obligations. The first pillar is the most important and is the profession of faith, known as the *shadhada* and is recited. It translates as 'I bear witness that there is no god but Allah. I bear witness that Mohammed is God's messenger.' The second pillar is prayers or salaat, when Muslims undertake washing rituals and face in the direction of the Ka'ba in Makkah to pray five times a day at dawn (fajr), midday (dhuhr), mid-afternoon (asr), sunset (maghisto) and at night (isha). In Saudi, most shops shut down during prayer-time and businesses do not answer the telephone. It is normal practice for a Muslim to pray anywhere and very often you would see people stopping their daily activities and praying wherever they were. I can recall walking past a couple of women in a shopping mall who had found a quiet corner to perform their prayers. The third pillar is zakat, whereby the less fortunate are provided for through annual religious taxes which companies and individuals require to pay. Alms and charity are also considered zakat. The fourth pillar is fasting between sunrise and sunset, abstaining from food, drink and sexual relations during the month of Ramadan as a method of spiritual self-purification. The fifth and final pillar of wisdom is the obligation to perform the annual pilgrimage Hajj to Makkah once in a lifetime for those who are physically fit enough and can afford to participate. The Hajj takes place during the twelfth month of the Islamic calendar. The end of the Hajj is marked by Eid al Adha, a festival celebrated by prayers.

One evening we took our eldest boy to one of the souqs on a quest to find him an Arabic costume so he could dress up as an Arab. This was something he had wanted to do ever since he arrived. Alan and I were amazed when he started conversing in Arabic with the stallholder. They had a long conversation, of which I could only understand a few words here and there. My knowledge of the Arabic language at the time was extremely basic to put it politely - *naam* meaning 'yes', *la* for no, *shukran* for 'thank you', *afwan* in reply meaning 'you're welcome', and of course *muta' assif* for 'sorry'. I had known he was learning Arabic at school and decided at that point that it was about time I made more of an effort, and start to learn a bit of Arabic too. I managed to find a decent Arab/English phrasebook in *Jarir's Bookstore*, which became well-used rapidly. My attempts at Arabic were always met with a smile and lots of conversation whenever I gave it a try.

I did find that because the Saudis roll their 'r' s and pronounce their 'och' or 'ach', my Scottish accent helped, and very often I would have a torrent of conversation thrown back at me, as my murmured guttural thanks were apparently convincing. (Or that is what I was led to believe). Whenever there were Arabs on a till they would always try and talk to me after I had said, "Shukhran," complimenting me on my pronunciation, or just trying to make small talk. Because I had long dark wavy hair very often they would initially think I was Lebanese until they noticed my blue eyes. I observed that many Arabic women seemed to partake in lengthy conversations and banter with male Arabs or shop assistants at the till while they were purchasing their shopping, and for many it was evidently part of a successful day out.

I was often taken aback at the number of times I would be at a till paying for something when a Saudi customer would just come straight over and demand to be served. Queuing was definitely something that was not widely practised. If I was queuing to pay, frequently another customer would just walk up to the cashier straight in front of me. Thankfully, most staff on the tills would not serve customers who behaved in this way until it was their turn, although you had to stand there and listen to their incessant conversation while you were being attended to which I considered to be the height of bad manners.

To put it bluntly, the roads and driving in Riyadh were an experience, but they were even more treacherous during Ramadan. It is illegal for women to drive in Saudi Arabia, although I had heard of a protest in which some women drove through the streets of Riyadh a few years previously, getting their husbands into severe trouble in the process. I must admit in my opinion the thought of veiled women driving on the roads would not do anything to improve Saudi Arabia's extremely high rate of road accidents and deaths on the road (not due to their driving ability, but because of the impact of the limitations on their vision, if driving while veiled).

I often saw young boys at the wheel of a car or 4x4, who could hardly even see over the steering wheel, driving their mothers and sisters wherever they needed to go. As women were not allowed to drive, while their husband was at work if they didn't have a driver, it would be common practice for their young sons to take to the wheel. I wondered how old many of these children were, driving their mothers round in expensive, powerful cars and jeeps. Some of them didn't look much older than nine or ten years old. Each time I was out in the car it was difficult not to remark on the children playing and clambering about in the cars, babies and young children on parents' knees or even on the dashboard, with no sign of seatbelts or child car seats. It was hard enough to see this first-hand, let alone answer our boys' questions on this matter, as I have always been extremely strict on how they behave in the car, and how they must sit properly with their seatbelts on. Our two boys couldn't believe their eyes when they saw children playing and having a carry-on with no seatbelts on, sometimes hanging out of the windows or sunroofs while the vehicle was moving.

The fact that seatbelts and child seats can help reduce injury and even save lives in the event of an accident just didn't seem to be generally acknowledged whilst we were in the Kingdom, or if it was it wasn't widely practised. Although it is against the law not to wear a seatbelt, there appeared to be no enforcement of this for the whole time that we were out in Riyadh. Child seats for the car were one of the first purchases we made when we came out as a matter of priority. Expat nurses we knew who worked in the hospitals in Riyadh get extremely upset and frustrated with the serious traffic accidents, particularly those involving young children. The numerous deaths and severe injuries that they face daily that could have been prevented, they find themselves having to deal with first hand. The Arabic 'Anshallah' means god willing, and applies to daily life here as everything is 'Anshallah' with a shrug and no questions, that's just how it is. If God meant it to be then that's how it is.

The driving in Riyadh (which is technically on the right hand side) has to be experienced to be believed - a four lane highway with cars overtaking wherever they can, zigzagging through heavy traffic, cars all over the road with their drivers on a mobile or adjusting their headgear at the same time (how they have any peripheral vision whilst wearing their headgear I do not know), cars pulling out all round you with no warning (indicators seem to be used rarely), cars driving the wrong way on the road, cars going off-road to jump a queue or just driving wherever they want to go regardless of what is going on around them, or where they are on the road - the list is endless and I was constantly baffled by what I saw on the roads every single time I ventured out.

Frequently drivers would stick an arm out of their car window, palm facing upwards, with the tips of the fingers and thumb together, making movements up and down, meaning patience, patience. I had seen the shopping bus driver gesticulate in this manner before whilst saying the words, "shway, shway." From time to time a driver would pull the point of his chin which would translate as shame on whoever it was whose actions displeased him.

At sets of traffic-lights, as soon as the lights change to green the horns would go full-blast and non-stop, even though traffic was barring your way in front of you with nowhere to go. Often Saudi drivers undertake what is known as a 'Saudi U-turn', a manoeuvre where instead of queuing at the left hand lanes to do a u-turn, they approach the lights in the right hand lane, driving through traffic queuing at the lights, and in the process stopping all traffic from moving. Most highways have between three and five lanes and it was common to see a vehicle cut from one side to the other in order to exit the highway or to get into the fast lane, usually performed without indicators. This manoeuvre, known as the 'Saudi sweep', seemed to be made at the last possible minute, regardless of where surrounding cars were on the road. I actually found myself wondering whether some of the drivers on the roads had any awareness of the other cars around them at all.

Many drivers didn't drive within the lane markings, and drove along obliviously without a care in the world, taking up two halves of two traffic lanes. There was also the 'Anshallah lane', aptly nicknamed by expats, because if you used it you literally took your life in your hands. It was a three quarter lane adjacent to the fast lane which would be used by impatient drivers as an extra fast lane, but because it wasn't as wide as a full lane, vehicles using this lane could easily become wedged between a fast lane of traffic and a concrete wall. Many accidents occurred as a result of cars being nudged or bumped into the concrete wall, which seemed particularly ironic as its purpose was to provide a route which allowed emergency vehicles quick access to wherever they were needed on the road.

Although motor insurance is available in Saudi Arabia, third party cover wasn't compulsory while we were out. Some Muslims have scruples over insurance principles and particularly third party cover. Expats are generally advised to check they are adequately covered, as even if driving an employer's vehicle on business, third party cover may not be provided unless you specifically request it first.

I had never seen so many near misses and so many road accidents before. In some parts of the city at certain times of day, three or five lanes of traffic turned into between five and eight and it literally felt like bumper-cars. I hated being in traffic like that as a passenger, and would have disliked it even more as a driver, as you're wedged in with nowhere to go with only inches between your vehicle and those surrounding you, having to concentrate constantly. If you're unlucky you can end up being caught up in congestion like this for an hour, which, even though all cars here have air conditioning, is not pleasant.

The highways themselves were in reasonable condition, and most signage in the city was in Arabic and English. However, signage relative to road-repairs was non - existent, and on some roads, the layout left a lot to be desired, where suddenly, without any warning several lanes would merge into one. Service roads run alongside the highways which can theoretically mean you have a four or five lane highway with two, two lane service roads either side, so there were rather a lot of lanes to choose from.

Off the well-maintained highways, the roads were generally not in such good repair - large potholes remained unmarked, numerous roads had areas of subsidence or very large gaping cracks in the tarmac surface. Huge speed-reducing sleeping policemen easily caught you unaware (especially when driving in the dark), as they were the same colour as the rest of the road, so any journeys off the highways tended to be rather bumpy. Road-works at night, where huge pits had been excavated deep into the ground/rocky sand were a sight to behold, very often with multi-coloured or flashing lights round them, sometimes with bulbs arranged to create an arrow. Away from the highways and the centre of the city, the road signage was only in Arabic, which made finding your way tricky, but many places you would expect to see signposts for had no signposts anyway. It was important to have a map with you when you went out in the car, no matter where you were going as you could not rely on road signs to get you to your destination.

As a female driver who legally was not permitted to drive whilst in Saudi, I must admit I cannot recall a single car journey (apart from in the morning after work has started when the roads are not too busy), where as a passenger I haven't found myself putting my foot down heavily on the floor to break on numerous occasions. Although I love driving, I had to admit I would not have relished driving round Riyadh, apart from at times when the roads were quiet. What I missed was not just being able to get in a car and physically drive myself where I wanted to go when it suited me, but at least there was the shopping bus which was something. I heard stories that some Western women on another much larger compound had previously got themselves and their husbands into a great deal of trouble when they were seen driving within the confines of their compound, and it was made very clear to all women that driving anywhere in Saudi was illegal and a very serious matter not to be contemplated.

American SUVs and pick-up trucks make up most of the traffic on the roads. Particularly common are pick-up trucks with tethered livestock in the back - usually goats and sometimes a camel or two. On one occasion I had a complete fit of the giggles when I saw a pick-up truck laden down with WCs in various shades of pastel colours in the back. I guess you had to be there to see the funny side, but I had never seen so many WCs in so many pastel colours before. To see them on the back of a truck, piled high was really comical. We all ended up in stitches, speculating where all of these WCs were going - was it to an Arab with lots and lots of wives, who each had their own bathroom, or were these the latest fashion, about to go on display in a showroom, or had some artist decided to buy them to make a sculpture to make some kind of obscure statement? From what I could make out there were peach, apple, avocado, cream, lavender, rose pink and dusky blue models, and I will never forget the boys arguing in the back of the car as to which colour was the best and why. It certainly made a change from the boys telling us that a camel or goat in the back of a pick-up truck next to us on the road looked as though it was going to escape from its vehicle. Boys being boys, we had to overtake the truck just in case the WCs had been used at a desert gathering and were all full and on their way to be emptied as they were balanced precariously in such a manner that it seemed they were due to topple at any minute.

Numerous white taxis operated all over the city and I had naively previously thought taxi-driving manoeuvres to be the same the world over. Many vehicles and 4x4s were covered in sand if their occupants had come from the desert, sometimes so badly you were unable to make out the colour of the car, let alone the number-plate. Most vehicles were white, silver or sandy coloured with damaged bumpers or old accident dents in their bodywork. I had never seen so many extremely expensive top of the range sports cars before, usually with the occupants posing inside trying their best to look cool around the centre of the city. Some had Arabic music blaring out of the window whilst others sounded as though the cars' inhabitants were listening to Islamic verses and recitations.

Many of the cars, taxis and jeeps had tinted film applied to the glass providing privacy as well as helping to keep the temperature down inside the car. A recent law had been implemented forbidding the tinting of the windscreen and front passenger windows for security reasons, but many cars still had their front passenger windows tinted. The rear windscreen is commonly tinted and very often also sported images of the King and allegiances to the Kingdom of Saudi Arabia.

Once a week, at around tea-time when some residents would be about to eat a barbeque outside, fogging of the compound would be undertaken. Although we were usually reminded when this was going to be undertaken on the compound notice-board, inevitably we did occasionally get caught out. Fogging involved a diesel smoke being pumped into the air round the compound to kill off mosquitoes and larvae and it absolutely stinks. It did seem to work, so there were never any serious complaints raised, although you wouldn't consider eating fogged barbeque food, no matter how hungry you were.

A few of the women on the compound set up a café which was situated ideally between the play-park and next to the pool. It opened for a short time at lunchtime, and again at teatime and did a cooked breakfast on a Thursday and Friday which proved to be very popular. Tables and chairs were set up beneath a shaded canopy area, and it was nice to have somewhere on the compound to go to sit down and eat something that someone else had cooked. Food that has been prepared and cooked by someone else always succeeds in tasting better than your own, especially if you do most of the cooking. I found this to be even more the case in Saudi, as the heat affected my appetite and put me off cooking, as I only enjoy cooking when I am hungry. The majority of families would meet up on a Wednesday at the end of the working week, for a leisurely meal and get together in the evening as the sun was setting, which meant the adults could have some adult conversation, while the kids played in the play-park after their meal. There were always parents at the play-park watching the younger children, and because everyone knew each other the children were kept in check if the situation arose. The atmosphere was always great, and it was good to have an informal get together with other residents that you could turn up to and retreat from whenever you felt like it.

Whilst I had got to know a few other parents I hadn't found anyone I clicked with and adapting to a new life in a foreign land would take my emotions to extreme highs and lows that I had never previously experienced. My first Ramadan on the compound was trying as I felt so restricted in so many ways, having no close friends round me, not being able to phone and speak to friends and family whenever I felt like it due to time differences and costs, and life took a bit of getting used to. I would frequently fly off the handle at Alan when he got back from work, having been cooped up on the compound all day, often having had little stimulating conversation with anyone but the children.

My husband told me that his first experience of Ramadan in Riyadh had been frightening. He was living in a bachelor apartment on his own and no-one had warned him to expect to hear lots of fireworks being let off very late at night. Waking up to what he thought was gunfire, he found himself thinking about implementing the action plan he had come up with if his compound came under attack. Phoning one of his colleagues who was also a good friend and who lived in the same apartment block at the time, they were able to joke about it a few minutes later.

Alan managed to secure visit visas for his parents to come out and visit at the end of October, which took an incredible amount of effort and time as there was an unbelievable amount of paperwork which required to be undertaken on his part, numerous government offices to visit, form filling and signatures obtained in order to gain the necessary approvals. In addition, Alan required a letter of permission from his bank in Riyadh to take the car out of the country to Bahrain, as he was paying for it on finance. Without this paperwork, he would have found himself stopped at border control.

Alan's parents flew to Bahrain, and he drove and picked them up from there. Alan was particularly pleased that he had managed to accumulate sufficient air-miles from all his trips backwards and forwards to cover his parents' flights. We had taken the decision that it would be better for my elderly in-laws to fly to Bahrain, as queues at immigration in Riyadh can be very long indeed and all the stairs and escalators would have been difficult for them to manage, especially after a long journey. Given that it was Ramadan when they arrived, and that they were tired, they stayed in a hotel in Bahrain for the night, before the drive back to Riyadh the following day. Alan's parents were both glad the rear windows of the car were tinted so no-one could see in, which meant they could drink some water without being seen, as they found the dry heat made them excessively thirsty. I had bought Alan's Mum an *abaya* from the supermarket which thankfully fitted her and was fine for wearing in the car. I had to take the hem up on it once she arrived, so I was glad she hadn't had to wear it out and about before then, apart from her brief walk to a toilet from the car, when she nearly tripped over the bottom of it. However, Alan been holding her arm at the time.

Unfortunately I had not had the foresight (and neither had Alan), of warning her about an Arabic toilet. For anyone who has not heard about Arabic toilets at service stations, a first experience comes as somewhat of a shock, particularly for my mother in law who was in her seventies. Alan had never stopped at the side of the road to utilise the facilities before, so had no real idea what they were like, although he had presumed that the ladies would be better maintained than the men's. The fact that she walked straight in and out and decided then and there to decline the use of the facility, even though there was at least another couple of hours journey to our villa, gives as good an initial description as any.

The Arabic toilet my husband took his mother to basically consisted of a hole in the ground, and a watering can. There wasn't even any paper or pipework. At service stations such as this one there was no drainage, and the stench was unbearable. This made for a great conversation piece as an unforgettable first experience of Saudi Arabia for my mother-in-law and not one she was likely to forget in a hurry.

The toilets in the large shopping malls, the airport and hotels were to a much better standard, with some of them having toilets as we know them, with cisterns and seated pans. However, the standard toilet comprised of a ceramic tray at floor level, with a hole in the centre, and a showering mechanism on the wall. Where there are shower arms for these facilities, I have yet to encounter a dry floor, but if there is a seat, you will probably see footprints on it at either side. I must admit I only use the toilets if I absolutely have to when out and about, and those are the ones in the shopping centres and hotels. I would strongly advise not to go near any toilets around saalat, (unless you absolutely have to), as water seems to be sloshed everywhere during the ritual washing that takes place before prayers. It is important to know that you must never eat or shake hands with your left hand, or pass anything to anyone with your left hand, as this is the hand they use for washing afterwards and is considered unclean.

I spent months constantly moving the soap dispensers at the wash hand basins in our villa from left to right, as George kept moving them to the left. As we are all right handed, they are no good to us on the left, but it took a long time for him to stop moving them to the left, even after I had told him I wanted them on the right and for a while it felt like the battle of the soap dispensers. George would always fold the toilet rolls into neat triangles at the end too… I must admit it felt like being in a hotel at times when he was around.

It was important to Alan to let his parents see where we were living, and it was the trip of a lifetime for them both. They were quite happy just to spend time with us and the boys, mostly in the villa and on the compound. Alan's Mum came out with me on the shopping bus a couple of times, which was an adventure for her. We also took the bus to a coffee morning on another compound, which was far more luxurious than ours. There was a plant sale on, which was interesting to look round, as the plants were so different to those back home. There were lots of coloured grasses and cactus-like plants with beautiful colourful flowers or spiky ornamental plants, many like nothing I had seen before. There were also some flowers in pots. I bought a couple of heather coloured grasses, which I thought would look great outside our front door.

My in-laws had just celebrated their Golden Wedding Anniversary with the rest of the family in Scotland earlier in the month, and we were sad we hadn't been able to share it with them. Our Golden Wedding Anniversary present to them was a holiday in Riyadh. Alan's Dad celebrated his eightieth birthday with us while he was out, which was a special occasion in itself, but even more so, as he had successfully come through cancer a few years before. He kept telling us that he would never have thought in a million years that he would make his eightieth birthday, let alone share it with us in Riyadh. We purchased an ice cream cake from *Baskin Robbins*. Once it had defrosted sufficiently at room and fridge temperature by trial and error it was delicious.

There was a Halloween party on the compound in the clubhouse for all the children. Calum dressed up as batman and Andrew dressed up as La La, his favourite Teletubbie. I remember going to some lengths with a piece of wire coat hanger, a ball of Blu-tack, and a needle and thread to make sure La-La's antenna stayed upright and didn't keep falling over.

The children had fun at the Halloween party and Alan's Mum was asked to judge the fancy dress. She couldn't believe it when she realised that some of the Asian women were pointing out their own children or children they looked after as having the best costumes. They took the fancy dress competition extremely seriously. The cultural etiquette for fair play that we were used to was unfamiliar to them, which was an eye opener. Scores of children swarmed round the villa doors of the compound in large groups afterwards. I think they all got a bit of a shock when they were all made to sing, recite a poem or tell a joke, before I gave them anything at our door. I did persuade them all to do something though and a good night was had by all.

Although it was lovely to see Alan's Mum and Dad and to have them to stay with us for a month in Riyadh, it just highlighted to me how much I missed my own family and my previous life back home. Despite being genuinely happy to see them and spend time with them, I found it made me even more homesick than I already was. I tried not to let things show, and always found things to do to keep myself occupied, to try and keep my mind off how I was feeling, but I did end up disappearing to the bedroom on several occasions when things had got to me, to have a good cry when no-one was about, which wasn't like me at all.

At this time an Egyptian paper reprinted the cartoons that had been published of the Prophet Mohammed by a Danish paper in September, and ambassadors from ten Islamic countries complained to the Danish Prime Minister about the cartoons. It caused a huge uproar at the time, as the Islamic prophets of God - Noah, Abraham, Moses, Jesus and Mohammed are to be respected and honoured in Islamic teachings, and to insult any prophet through any medium is a major sin, so the publication of the cartoons gave grave offence to Muslims round the world.

Calum returned home from school one day and called me a 'bint'. I was absolutely affronted and told him that that kind of language was unacceptable, and demanded to know where he had picked it up from. Keeping a straight face, he advised me that he had been taught it at school during his Arabic lesson and that 'bint' is Arabic for woman or girl and translates as 'daughter of'. Given my limited understanding of the word, I didn't believe him, but he was so adamant that he was telling the truth that I looked it up online, only to find that I was in the wrong. If anyone was to use that term at home, I would take it as slang to mean a young girl or woman with loose morals, or a sexist term for a stupid or naïve woman to put it politely. I learned that it is also a term widely used in the British armed forces as an alternative word for 'bird', and is used in the midlands as an affectionate word for young woman or girl.

Arabian women in *abayas* are occasionally referred to by some male expats under a number of derogatory slang names, including ninjas, Guinness bottles, oil slicks, bin liners and BMOs (black moving objects),which I took to refer to the shape and colour of their anonymous clothing worn in public, rather than anything personal. Whilst I was not particularly comfortable when in company whenever this kind of language was being used, goodness only knows what the Arabs called Western women in *abayas*. I am sure for Arabian women who have grown up in Saudi, adhering to the strict modesty of the veil and *abaya*, some of them must feel that Western women were exposing themselves when wearing what are to us ordinary clothes (and that would be clothing that we do not consider to be revealing).

We attended our first parents' night at school, which was informative on a whole series of levels, educationally and culturally. I was determined to make sure I had sufficient knowledge to bridge any gaps between the English and the Scottish curriculum. This was high on my agenda as I wanted to ensure that on Calum's return to school in Scotland he would be able to slot back in again without too much difficulty. I was also keen to find out what he was being taught within the Arabic lessons, which covered culture in addition to language.

Adjusting to a considerably larger school than the village school he was used to at home was challenging, but Calum seemed to be adjusting well, which was reassuring. To have gone from a composite class in a small village school with a school role of less than a hundred pupils to a school which provided education from nursery children to the age of sixteen was a big difference. In his year there were six classes of children, and the school was huge in comparison to what he had been accustomed to. In addition, although he had a class teacher and a classroom assistant, he had many other teachers too for subjects such as music, art, swimming, physical education and Arabic. I later learned that there are no music schools in Saudi and PE is not on the curriculum for girls attending national Saudi schools.

The facilities in the private school in Riyadh far surpassed what he had been used to in Scotland. The school had its own pool and swimming was part of the curriculum every week. Our child's teacher remarked on how independent our son was, and that he was particularly good at doing things for himself. I asked her what she meant, as I thought it was a strange thing to say. I had deliberately made a point of involving both boys in helping out with household tasks and doing things for themselves, as and when they were ready. In Scotland, I hadn't considered our children to be any more independent than others their own age. She put what she had told us in context when we were made aware of the fact that most children attending the school have nannies or maids who cater for their every whim, and that included many of the expat community. Providing us with just one example from school life, that for many children, when they come out of the swimming pool, they actually expected the teachers to towel them dry and dress them clarified what she meant. She described the scene that the teachers have to deal with after swimming lessons at the lower half of the school at the start of a term as wet children standing with their arms and legs wide apart, waiting and expecting assistance from their teachers to be dried and dressed, then and there. The children have a very quick lesson to learn and are all expected to dry and dress themselves if they haven't previously done so.

Despite the fantastic facilities at the private school Calum attended in Riyadh, he retained a special fondness for his primary school back home. Whenever something was done differently at school in Riyadh, he would always say, "That isn't the way it is done in our primary school in Scotland," and I am sure the teachers must have wished he would stop saying it, as he said it so often.

CHAPTER 5

Countdown to Christmas

At the start of December we started marking off the days on the calendar until we were due to fly home. Never previously having been away for more than a few weeks on holiday, we were looking forward to getting back, and the prospect of seeing friends and family was exciting. Time seemed to have gone by both slowly and quickly simultaneously since we had arrived in Riyadh in August.

I couldn't believe it when we woke up to frost on the third of December. Until the heating system came on automatically I hadn't even noticed we had heating in our villa previously. It hadn't been used in a while as the kerosene smell from the oil-fired heating system permeated strongly throughout the villa for the first few days after it rumbled into action, but at least it was in working order.

Alan had not warned me that it would get cold, and I was extremely miffed to have to go and purchase clothes for cold weather in Riyadh (which was a task in itself, finding some) when we had left a more than ample supply in Scotland. It didn't seem right to be wearing fleeces and jumpers, but by the beginning of December, the temperature had dropped substantially both during the day and at night. I had noticed that many of the Asian expat workers had been wearing woolly hats, jumpers and scarves since the end of October, when we started wearing long-sleeved shirts and trousers in the evening, so they must have felt the change in the temperature. By the time we turned the heating on they had started wearing gloves too.

On my hunt for winter clothing for us all, I persuaded Alan to take us to Kingdom Shopping Mall, as there was a *Marks and Spencer's* there which I hoped would have something suitable for all of us without having to trail round lots of different shops. Alan and the boys were looking at men's and boy's clothes, so I decided to look at women's clothes on my own in the shop, a short distance away from them.

A Pakistani store security guard I hadn't seen before started following me round, a bit too closely for comfort, trying to engage me in small talk, telling me how I reminded him of his sister. I had been in *Marks and Spencer's* on many occasions before with other women and had never had any problems before browsing on my own. As I made my way briskly towards my husband and children, the security guard was still attempting to engage me in conversation, following my every step, making me even more uncomfortable by the second - he was still at it when I promptly introduced him to my husband and children. Clearly he didn't understand, or didn't want to comprehend what I was saying, whilst Alan initially found the whole situation hilarious. I only just managed to persuade him not to make a scene, purely because we had the boys with us, but we didn't purchase our winter woollies we had gone in for, and promptly left the store empty-handed.

We walked down the mall a little way, and I turned my head, only to immediately look straight ahead again, not believing what I had glimpsed behind me. The security guard was still following us down the shopping mall, albeit that now he was a few paces behind us. Having advised Alan that he had followed us out of the shop, and was still behind us, my husband promptly told us to keep looking to the front and not look back. Alan then turned round and gave him an extremely long, hard stare. He told me afterwards that it was his Glaswegian 'don't mess with me' stare. We all walked to the lifts to the car park without turning back round. When I returned the following week on my own, having taken the shopping bus, I was somewhat relieved to find the security guard was nowhere to be seen, and I finally purchased our winter clothing without any hassle whatsoever.

Lifts in Riyadh came in many guises. In shopping centres and shops, sometimes they were staffed by staff inside the lifts, sometimes they were staffed by staff outside the lifts, sometimes they were for women only, and some lifts had no personnel supervising them. There were lifts that were encased in glass, enabling a clear view to all outside, there were lifts that were partially enclosed and there were lifts that were totally enclosed. Whilst out and about with my husband and the boys, Alan would always give me a sneaky kiss or grab my hand for a few seconds if it was only us or us and the boys in a lift where no-one could see in. On one occasion, the lift doors opened quicker than anticipated and there was an Arabic couple outside waiting to get in who gave us a knowing smile at our flustered embarrassment before they joined us. I wondered how many other couples had done the same and how many of the lifts we had been in had hidden cameras. Alan told me that one of the first pieces of advice he had been given was that while he was out in Riyadh he was to never get into an elevator on his own, even if there was no-one inside. There were several reasons for this, but the main reason was that doing so could potentially land him in all kinds of trouble. If he was seen in the company of a female national (due to the local segregation laws) and if a Saudi woman or any other woman for that matter was to join him on another floor he would be seen as doing wrong, being alone in a lift with a woman who was not his wife. This way of thinking on this cultural issue was beyond my Western comprehension, but it made sense for Alan to conform without question for his own good.

Saudi ways were so different from back home at times that it was not unusual to find yourself caught off-guard. I had heard that Riyadh's zoo was worth a visit, so decided to find out more. The women I knew that had gone had enjoyed the landscaping and huge grassed areas where their children could run about and advised that there were lots of animals to see and that they seemed to be kept well. After asking more questions, I ascertained that women and children could visit, or men and children on different days, but a whole family couldn't go together because of the segregation laws. Due to the opening times, I would have only been able to go with both boys at the weekend, and Alan would have had to drive us all the way there and drop us off, only to drive back again to pick us up later, so we decided to give it a miss. After years of being apart, weekend time was family time which was precious to us, so as far as we were concerned there was no decision to take as to who would go and who wouldn't. It just wasn't up for debate.

The traffic police conducted a massive campaign to clamp down on speeding motorists at the beginning of December. The maximum speed limit in Riyadh is 120 km/hr. A company notice was issued to advise that financial and jail sentences were now to be issued as speeding penalties, making it very clear that individuals were responsible for their own actions and that company traffic brokers would not be able to assist in an employee's release from jail or trips home for Christmas, if a fine was left unpaid. Non-payment of debt is a crime under Sharia Law and sufficient reason for imprisonment. Some friends had told me of situations where their husbands had found themselves having to pay fines at the airport before being allowed to fly out of the country, but they were the lucky ones who still managed to get away. For those unlucky enough to find out that they had committed traffic offences when they reached passport control at the airport, they are only able to pay them at the airport during Saudi office hours. It therefore makes sense to check whether you have any outstanding motor fines due a few days before planning to leave the country, otherwise you may find that you may not be allowed to leave.

Nightlife as we know it after sunset prayer does not exist in Saudi Arabia. Evening entertainment is what you make of it, as there are no public cinemas or bars, nightclubs or discos. For expatriates, typical evenings out are spent walking in the cool evening air, savouring a meal out, having a barbeque with friends, or attending a party or event on one of the compounds. There are many events at the embassies, but entry is by invitation only if you mix in the right circles. Shops, malls and souqs are open till around eleven at night, but you have to bear in mind that prayer-time will cause inevitable disruption to your activities, unless carefully planned. Coffee houses and shisha bars on the outskirts of Riyadh are for men only, and engaging in lengthy conversations until the early hours is a popular pastime amongst the locals. The largest and most well-known is Al Shallal, which has indoor and outdoor spaces for socialising with Middle Eastern snacks, tea and the traditional shisha water-pipe.

Alan took me out for an Italian meal at the Sheraton Hotel, which was the first night out together we had had in a long time. One of the maids of a family on the compound I knew well (as she spent time at the play-park with the children she looked after when I was there with my boys) had been available to look after our two, so we decided to take advantage of this and have an evening out. In the traffic, by the time we reached the restaurant and savoured our meal, it was time to go home again. The next day it transpired that Calum had spent most of his evening learning to recognise, write and speak the letters of the Arabic alphabet, as he had asked the maid to write the Arabic alphabet down, together with the sounds underneath. This bit of paper became well used in a short period of time. It was educational to learn a different alphabet, with some slightly different sounds, and not so many letters. This was to become a challenge at a later date when Calum had to write his name in Arabic for school homework, and there wasn't a corresponding letter. However, we managed to work it out phonetically after a bit of head scratching.

It had taken me a while before I felt comfortable leaving the boys with someone else in the villa in the compound. Although I knew the maid well, and knew she was quite capable of looking after the boys and would do so until whenever we got back, we were in another country a long way from home, in a part of the world where terrorism was a perceived real threat.

There were a couple of women on the compound I knew of who only went out with their husbands and children because of this, as they felt they had to be there for their children at all times, and never let them out of their sight apart from when they were at school or nursery. I must admit I had my doubts at the back of my mind when I was out with Alan, but everyone on the compound looked out for each other, and I knew that should anything untoward happen, the boys would be looked after. It was horrible to have such thoughts whizz round your head whilst attending a meal out, but I couldn't help it. We didn't venture out together without the boys very often, but when we did, I was always glad to find them tucked up in bed when we got home.

There are all kinds of restaurants in Riyadh, from fast food outlets to high class restaurants within hotels, which offer excellent worldwide cuisine catering for all tastes and pockets, take-away or sit-in. Middle Eastern food is served in shami restaurants, which usually have lamb and chicken spits on view, selling schwarmas, flat bread freshly squeezed juice cocktails (all non-alcoholic), an assortment of dips including hummus and mutabbal, meat samosas, spinach pastries and kibbeh, minced meat with pine kernels and stuffed vine leaves. Skewered meats are also available. Al Nakheel, housed within the Al Khozama Hotel was considered to be the best Arabian restaurant in Riyadh amongst those we knew. The influence of Western culture was particularly noticeable in the fast food industry, with numerous *Starbucks, McDonalds, Subway, Kentucky Fried Chicken, Dunkin Donuts, Cinnabon, Domino's* Pizza, *Baskin Robbins* outlets across the city, located in shopping malls and in some local shopping areas.

Saudis love to eat out, and there is ample opportunity to do so in shopping mall food courts, hotels, city centre and residential areas. However, like many other things in Saudi, eating out is an experience as it is done differently. Many budget priced restaurants only cater for men, and in a food court there are separate sections for men and families, and separate sides to order food from at each food establishment. Alan and I were never able to ascertain which side was which, and would usually end up at the wrong counter, unless there was a queue which solved the dilemma for you as you could tell by the single men standing at one side or the women or families at the other. Men eating alone, or with other men eat together in the men's section, while women and children and close male relations can eat together in the family section. Sometimes in a family section there are screens or curtains round each table, which can be drawn for privacy. In some restaurants there are individual rooms for families to have their meal, enabling veiled women to unveil while they eat in private, upholding and respecting cultural values and tradition.

The very first time I ate a takeaway in an open family area, I was astounded to watch fully veiled women consuming their food under their veils. This must have been an art in itself, and I couldn't help thinking about all the food covered veils that must, no doubt result from this, although the thought of walking round with a food covered veil afterwards would be enough to put me off a takeaway in the first place. I am a messy eater at the best of times and usually end up spilling something down my front whenever I go out for a meal, but at least I don't have to breathe in food smells from a veil afterwards.

Unmarried couples who socialise publicly by going out for a meal or shopping together are in breach of local moral laws. It was not uncommon while we were in Riyadh for the Muttawa to undertake spot checks at restaurants or supermarkets, and foreigners were not exempt. If caught in this situation foreigners were jailed or deported in addition to being lashed in public. There were stories in the papers of unlucky unmarried couples who had been caught (mostly Asian), and their fates told to set an example of them and to discourage such behaviour.

When visiting *IKEA*, we would usually time it to allow us to have a meal while we were there. We would close the curtains round our table for privacy before the boys tucked into their meatballs and chips. Alan and I would opt for a chicken or fish and rice dish, which was always full of Arabic spices and tasted delicious. I have never seen the same chicken and rice dishes in *IKEA* in Scotland, which is a pity.

Schwarmas are a Saudi speciality, and can be obtained from many local Arabic takeaway establishments. They consist of thin, flat, unleavened bread rolled into a wrap which contains chicken, onion, chips, lettuce and other ingredients and a choice of hot or spicy sauces, tomato and tahini or parsley depending on the shop you purchased it from. Indian curries were tasty, but bore little resemblance to those we knew at home, which are sweetened to meet Western tastes. We had to wait until our next visit home to eat pakora which is the staple starter at Indian restaurants in Scotland.

Alan and I managed to secure the child-minding services of another friend's maid one Thursday (the equivalent of our Saturday), and we went to Al Mamlaka, or Kingdom Tower as we often called it. I had been to the shopping mall several times before on the shopping bus, which was three stories high, with the top storey offering shops staffed by women with access to women only. Ladies Kingdom had over forty stores, ranging from a women's bank, maternity, lingerie, *abaya*, beauty, fashion, jewellery, perfume coffee shops and a mosque. However I had still to experience walking over the sky bridge.

Alan drove us through the security checkpoints and parked in the underground car park. From there we took one of the lifts to the shopping mall and made our way to the hotel and business area of the building towards the elevators for the upper floors. There was even more security to walk through, and my bag was scanned through an X-ray machine. There was a scale model of the building in the central hall which led to the lift, and everywhere we looked seemed to reflect the unique image and shape of the tower, from the lights, ceiling panels, and waste-bins to the engravings on the front of the lift doors. In plan form, the building resembles an eye, and comprises a three floor shopping mall, state of the art offices, a business centre, luxurious residential apartments and the five-star Four Seasons Hotel, for which there is a separate swanky entrance externally where you can leave your car and have it parked for you.

We entered the first dark, fibre-optic, twinkling, star-lit lift, which transported us up to the transfer level for the tower which took fifty seconds, leaving our feet on the ground floor and our bodies somewhere in mid-air, and got out to walk to the second elevator which took forty seconds to take us up to the sky bridge on the ninety-ninth floor. We were told by the lift operator that the lift travels at the speed of one hundred and eighty kilometres an hour, so it was no wonder the lifts had left us feeling as though we had been silently and smoothly blasted into space. The building won the 2002 Emporis Skyscraper Award and measures three hundred and two metres and thirty centimetres to its highest point. We had gone at dusk, and found ourselves looking down at a view of the numerous air conditioning plants on the mostly flat roofed buildings around us, taking in the block plan layout of the city. We had timed it perfectly and as it became dark, the views of the city, the roads and the traffic from such a height were an amazing blur of neon lights, forming two moving lines, some stationary and some moving at different speeds on the two main roads either side of us.

The experience of walking over the fifty-six metre long bridge was out of this world with the curved walkway underfoot particularly steep as we made our way onto the bridge. At two hundred and ninety metres and forty centimetres to its highest point from ground level the panoramic views across the city through the toughened glazed panels were unforgettable and breath-taking. Leaning over the hand-rail had to be done to gain the heightened thrill of the experience. Although I did so, I did not choose to lean backwards, as a few of the others on the bridge were doing at the time. Some Arabs were taking pictures of themselves on the bridge, and there was an official photographer there who took our picture for a fee. The photographer had lined up his tripod so that pictures taken on the Kingdom Centre's Sky Bridge showed the Al Faisalia Tower, or the Globe, as it is more commonly referred to in the background, which is the other main landmark in the city. They lie on the same axis, between the two main thoroughfare roads in the central part of town. Kingdom Tower, or Al

Mamlaka is strategically centrally located at the crossroads of King Fahad Expressway, Olaya Road and Orouba Road.

Al Mamlaka, I am reliably informed was designed to appear like a woman's veil. However, in a country where alcohol is strictly off limits, it has ironically been nicknamed 'the bottle opener' by expats due to its shape. I couldn't help but wonder whether those responsible for its design concept were aware of this. During the day its external glass skin reflects its surroundings, which due to its height depends upon the weather, reflecting the sun and clouds. The tower is lit up externally at night and goes through an awesome series of gradual colour changes - purple, blue, green, yellow, white, orange and red. When the offices within it are occupied, they are lit up around the central gap at the uppermost part of the tower. It was the tallest building in Saudi Arabia when we were out, but will be superseded by the new Kingdom Tower in Jeddah which is currently under construction.

We walked round the shop and bought some expensive postcards of Al Mamlaka (it was a rarity to find postcards in Riyadh), before stepping into the upper lift to take us back down to the sixty-seventh floor. Alan had booked a table for us at Spazzios which is located on the sixty-seventh floor of Kingdom Tower, and our meal out was a complete treat. I was even allowed to remove my *abaya* and it felt like a proper meal out. Alan ordered us a pitcher of Saudi champagne, and we made our choices from an incredible fine dining menu. When the champagne arrived it had chopped up apples and assorted fruit in it and tasted absolutely divine with our starter, but unlike any champagne I had ever tasted before. Eating out in such an exclusive restaurant, it was only when our main course was served that I remembered that where we were alcohol is illegal. My taste buds told me that the Saudi champagne I was drinking contained apple juice and fizzy soda or mineral water but to be truthful, up until I realised what I was drinking was not alcoholic, my mind had unconsciously tricked me and made the assumption that it was, due to the opulence of our surroundings and the fact that there were no *abayas* in sight.

Although alcohol is strictly illegal in Saudi Arabia, it is available. The penalties for being caught in possession of it are jail, flogging and deportation. However smuggling alcohol into the country or distilling alcohol carry even more serious punishments. Expats in Saudi each have differing views on the subject, some choosing to abstain out of respect for local beliefs or the law. A few expats made their own wine or brewed their own beer for their own personal use and some sold it to fellow expats. I have to admit that the majority of wine available that I came across was absolutely disgusting, but if you were lucky you could find someone whose home brew was palatable with a meal or tasted better when diluted with sprite or diet 7-Up.

One of the expats on our compound brewed his own red wine, and unfortunately one day it exploded without warning all over their villa. He had to get the maintenance men on the compound to repaint two of his rooms, so his profits must have been somewhat reduced, as I'm sure they would have been charged well over the odds for the re-painting required on that occasion.

Sid is a locally distilled clear spirit, which is short for *siddiqui* in Arabic, which translates as 'my friend'. Un-cut sid requires to be diluted with one to two parts water and is absolutely lethal. There were numerous cases of alcohol poisoning and deaths which had occurred from drinking un-cut sid, as it is so powerful when concentrated it is impossible to tell the difference just from looking at it. Sid is drunk with coke or tonic as a mixer, but smelt to me like methylated spirits or turpentine, and as I do not like vodka anyway, it wasn't to my taste at all. Bottles of original spirits are available on the black market at incredibly inflated prices, but the penalties of being caught in possession of it deter most. Clearly drink driving is unacceptable and not advisable, but whilst in Saudi even more so. It did get me thinking about what happens if anyone is caught driving while under the influence of drink, in a country where drink is illegal, and whether in an officially dry country what laws exist to deal with this situation.

Whenever items were reduced in large sales in the bigger retail chain stores the malls were mobbed. Everything was substantially reduced in price and there were plenty of bargains to be found, at much reduced prices from in the UK. However, it was only worth going at the very beginning of the sales period, as the shelves would be cleared out in no time. It wasn't uncommon to see groups of *abaya*-clad Arabian women loading up their trolleys with everything they possibly could cram in as quickly as possible, emptying whole shelves as they went. When I saw this with my own eyes, it reminded me of the jumble sales I used to help out at as a child, and how some women would try and clear clothing straight off the tables and into the black bin bags they were carrying. I knew some Western women who were sale experts, and would always know when the sales were on. They would identify the clothing, house-ware or furniture they wanted to purchase beforehand, and would go to the sales with a list of the items they intended to buy together with a rough guide as to their locations within the shop. What was more, they seemed to be able to manage to buy what they had gone in for.

Although it was December, and the countdown to going home for Christmas had started, it didn't feel like it. There was no run-up to Christmas in the shops (of course there were no Christmas items in the shops and no decorations or Christmas trees, carols or Santa's Grottos in the malls) and it did not feel like December, even though the weather had turned cold by Riyadh standards. Feeling like I should get into the Christmas spirit, I started making homemade snowflake glittery Christmas cards with the boys for friends on the compound, having found some glitter in *Jarir's Bookstore*. I then had a flash of inspiration and embarked on making a wreath for our front door out of washing line rope, a wire clothes hanger and some tinsel which I had found tucked away in the corner of the shop on the compound (no, I had not been watching Blue Peter in Riyadh and I had no sticky back plastic). I was determined that even though it didn't feel like it was nearly Christmas, we would put some Xmas decorations up in the villa.

I ventured out on the shopping bus to a couple of coffee-mornings on other compounds where there were items for sale. There was a mixture of stalls, from sweets, bread, *abayas*, accessories, jewellery, artwork and crafts. In amongst the stalls there were some beautiful homemade Christmas decorations and goodies - felt stockings, Santas and decorations and treats. The bread was a feast, as I hadn't managed to find bread that resembled the wholemeal sunflower or crusty bread I would buy from our local bakery at home anywhere. It wasn't as good, but being French bread, it was delicious and tasted amazing due to the fact that I hadn't tasted proper bread like it in months. There was even tinsel on sale, and some Christmas cards, but I didn't see any Christmas trees.

By this time I felt more in the Christmas spirit and made the decision then and there that we would have a Christmas tree in the villa somehow. The hunt for a Christmas tree was far from easy. A tinsel tree seemed to magically appear, fully decorated in the clubhouse, and some expats managed to bring Christmas trees over in their luggage without them being confiscated. I had set myself more of a challenge than I had originally thought... and looked everywhere I could think of to no avail for the next ten days. I eventually made a small three dimensional Christmas tree out of two sheets of cardboard slotted together, and although we had painted it green and covered it in glitter it just wasn't quite right. It looked awful.

Undertaking our food shop at the supermarket, there were no chocolate Santas, mince pies or Christmas trees, Christmas cards or even tinsel, but we had been busy making Christmas cards and decorations that week and it was beginning to feel a bit more like the run-up to Christmas. I will never forget starting to load the shopping from the trolley onto the conveyor belt when Calum started singing, "When Santa got stuck up the chimney." I discretely told him that perhaps it was not the best thing to sing in public with Saudis all round us in a country where any other religion than Islam is prohibited. He was quiet for a couple of minutes and then he started singing, "We wish you a Merry Christmas" rather too loudly.

There was an Arab family right next to us in the queue behind us, starting to load up their shopping who were definitely close enough to hear every word. With Arabs queuing at the checkouts on either side of us, and not another Westerner in sight, I told him in no uncertain terms that he had to stop singing now, as some people might find it offensive, and we could get into serious trouble if he continued. Thankfully he did stop, but then he started humming the tune, and he started to ask some very difficult questions rather loudly, about why it was unfair that he couldn't sing Christmas carols and songs if he felt like it.

I felt awful in the first place having to tell him to stop, but I felt even worse telling him he was to be quiet and that we would talk about it at a more appropriate time. Having to explain to a child of nearly six in terms he can understand, why he cannot sing Christmas carols and songs while out and about in public in Riyadh in December and getting him to comprehend the importance of this was far from easy.

There was a bazaar on the compound next to ours at the weekend, and I went with the boys. There were camel rides, and lots of local crafts on sale and the usual stalls, but no Christmas trees to be seen. Being thirsty and having run out of water I decided to go to the compound shop to buy some, as although there were plenty of things to drink at the bazaar, it was water I needed to quench my thirst.

When I got to the shop, I walked past, and did a did a double-take as there in the window (the last place I would have expected to see one) was a pathetic looking, bent and straggly fake Christmas tree with no decorations, hidden away in the corner. The compound shop wasn't too busy and I walked round every aisle scouring the shelves looking for Christmas trees. There were none to be found. Going up to the till to pay for the bottles of water I had originally gone in for, I asked the shop-keeper about the Christmas tree in the window and whether it was for sale. A few minutes later, I left the shop, having paid rather more than I should have done for my bottles of water and the little bedraggled Christmas tree, which was now hidden away completely in rolls of bin-bags under my arm. Nevertheless, I had a rather big smile on my face on my way back to our compound in the car. Mission accomplished.

When we got back from the bazaar, the boys and I spent ages cutting out white paper snowflakes and covering them in glue and glitter. I had fixed the tree so it was no longer lopsided and spent some time adjusting the branches so it looked much better. By the end of the day we were all covered in glitter ourselves, and had put up the Christmas tree in the villa (we put it on top of a coffee-table to make it look bigger than it was), covered it in homemade decorations, and were feeling more festive. I had never before considered a Christmas tree to be such an important part of the run-up to Christmas.

As we were due to arrive home on 23 December, I undertook an online grocery shop and booked a slot. We had the whole family descending on us over Christmas, which I was looking forward to, and I was doing the cooking. It was going to be great, catching up with everyone and having them all over together. I found myself taking immense pleasure in adding things to my online shopping list that I couldn't purchase in Saudi - mince pies (even though I wasn't partial to them), chocolate Santas for the boys, marmite, pork sausages, pork stuffing (when I would usually make chestnut), bacon, and a gammon joint. I even found myself adding bottles of red, white and rosé wines to my order, almost tasting them in my head as I did so. I rarely drink, but do enjoy good wine when I do, and I had gone for nearly five months without having tasted any decent wine.

I couldn't help chuckling to myself as I placed the order online, thinking about the bizarreness of what I was doing - I was ordering things that were illegal, or we couldn't purchase in Riyadh, whilst in Riyadh, only to be able to appreciate them all the more when we got home. It was surreal. I hoped that all the items on the list would be available, as the last thing I wanted was to have to go near the shops at home as soon as we got back - the priority would have to be putting up another Christmas tree and the decorations at home in Scotland on Christmas Eve.

In the Kingdom Shopping Centre, there are a couple of amazing shops which sell Arabic biscuits, sweets and dates. I paid one of them a visit, as they had the most exquisite fabric and bead boxes that when filled made wonderful Arabic gifts to take back, even though they were rather expensive. I had them filled with dates - it was difficult to choose from the vast selection of stuffed dates available - lemon, lime, orange, almond, hazelnut, pistachio to name a few, but take it from me, they are all sticky, sweet and a treat. Dates here are far tastier than the little box of dates that would traditionally appear on the table to end a celebratory meal at home. In one of the souqs I had already bought some pretty wooden boxes, decorated in Islamic patterns with different coloured wood and mother of pearl inlay strips. I also had bought some mini prayer mats which made perfect coasters.

Walking round the shopping mall, there was always one shop which sold very expensive Arabic perfume, which one of its sales assistants would try (unsuccessfully) to get me to sample on my way past. It wasn't that I didn't like it, as slight wafts of it were pleasant, but for me it was too strong to consider wearing. In any case, it was far too expensive. In Saudi, men are encouraged to wear scent, however women are required to be a bit more discreet, as they would not wish to be seen as trying to attract members of the opposite sex. Many Saudi perfumes have an oud base, which is a strong and unique scent. The oil can be dabbed on hair, wrists or neck, and the incense is frequently used to perfume clothes. Oud comes from a fungus on Aquilaria trees, and is available as chips or oil. Chips are lit and burned as an incense and the oil is used as a perfume (note no alcohol) for women, which can linger in a space for a long time after its wearer has left. Oud is incredibly expensive and if you are a special guest or at a special function, then it will be burned, and the burner passed round between guests, wafting its scented smoke from person to person.

I made last-minute online present orders for close family, as I wouldn't have time to think about or shop for presents when we got home. Thankfully I had been organised before we left in the summer, and had already written Christmas cards and bought a few presents in July and given them to my Mum to post in December. I had also bought the boys' Christmas presents five months in advance and wrapped them so they would be waiting for us when we got home. I couldn't even remember what I had bought for them now and just hoped that in the five months since I had chosen them, they would still be suitable. The few friends I had shared this information with back in July, had looked at me as if I had finally lost it when I had told them I was writing Christmas cards and buying and wrapping Christmas presents in the summer. It seemed absolute madness at the time, but I was very glad I had been so organised and forward thinking, as it was one less thing to do once we got home. My project management skills were still coming in useful, albeit in an entirely different area and manner than that which I had received training in.

Riyadh in particular is developing rapidly, and the hotel industry taking off. Traditionally, Saudi hotels only catered for tourism centred round the pilgrimage to Mecca. Business demands in the capital were expanding to cope with training, seminars, conferences and providing for the needs of business travellers from all over the world. There are many well-known hotels in Riyadh which include the Al Faisaliah Hotel, the Olaya Holiday Inn, the Four Seasons Hotel in the Kingdom Centre, the Radisson Hotel, the Intercontinental, the Sheraton and the Golden Tulip.

All of the hotels we visited had airport style security in place which we had to go through in order to gain entry. The buildings themselves were cordoned off with huge rows of concrete bollards round their perimeter, joined together to form an impenetrable barrier to vehicular attack. If parking in their car parks, it was necessary to drive and navigate through manned roadblocks and security checkpoints before being allowed access. While we were there, women would require to be accompanied by their husbands or guardians if staying in hotels. In addition, local segregation traditions meant that although most of the well-known hotels had swimming pools and gyms, many did not provide access to these facilities for women, whilst others had specific times for ladies only, or completely separate facilities for women altogether.

All of the hotels have fantastic restaurants within them, with exceptional worldwide cuisine available in pleasant surroundings. Some of them permit women diners to enjoy their meal in areas where you are allowed to remove your *abaya*, which when out for a special occasion can make a huge difference. To be able to go out for a meal without being covered up was a treat. Some of the hotels have individual rooms, where a party of you can be seated and eat, or curtained off table areas, or even restaurant areas designed in such a way as to allow privacy for each table. In some hotels the set-up is more what we are used to in the West, and occasionally you may be allowed to remove your *abaya*, but you are advised to keep it right next to you in case you have to suddenly cover up if the Muttawa make an appearance. It is commonplace for the religious police to carry out spot checks on couples dining out, or groups of men and women out for a meal, as it is only acceptable for married couples to eat a meal together or a woman to dine out with her guardian or close male relatives in public. Should a man and woman be caught out for a meal (romantic or otherwise) and they do not have proof on them that they are married, the consequences can be extremely serious. Yet another reason to ensure I carried my iquama and my company identity card with me at all times.

I went out with Alan, his work colleagues and their wives for a Teppanyaki at the Radisson Hotel, which was a treat. The food was cooked for us by a chef who tossed, turned and juggled the ingredients and sauces right in front of our eyes whilst the tantalising smells wafted over to us while they were being cooked. Sizzling clams, oyster, chicken, beef and differing accompanying sauces brought out taste-buds I didn't even know I possessed to make it a memorable evening. I knew several of those round the table already, so it was an enjoyable night, and a chance to meet some of Alan's colleagues I had heard about previously but not met, together with their wives. It actually made a change being out in adult company, but I found it strange and somewhat stilted with the majority of the conversation revolving round our husbands' work. I found I missed talking about my previous professional life's day to day accomplishments and frustrations, and it really brought it home to me that my life had been totally centred round the children since I had arrived in Saudi.

On the last day of school before breaking up for Christmas, Calum returned with a chocolate Santa from the bus monitors, women who accompanied the children to and from school on the bus every day. It emerged that they visit Bahrain for the weekend to do their Christmas shopping every year, and on their list were chocolate Santas for all the children on the buses. The chocolate Santas were much appreciated, but I am sure the children had absolutely no idea of the efforts that had been involved in getting them.

We checked our baggage in at King Khalid Airport (an experience in itself of being in the midst of hundreds upon hundreds of bodies, mostly Asian, many giving off odours of strong Arabic scent or perfume, spices, sweat, or food, endlessly queuing in a small confined area, where many do not queue, but simply barge in). Having put our hand baggage through the X-ray machine, I found to my horror that I was being asked to step to the side, and go into a separate curtained off area. I waited till Alan was through, so he could take the boys, and proceeded through this black curtained area, not knowing what on earth to expect. I followed the passageway between the black curtains through until it stopped at a black curtain, which barred my way. I said, "Hello" cautiously two times, but there was no reply, so I decided to proceed through the black curtained door which led to another passageway and a small room. There was an Arabic woman standing there, in *abaya* and veil, who nodded to me, and proceeded to sign to me to stand with my arms and legs spread open. She then checked me over, made a clicking of her teeth, gave me a nod and a grunt, and pointed to another black curtained door, which took me out to an area just past the X-ray scanning machines where Alan and the boys were standing waiting for me. I grabbed my hand luggage and joined them. (Thinking about it now, every single time I left Riyadh, I had to go through this curtained - off area, sometimes on my own, and from time to time with the children. Usually the woman on duty was veiled and I could only see her eyes, but I can recall one occasion when the woman undertaking the security check was not wearing a veil).

Knowing what was in front of us, as we had been forewarned in terms of what a wait at the airport in Riyadh entailed, I had made sure the boys packed things in their small rucksacks to keep them busy. There was absolutely nothing to do apart from watch the planes, look at the water fountains changing colour, grab something to drink and avoid using the facilities if at all possible.

King Khalid Airport was completed in 1983 and has four main passenger terminals and a royal pavilion. Its central mosque is hexagonal in plan, covered by a large dome. I noted that the mosque only had one minaret which stood out, as a mosque would normally have two. The structure of the airport was triangular and hexagonal, with curved triangular roof panels supported on steel archways, braced by more triangles, containing window panels within. Looking closely, everything was reduced to triangular shapes and patterns, even down to the pattern on the carpet and the triangulated ceiling, but the colour-scheme was overly brown which concealed much of the amazing building structure which I was enthralled in.

Thankfully, as the airport was full of expats leaving Riyadh and returning elsewhere for Christmas, there were several families we knew who were boarding the same flight as us, before changing planes for their holiday destinations, or going back to the UK, so the boys had some friends to keep them occupied while we were waiting. This made an immense difference (especially given the fact that our flight had been delayed), in terms of passing the time at the airport. It seemed strange to be getting the same plane as many of the teachers from our sons' school, mostly who were also going home to celebrate Christmas with their families in the UK. We then boarded our Saudair plane bound for Dubai, with the aim of grabbing a few hours kip at the airport hotel in Dubai if we were lucky, followed by an early rise to get the plane home.

.

CHAPTER 6

Sandstorms and Rain (January '06)

We returned to Riyadh in January, with much lighter suitcases than we had left with in December, as we had very little to bring back out with us. I had made sure I purchased several boxes of tampons while back home, as there didn't seem to be any in the supermarkets in Riyadh. There was no way I had even contemplated explaining what I was looking for to any of the male pharmacists in any of the chemists in Riyadh, as stocking up on necessary medicine remedies and antiseptic cream had been a task in itself. Making the pharmacist understand exactly what you were looking for, when most medicines came in unfamiliar packaging and Arabic writing was a bit daunting, especially as more-often than not, equivalent items did not appear to be sold in Saudi. However as we went through customs, I found myself hoping that we didn't get stopped, as knowing my luck tampons could be banned, and the idea of explaining myself over a few boxes of them to male Saudi customs officers, or female ones at that was far from appealing.

I had given Alan our passports, and the boys and I were standing right behind him at the passport desk. We had made our way to passport control as soon as we were off the plane, to avoid the long queues. The Arab checking the passports signalled for Alan and the boys to go through, but started making gestures to me to go in another direction. Two officials appeared from nowhere, and it was all that I could do to make sure Alan knew that I was being separated from him, and to make him aware of the fact that I wasn't happy about it one little bit, as I had no idea what was going on.

One of the officials had my passport and was waving it about over his head, jabbering away excitedly and talking non-stop. I was ushered into an office, shown a seat and left there for at least fifteen minutes on my own. I found myself going through the contents of my suitcase in my head, wondering if I had packed something I shouldn't have done inadvertently and began to consider whether I should have left the tampons in Scotland. At this point, the same two officials came back in, handed me my passport, and signalled to me to go back out, with no explanation whatsoever. Alan and the boys were waiting for me, and to this day we have absolutely no idea what all that was about. Thankfully I had my husband there, who had been demanding to see me for the whole time I had been ushered away. I had felt extremely vulnerable sitting on my own, not having a clue as to why I had been separated from my family, and not being able to understand what was going on, or being said around me. I was certain that I hadn't packed anything that I shouldn't have done (apart from the tampons which on reflection I still wasn't sure about), or anything that would contravene the strict customs laws in Saudi. To go through a situation like that at the end of a long journey is not good for your nerves.

Returning to Riyadh after a wonderful - but what felt like a colder than usual - Christmas and New Year at home (even though it wasn't, having become acclimatised to higher temperatures), we were looking forward to better weather. It was much warmer than it had been in Scotland, but we were not prepared for weeks of rain and sandstorms on our return. When it rained in Riyadh, everything seemed to become filthy easily as the rain picks up the sand in the air which smelled foul at times, and I found myself longing for fresh clear air as we know it.

Outside the city centre, there didn't appear to be any surface water drainage, and large areas of Riyadh became covered in water which sometimes stretched over all the lanes on the road when it rained heavily. A must in this weather were 4x4s, as you could get stuck easily in a car. The water became a breeding ground for mosquitoes, and there had been several cases of Dengue fever reported recently in the *Arab News*. I certainly didn't like the sound of contracting that, as it was particularly nasty by all accounts.

Saudi drivers, not being used to driving in wet conditions, are terrified of driving through water, and will try and avoid doing so if at all possible. In these conditions vehicles swerved all over the road to avoid puddles - even driving in rain seemed to make them nervous at the wheel. Consequently, driving in wet conditions was a slow process and traffic congestion was to be expected at the first sign of rain. We soon became accustomed to seeing many cars taking shelter under an overpass as soon as it started to rain, which we found particularly comical when many were high spec off roaders,

4x4s or jeeps, particularly as driving in the rain in Scotland is such a regular occurrence.

The weather in Riyadh can literally change within minutes without any apparent warning. Sandstorms vary tremendously between a slight sandstorm, which doesn't stop you getting out and about as normal, to strong sandstorms, which you wouldn't even consider going outside or being caught out in the car in. Usually sandstorms signify a change in the weather following them. Apparently twice a year, the weather is more overcast and dusty than normal, for around one to two weeks at a time. The dust storms can occur as a result of the *shamal* - winds from the north-west, which can make visibility extremely difficult. This marks a change of the seasons, signifying the beginning and end of winter, with the rain often coming at this time too. I was told that the weather we had experienced was unusual, as the rain came before the dusty and overcast, sand-stormy weather.

The Saudis sensibly covered their faces in this weather, and the workers on our compound even wore masks. I found myself coughing only walking as far as the bus stop and back on the compound, five minutes from our villa, due to the dust in the air. At this time there were a lot of very nasty throat/ lung and chest infections going about. Although I am not a medical expert, I put it directly down to the air quality.

There was huge controversy when it emerged that Riyadh was hosting an international football match with Sweden, but that in accordance with Saudi segregation laws, women would not be allowed in the stadium to watch the match. There were protests in the Scandinavian country, one of the leading nations on gender equality worldwide. Saudi Arabia backed down at the last minute on this issue following intervention by Swedish diplomats, to allow those women who had come over with the team to watch in a specially segregated area. From what I understand, if the Kingdom hadn't backed down on this issue then the Swedish team would have refused to play and the matter would have made world news headlines. The match went ahead on 18 January, but the venue was changed at the last minute.

The Saudis are very much into their football, and it is a national pastime. In 1987, the King Fahd Football Stadium was completed, a unique circular structure with a tent-like roof which crowns it, supported from twenty-four columns in a circle. The two hundred and forty-seven metre diameter structure has a capacity of sixty-eight thousand and is also used for athletics. The Saudi Arabian National Football Team is known as 'Al Saquour' which translates as 'The Falcons' or 'The Eagles' and is also referred to as 'Al Achdar' which means 'the green'. The stadium was designed to meet international FIFA requirements by Ain Friezer and Partners. Riyadh hosts four main football clubs - Al Shabab, Al Nasr, Al Hilal and Al Riyadh.

I would continually find myself worked up over small things, which in themselves were usually of no great significance. I was finding it increasingly hard to adjust to living in Riyadh as an expat's wife in so many ways, as it meant I had no alternative but to be so reliant on Alan, in terms of money, driving and going out, and I didn't like the feeling that I no longer had the independence I had previously taken for granted in Scotland. I did not have a local bank account I could access and I wasn't working and earning money. Simple things I needed required to be justified so that a shopping trip could be planned, and absolutely everything took so much effort. To achieve or get anything done I had to be reliant on other people in one way or another, which I did not adapt well to. On one occasion when I ran out of the perfume I use, I became upset as I was unable to just pop out to the shops and buy some. It sounds ridiculous writing about it, but the fact that I was unable to just go out and do something for myself when I wanted was incredibly frustrating. After several shopping trips over a few weeks I was unable to find it in any of the recognisable Western stores in Riyadh that sell it in the UK. Although my perfume did contain alcohol, only a few select perfumes were on sale and unfortunately for me, mine wasn't among them.

Whilst I was struggling to deal with coming to terms with some of the cultural adjustments that were required of me, having gone from an independent life in Scotland to my life in Riyadh, I found things particularly hard. Life wasn't easy on Alan either, as he had become accustomed to living a relatively orderly life, without the constant demands, mess and haphazard ways of children and a wife living with him, so we were all having to adapt in different ways. We had spent so much time apart over the last few years that whilst we were happy to be together, we were finding that learning to live together as a family again was definitely not going to be easy. The hot weather made us all impatient and due to the differing stresses and strains we were under we would inevitably react at times.

Alan was used to living by himself with time to unwind when he had finished his working day and doing what he wanted when he wanted without demands from family. He went from having time that was his own to having very little time to himself, and in addition being responsible for most things outside the home. He also had to adjust to the routines of living a family life, whereas previously he had lived in bachelor accommodation and gone out with the guys whenever it suited him to do so. He was tired when he came back from work and his previous routine of a siesta or a quiet snooze by the side of the pool had been instantly knocked on the head as the boys were desperate for his attention as soon as he returned. The last thing he wanted when he came in was to have the children making demands and me telling him that I was desperate to get out of the compound as I'd been cooped up there all day, or that he had to drive us to the shops as there was something that we needed that wouldn't wait until the weekend.

Driving in Riyadh was especially stressful in the evenings as the roads were so chaotic and the driving so unpredictable. A trip out for Alan with us in the car would mean fighting his way through the traffic, keeping his wits about him, finding a safe parking space in the right area, attempting to reach our intended destination before prayer-time and thinking a couple of steps ahead the whole time. For him, this meant constant pressure he didn't need and a late night after having been at work all day and having such an early rise for work the next morning. We all found life difficult in different ways and I found that Alan would blow a fuse far more frequently than he used to. Living in Saudi with us definitely made him more impatient and irritated than he used to be at home.

During all the bad weather I embarked on making a scrapbook with Calum so he would have a record of things he had done and places he had been while living in Riyadh. I also started another scrapbook for Andrew, more than doubling the effort required on my part. It had taken a while, but I had finally succeeded in getting my youngest son into the routine of having a nap after lunch, once I had picked him up from nursery. If I was lucky, this meant Calum and I could have some quality time together, just the two of us when homework and piano practice was finished, and this was an ideal project for us to undertake.

Crosses are considered to be religious symbols in Saudi, and crucifixes are confiscated if discovered when going through customs. Calum had received a Scottish T-shirt for Christmas with 'Scotland' written on it and a St Andrews saltire cross. It was his favourite top, and he insisted on taking it back with us to Riyadh. He wore it on every single opportunity he could - school sports day, children's parties and when he wore a top over it he even managed to get past me and wear it when we left the compound. By the time we were out and about in Riyadh, the cardigan or top which concealed it would be off and it would only be when I noticed we were being stared at more than usual that I would realise why.

I had a long necklace, with a central 'x' engraved on the wooden pendant, which was strung on a thin brown leather cord that I had taken out to Riyadh, without thinking anything of it. I always wore it underneath my *abaya* when outside the compound. I had no idea that there could be so many perceived hidden meanings behind what I understood to be a cross, a simple addition or multiplication sign, the letter x, a necklace or a Scottish saltire until I read a lengthy article on the subject in the local paper. I heard a rumour that at one stage the Ministry for Promotion of Virtue and Prevention of Vice put forward an idea to replace addition and multiplication symbols throughout the Kingdom, but clearly it never came to anything and common sense prevailed. Certainly it would have been interesting to see what the consequences would have been for retail stores or businesses containing the letter x, as there are quite a few of them.

George held down two jobs, one for us as a house-boy, and another as a driver, driving some of the house-boys on our compound to and from their living quarters to work, and some additional driving with the company mini-bus he had. Alan had a brain-wave and managed to square things with George's boss so that he could also drive for us, providing it didn't conflict with his other job, which was fantastic news for me. It took a while for the paperwork to be sorted out, but it was well worth it - the difference that it made to my life and to Alan's as a direct result was huge. If Alan hadn't managed to obtain George's services for me as a driver in the mornings, I don't think I could have stayed in Saudi for much longer and would have returned home for good with the boys.

Alan told me years later that before allowing George to drive for us he told him that he was to look after us as if we were his family, he trusted him to be a good driver, but that the boys and I were far more important than the value of the car. It wasn't until years later that I found out that Alan took a lot of stick for allowing me to have access to a driver and his car while he was at work. This would mean that he would sign out a company pool car whenever he needed to get out and about for his work during the day, and put up with any comments that he got as a result. Alan knew what it meant to me to be able to get out of the compound and have a bit of freedom with a driver although he also liked having George to drive him about when it suited him too.

After my first journey in the car with George driving, it took another woman on the compound to advise me that only a husband and wife can travel in the front seats of a car together in Saudi, and I should travel in the rear passenger seats when my driver was driving the car and not my husband, if I didn't want to get into trouble in future. I was not privy to this information beforehand, and George would not have seen it as his place to tell me what to do. I hadn't previously given any thought whatsoever as to when I could and could not sit in the front of a car, depending on who was in the car with me. I hadn't even noticed that as a rule, women would sit in the back of the car when their driver was driving, and only sit in the front seat when their husband was driving.

As my youngest son had recently started a new nursery on a neighbouring compound, it worked out well that I had a driver to take us, so I no longer had to cadge a lift backwards and forwards from a couple of other families who had a driver, whose drivers drove their Filipino nannies and their children to the same nursery. There was a hairdressing salon and beauty clinic on this compound, so I was finally able to get my hair cut while Andrew was at nursery, and from time to time I would get a French manicure on my toenails for a treat. As my feet were always in sandals, my toes were permanently exposed, so I usually had painted toenails while in Riyadh.

George had been working in Saudi for over five years. He was an amazing person who worked all the hours he could to support his family in Sri Lanka. He paid for his two sisters' weddings while we were in Riyadh before finally being in a position to think about settling down himself. He was always optimistic and managed to see the positive side to everything, even when things were not going well for him or his family, and always had a broad smile on his face. He was entitled to a ticket home every two years, which was considered a good contract for someone in his position. The fact that we gave him additional work and responsibilities and additional money made a big difference to him. He always turned up for work on time and once turned up when he was really ill as he didn't want to let us down. I gave him the day off, told him to go to the company doctor and that I didn't want to see him until he was better as I wanted him to get better and I didn't want anyone to catch what he had. Unfortunately this was not the kind of behaviour he had been used to, and he was taken aback at my concern for his health and extremely grateful for time to recuperate. He only took two days off to recover from the fever he was suffering from, which was particularly nasty.

One Saturday morning, George looked tired. I asked him what he had got up to during his weekend. I was not prepared for the answer I received. He told me that he had gone shopping with a group of friends in Batha, in the old part of the city which houses numerous souqs. It was prayer-time and because they were not attending the local mosque to pray, him and his friends had found themselves at the mercy of the patrolling Muttawa and were rounded up and bundled into a van. They were taken to a local prison cell and locked up to teach them a lesson. From what George told me, this occurrence happens frequently in this part of the city, which is near the Muttawas' headquarters.

Batha forms part of the old centre of Riyadh, and is a maze of alleyways containing differing souq markets, frequented by most of the Asian community. There are many different shopping areas, but it is practically impossible not to get lost amidst the hustle-bustle and confusion of colourful souq life. The area is always mobbed with crowds of Asians and Arabs, and only a handful of Westerners.

There is an electronics area, known as the five buildings, a tent souq, where canvas products from bags to Bedouin tents can be purchased, and a spare parts souq where car parts are sold. In the tailoring area, tailors can copy any clothing item for a fraction of your original item's price. I had heard of a wonderful bead, button and fabric shop, and was thrilled when I managed to find it on my first visit. In another area you could purchase knocked off Rolex watches, which looked the part; in another, designer handbags. My husband told me of a road where you were able to buy pirate DVDs of DVDs prior to their release in cinemas in the UK. A friend of his would regularly obtain the latest films due for release, but very often they were poor quality and cinema copies that looked as though they originated from Russia and China. Nearby you could take your gaming console to be chipped to enable it to play the pirated most up to date games on sale. It seemed awkwardly contradictory to be in a country where due respect and adherence was required for local religious customs, laws and traditions, but at the same time there appeared to be little respect for international copyright. Parts of Batha were clearly a thriving industry in fake designer goods.

The junk souq has all manner of things for sale; there is also an antique souq, a clothes souq, and of course the gold souq. The gold souq comprised numerous gold jewellery shops displaying their wares behind glass shop-fronts inside a covered marketplace amidst a rabbit-warren of similar shops. Here it was possible to buy custom made pieces of jewellery for a fraction of the price in the UK and most expats would have jewellery made that they designed themselves, or was copied from a picture whilst they were in Saudi.

We went back a few days later, early on a Thursday morning when it was a bit quieter, and discovered that the two Thumari gates weren't far away. The original city had nine gates round its walls, before the wall was torn down in 1950 to expand the city. The original east entrance gate had been restored to its original state and a portion of the adjacent wall to the south had been re-built together with a tower on its right hand side. The gate signifies the entrance to the historical area of Qasr Al Holm District in the area south-west of Batha known as Dirrah. The newly built Thumari gate is over the road.

We walked round the famous 'chop-chop' or Justice square, which is also known as AsSufaad or Deira Square. Punishments are inflicted in front of on-looking crowds on a Friday after midday prayers. As I walked round the square I looked up at the famous clock tower, and came across a water fountain and an area where there were drainage channels set into the paved square. It dawned on me that it was highly likely that I was standing right where the public executions took place, and I found myself pondering over the stories of those who had been executed or punished. I wondered when the last execution took place and when the next one would, as contrary to popular belief, beheadings do not take place every Friday. Although standing there made me feel extremely uneasy, I could at least say that I had been there and seen the place with my own eyes. If I had visited the square with no prior knowledge, I would have left not knowing what goes on there, as there were no blood stains on the ground that I could see. Morbid as it was, I couldn't help but look rather closely.

Coming to terms with the fact that I was actually in a square where such extreme punishments are undertaken in this day and age made me feel distinctly queasy. For a country which is one of the fastest developing in the world, which sees itself as modern and forward thinking in many ways, its contrasting barbaric ways are questionable to many, especially Westerners. For anyone who risks undertaking criminal behaviour in Saudi, they do so whilst being fully aware of the possible consequences of their actions if caught and convicted - be it stoning, lashings, beheadings or the severing of limbs. What I fail to understand and find so disturbing is the entertainment and public spectacle factor in routinely going to watch convicted criminals suffer or to lose their lives. To me, just imagining it is upsetting. Westerners are strongly advised not to visit chop-chop square on a Friday after prayer as they would find themselves pushed to the front and made to observe the proceedings with an uninterrupted view. Whilst the severest punishments are not inflicted every week, there was no way I was going to risk becoming an onlooker of such practices.

Leaving chop-chop square and going back into Batha, there was a large area of ground off Batha'a Street which had no buildings on it, but was heaped with individual piles of stones. Thinking about it for a minute I realised that this must be oud cemetery, where King Fahad had been buried the summer before, in an unmarked grave in accordance with Saudi tradition, with no national mourning period or flags at half-mast.

Muslim burials take place before sunset on the day of the death, but if the death requires investigation by the authorities, or the identity of the deceased requires to be established, the burial takes place as soon as possible thereafter. When the burial order is issued the body is cleansed, perfumed and wrapped in white cloth. A surah or verse from the Quran is read and close male friends or family carry the bier. Graves are unmarked and are aligned to face the direction of Mecca. Women do not attend the burial.

After the burial, men and women from the bereaved family receive condolences separately for three days. A widow is socially isolated for four months and ten days to ensure she is not pregnant. If she is pregnant, then her period of mourning lasts until the birth of her child. Inheritance is dealt with under Islamic Law, and any debts are paid off straight away. Personal possessions belonging to the deceased are disposed of and not passed on, which is a very different approach to the way we tend to do things in the West.

I found out about two massive redevelopment projects in the Qasr Al Hokm district that had taken place to preserve the centre of old Riyadh - the Qasr Al Hokm project and the King Abdul Aziz Historical Centre, after having already walked round part of them. The aim of the plan was to preserve the old district and build new streets and pedestrian areas within newly landscaped urban areas. The project set Musmak Fort within a pedestrianized square and rebuilt the city's main mosque in its original location. The great mosque which has no domes had been orientated to indicate the direction of the kiblah on the skyline with its two square minarets, and its courtyards and open squares had been designed to permit them to be used as additional prayer areas at busy times. Justice Palace has also been rebuilt on its original site and has two covered walkways between Qasr Al Hokm and the mosque which marks the bridged route that the King would have traditionally taken over the souq below. Two of the city gates, one of which we had visited earlier, some of the wall and a watchtower had also been rebuilt as part of the project.

If I had been better informed at the time, I would have followed the path of early twentieth century guests arriving to meet the King, by going through the east Al Thumairi Gate to Musmak Square, with the fort to the right and Qasr Al Hokm right in front of me. This was one of the ideas behind the redevelopment, but unfortunately there was no information available on this when I walked round, so my route was different.

In January, unfortunately several other countries reprinted the cartoons of the Prophet Mohammed, sparking protests and violence in some Islamic countries. Huge offence had been caused, but the Saudi line was to condemn the violence elsewhere, and to focus on a more peaceful form of protest. The Saudi ambassador was recalled from Denmark, but it took until the end of the month for an apology to be released from the original paper that had published the cartoons.

Calum had made good friends with another boy in his class at school, and I received a note from his mum, asking me to give her a call to arrange for him to go and play one day after school. They lived on the same compound as the school our children attended. Not knowing her, and being where we were, I made arrangements to go along too. It was always good to make new friends and visit other compounds, and the boys played at each other's villas a few times. They were a lovely family from New Zealand, who had Scottish roots, but unfortunately, as was often the case here, they moved away from Saudi several months after we became friends. People and children are always arriving and leaving, which is life, but it was at a greater level than we were used to back home, and my eldest son in particular found it hard when friends would leave school for good with little or no notice, when their families were leaving Saudi.

The Caledonian Society in Riyadh hold an annual Burns supper, which my husband had attended in previous years, having taken his kilt out specifically. Unfortunately the tickets ran out before Alan could get his hands on any. I couldn't find any haggis or vegetarian haggis in the supermarket, so we didn't have a Burns supper at home either. I did, however, come across tinned haggis several months later and we had haggis and tatties then without neeps, as I was unable to source turnip.

With bird flu making headlines in the news, and large numbers of small birds on our compound, I became concerned when I noticed a few dead birds on the path at the side of our villa early one morning. Many of the birds would roost in the trees adjacent to our villa or on the roof. As our air conditioning system had an external unit on the roof, I did wonder whether the unit was spreading airborne pathogens through the air conditioning units and into the house, and if it was a potential health hazard. I asked my husband to raise the issue with maintenance, but we never got a convincing response. The air conditioning gave me sinus problems in any case, which led to numerous nosebleeds throughout my time in Riyadh, but thankfully no bird flu.

In February, we organised a birthday party for Calum in the basement of the offices where my husband worked at the time. These offices were shrouded in security, but the children we were asking to the party had fathers who all worked for the company, so that wasn't an issue. In the basement of the offices there was a swimming pool, a bowling alley and a snack-bar. We hired the bowling alley and had a bowling party, followed by some good old-fashioned party games, and the snack bar provided the food. The venue wasn't far from some of the best shopping centres in the centre of the city, and the parents were all happy to leave their children with us for the party whilst they went shopping, so everyone was happy.

Valentine's Day is not celebrated in Saudi Arabia, as it is perceived to have Christian links with Saint Valentine and to promote immoral behaviour. I was astounded to learn that most flower shops shut down at this time of year, and the few that do remain open remove any red roses from their stock to avoid harassment from the moral police, the Committee for the Propagation of Virtue and Prevention of Vice. I found it even more bizarre to discover that *IKEA* were selling cards with love-hearts on the front, and a red heart-shaped cushion as part of their usual stock when we wandered round a week before Valentine's Day. I am sure their sales figures from these items alone must have looked impressive for February.

The Muttawa, or religious police are responsible for ensuring the public's observance of Saudi Islamic religious behaviour, such as fasting during Ramadan, the five daily prayers, prohibitions against alcohol and the modesty of women. Muttawa study at the Islamic University and are salaried government employees.

As a Western woman in Saudi I required to cover up by wearing an *abaya* and to cover my hair when requested to do so by the Muttawa, who would patrol the shopping centres, particularly at prayer-times. However I couldn't help finding their contrasting appearance somewhat amusing. All the Muttawa that I set my eyes on were excessively hairy, with plenty of hair on show themselves, usually long haired and bearded, with shortened *thobes* which revealed hairy ankles. Given that they spent a large proportion of their time telling women to cover their hair whilst at the same time flaunting theirs, I found their role somewhat contradictory, as they seemed to be obsessed with hair.

I did see a Muttawa vehicle that was particularly dusty parked in a car park outside one of the shopping centres once, on which someone had drawn a love-heart with some Arabic writing, together with a cupid's arrow. I would have been most interested to decipher what it said.

Out of respect when out and about without my husband at prayer-time I would usually cover my hair to avoid confrontation and drawing unwanted attention to myself. However I can recall one occasion during the call to prayer when I was walking ahead of Alan and the boys, finding myself being shouted at to cover my hair by a fierce young Muttawa wielding a stick. He was shouting at me in Arabic, gesturing to me to hide my hair, but hadn't realised my husband was behind me, as Alan was at the other side of a column with the boys when he approached me directly. Alan was furious, as the Muttawa should have approached him as he was with me at the time.

Alan was convinced that I would walk ahead of him more frequently than I used to do back home, when out and about in Riyadh. The reality of the situation was that when we were out we usually had the boys with us, and they would normally position themselves on either side of him, each grabbing one of my husband's hands when we were out without the buggy, slowing down his natural walking pace. If, on the rare occasion we were out without the boys Alan would usually try to take the lead and was convinced I had a chip on my shoulder about it. As far as he was concerned I wasn't happy either way, but I couldn't see how we just couldn't walk side by side. I suppose it was a reaction to where we were, but I do admit on reflection that perhaps I did deliberately make a point of not walking behind Alan whenever we were outside the compound, even if it was subconsciously.

My most memorable encounter with an extremely nice Muttawa once occurred as I was leaving a shopping mall and my driver was directly outside. I put my hands up to my neck and reached for my scarf, getting ready to cover my hair as soon as I saw him, when I was approaching the exit doors to get into the car. He smiled at me politely and gestured his beckoning fingers downwards (beckoning with fingers is done downwards here - fingers pointed upwards in this way is extremely offensive), saying in perfect English that as I was getting into a blacked-out car, on this occasion there was no need to cover up as no-one would see me in a minute. That really did make me smile and gave George and I something to talk about for a few days afterwards, as this kind of behaviour was unheard of.

I have long dark wavy hair which is frequently unruly and whilst it had never previously been in my character just to accept things I fully understood that there would be times when I would be expected to cover my hair whilst out and about in Riyadh. The time of day and the temperature would usually dictate whether I decided to wear my hair loose, tied back, or partially tied back. I did not cover my hair often, but I always wore a black scarf round my neck which I could swiftly pull over my hair when necessary. Whilst accepting this was something I had to do without question on occasion, it seemed completely alien to me that the very act of showing my hair was unacceptable at certain times to some more than others. In Scotland, the only time I would cover my hair would be to wear a woolly hat when out in the cold, or a hood in the rain, and even so my hair would not be fully obscured when I did so. When told to cover my hair I felt as though I was being asked to erase my visual identity and submit to being an anonymous woman in black from head to ankle, so it was a good thing it was not necessary for me to don the veil as well. Interestingly enough, due to my stubborn nature if I took the decision to cover my hair I did not feel that way at all. I have never liked having to do something because I have been told to do it, but in Riyadh this issue was black and white, with no room for compromise when accosted by a Muttawa. All women were expected to conform when requested, regardless of their religious background and whilst my feelings on the matter did range from one extreme to the other depending on the circumstances, I had no problems with acting out of respect for the culture of the country in which I was in when walking out and about in public areas in Riyadh.

Throughout the numerous extreme protests from Muslims around the world in reaction to the cartoons, the *Arab News* had many interesting articles on the subject. I was interested to learn that the Quran permits retribution equal to the crime, so in theory the retribution for drawing caricatures of the Muslim Prophet Mohammed would be drawing caricatures of the cartoonist's prophet. The old saying 'An eye for an eye and a tooth for a tooth' is an Arabic saying. However, in this instance, as Jesus is also a Muslim prophet, this was unthinkable. There was an excellent letter published in the *Arab News* that suggested that boycotting goods punishes those who have done nothing wrong, and that perhaps articles showing the high esteem Muslims have for Jesus would help educate people on this matter. I have to admit that before I came out to Saudi I knew very little about Islam and did not know that Muslims believed in Jesus, or that he is a Muslim Prophet. I cannot imagine cartoons depicting Jesus in this way having been published by any paper. Whilst not condemning or backing a case for or against free speech in the West, it is only right that some behaviour is not tolerated and it was right that no British paper decided to publish the controversial cartoons. Religious ignorance and misunderstanding has a lot to answer for worldwide and recently in Scotland and the United Kingdom, laws had been implemented to kerb racial or religious incitement.

It was interesting to note the large numbers of letters that had been sent in to the editor, condemning the violent protests elsewhere in Islamic countries. Saudi's stance on this issue continued to be peaceful, with repeated requests for their people to remain so in the press and news. A ban was implemented on Danish products and imports and for several months many of the shelves at the supermarkets which would usually contain Danish and French dairy products were completely empty.

At this time the annual Riyadh Book Fair took place, and it was well covered in the press. Unfortunately throughout the fair protestors and some Muttawa made their opinions known on various issues and disrupted readings and poetry recitals. In one instance women were stopped from reading out loud, as the protestors made their views on this issue clear as being contrary to acceptable behaviour for women.

The Muttawa do not have a popular job, putting a stop to anti-Islamic behaviour, primarily because there have been instances where their behaviour is circumspect too. Sometimes punishments are administered for things that are not clearly stipulated within Sharia Law, or unfortunate victims find themselves on the wrong side of an extreme Muttawa. I read an article in the paper of one woman who had been punished at this time because her son's hair was considered to be too long.

However, their worst press coverage came back in 2002 when a fire broke out at a girls' school in Mecca, and because the girls were not veiled, the Muttawa refused to let them leave the premises, as they believed it was wrong for the firemen to see their faces. At the time it was reported that the girls were locked in, and that the firemen were forcibly stopped from going into the building. Fourteen girls perished in the fire and many more were injured in the stampede that arose. Even though girls' dignity is everything in Saudi, quite rightly life is more important and the incident caused huge uproar throughout the Kingdom, with widespread public criticism and condemnation of the Muttawa involved.

Some of the supermarkets where we shopped were within large shopping malls that also contained play areas and fun parks for the children, with soft foam indoor play areas, fun rides and rollercoasters. Modern air-conditioned shopping malls have replaced many of the traditional souqs. Inevitably whenever Alan drove me to one of these supermarkets to do the shopping at the weekend, he ended up having a much more entertaining time than I did, as he had fun with the boys while I traipsed round the supermarket. Although he had to look after the boys, I found out the full extent of their fun several years later when they admitted that they usually ended up scoffing ice cream or doughnuts while I was oblivious to what they were up to. At around this time, Alan and the boys became overly excited when they found a fish and chip shop had just opened in the shopping mall nearest to our compound. Given that it also sold baked potatoes, we were all happy.

The school had a long weekend coming up, and Alan managed to obtain the necessary visa paperwork only just in time, allowing us a weekend in Bahrain towards the end of the month. Many expats and Saudis regularly drive to Bahrain for a weekend break for a change of scene and to escape some of the restrictions of daily life in Saudi.

The journey to Bahrain was an experience, once we had made our way out of the centre of Riyadh. In the suburbs, there seemed to be miles of vacant building plots that had roads and lampposts erected on them, and some families having picnics, presumably where their houses were going to be built. We drove past the camel souq, where camels of every shape and size were grouped and herded into numerous areas, surrounded by tents, some grass bales and lots of pick-up trucks. The landscape was a mixture of sand and camels for most of the journey with many wired fences, earth walls and thorn bushes. I had never known that camels came in so many colours, ranging in tone from almost black to browns and reds and terracotta down to a very light, almost white but still sandy colour. The sand changed colour considerably along the way, and the colouring of the camels seemed to help them to blend naturally into their environment. Many of the camels were roaming round themselves, others were tethered, and some had a shepherd walking with them and were saddled up. I was glad Alan had decided to drive during daylight, as I didn't fancy coming across camels on the road when it was dark. It was bad enough when you could see, as due to their colour, you had to keep your wits about you, as they tended to disappear into the landscape, which when the road you were driving on was partially covered in sand at times made things interesting. Not only would they do a substantial amount of damage if a car ran into one, but the fines for hitting a camel are extortionate and have been known to reach up to 70,000 riyals.

Further along the road, Alan drove past some farms and a camel racing track. At times, the road had had large amounts of sand which had been blown all over it, and we came across several sand blowers on our way, moving sand off the road. There were also sand moving machines moving vast quantities of heaped sand from the side of the road at various locations en-route. Alan and I kept our eyes open for speed traps, which tended to be located in the shade underneath the overpasses on the road, or for police cars which had positioned themselves in well hidden locations which you would only become aware of at the last minute.

On the way to Bahrain we saw numerous Bedouin camps from the road - some much larger than others. Most seemed to comprise of tents, goats or sheep and camels and some pick-up trucks and water in containers or tanks and wells. Occasionally there were a few mobile or static caravans as well. What was surprising to me though, was that most tents had a satellite dish right outside, so the extremes of desert and modern life were side by side. I couldn't help but ponder over the contradictory visions that formed in my mind, of Arabs watching satellite television on the latest plasma screen inside their nomadic tents. I couldn't help considering whether guarantees on televisions in Saudi had a clause exempting them from claims arising from exposure to sandy conditions, and what the average life expectancy was for a television in the desert.

The Saudis were nomadic until around only fifty years ago. Now the majority of the population live in towns and cities, although there are many who choose to continue their nomadic lifestyle. It is common for Saudis to erect tents within their walled gardens or courtyards, or to spend some time away from town and city life when they can, in a Bedouin tent, remembering their cultural traditions and roots in the desert. Saudis are renowned for their hospitality, which stems from their nomadic lifestyle of only a few generations ago, when food and shelter could mean the difference between life and death in a harsh desert climate. Food and shelter were traditionally offered to anyone who came in peace, regardless of whether they were from an enemy tribe or not.

In today's modern urban society, personal honour is of importance.

Saudis do not like conflict and will go to extremes to get themselves or others out of an awkward situation rather than argue or become confrontational. They will rarely say no directly, as they do not like saying something someone else does not want to hear, so in this part of the world it is best to have realistic expectations and to understand when they mean no without trying to force the issue. This is known as saving face. It is also not a good idea to admire a Saudi's possessions too much, or they may well then feel obliged to give it to you.

Saudis are descended from Bedouin, tribes of sheep and goat herders, dignified old tribes known and respected for their strength, courtesy and hospitality under extreme desert conditions. For centuries their food was purely from the desert and oasis - predominantly milk and yoghurt, meat and dates with imported rice and flat bread. Although many Bedouins today have Toyotas or jeeps parked beside their tents, they still follow their traditional lifestyle.

A Bedouin had milk and meat from his camels and goats, and dates picked from date palms. If he was reasonably well off, then food could include rice, flour and coffee. Making coffee in the old tradition is considered mans' work and is taken black, unsweetened and flavoured with crushed cardamom. The Bedouins have a saying for a generous man which is 'he makes coffee from morn till night', which is one of the best compliments that can be given. When an important visitor was received a Bedouin host would slaughter a sheep or goat and lay on a traditional Arab feast. This would consist of mutton and rice and flat unleavened rounds of bread, sometimes with bowls of dates and butter.

In a settlement or town, an important visitor to the home could expect baby lamb stuffed with rice, nut and raisins, rubbed on the outside with a paste of onion, cinnamon, cloves and cardamom. Cucumber, tomato, cooked pumpkin, apricot and melon may also be placed round the central tray on plates. Coffee and incense would be passed round at the end of the meal.

As my husband drove us further north, we could just make out the oil refineries at Abqaiq, and we could see the buildings in the distance of Al Khobar on the coast. Unfortunately Al Khobar had been victim to a number of terrorist attacks previously, collectively known as the Al Khobar massacres, which left twenty-two dead and twenty-five injured, but from which hundreds were evacuated safely. Victims were Indian, Saudi, British, Sri Lankan, American, Egyptian, Swedish, Italian, South African and Filipino. Evacuees also included Dutch, Lebanese, Japanese, Jordanians, Bengalis and Pakistanis in addition to people from those countries previously listed.

At around six forty-five in the morning on Saturday 29 May 2004, four terrorists shot guards and employees from a vehicle at the front gate of the Al Khobar Petroleum Centre. Police killed three of the men, but a fourth escaped, through a neighbouring compound to the Holiday Inn, where he fired several shots and hijacked a car. At about quarter past seven terrorists in a vehicle launched a rocket propelled grenade at the gatehouse of the Arab Petroleum Investment Corporation Building, killing two security guards and a boy on a school bus. Gunmen dragged a British man out of his car after they shot it and tied him to the back of their four wheel drive and drove off. A Saudi civilian rammed their vehicle off the road when they stopped at the intersection lights when he saw what was going on, but he was shot by the terrorists. When the police caught up with the terrorists shortly afterwards they shot them on sight.

At around half past seven six terrorists scaled the walls of Oasis Three compound while five others were in a vehicle at the main vehicle check point, with a civilian car in front and a school bus behind. The terrorists drove straight through behind the car, killing two armed guards with a machine gun through an open sun-roof, then fired at the school bus, killing two children and injuring four. They drove into the residential area before walking round the compound on foot, kicking in doors and asking residents if they were Muslim. Non-Muslims were shot or had their throats cut. The terrorists made their way to a restaurant on the compound, where the siege continued. They ate breakfast, after which they continued shooting and killing people on the first floor of the building. They took over fifty hostages taking them to the sixth floor of a hotel on the compound, placing devices which could be detonated at the exits, before holding other hostages at gunpoint as cover enabling them to make their getaway.

Saudi Special Forces surrounded the compound and rescued the children who had been on the school bus who had hidden in an underground car park. Over two hundred expats were evacuated. Saudi Special Forces attempted to enter the hotel at two in the morning, but retreated after several were injured having set off the booby trapped devices and following threats from the remaining terrorists that they would kill the hostages they had taken. American military officers were injured at two thirty in the morning. Support was given to the Saudi forces after British support arrived at Dhahran military airbase. By six thirty in the morning Saudi National guard helicopters were on the roof of the hotel at the same time as attackers on the ground fired into the building in an attempt to divert the terrorists inside.

Following the operation, most of the terrorists had already fled and the authorities confirmed that the hostages had been freed, two terrorists killed and one captured. On the same day however, eleven security and military personnel were killed from five other compounds in the Khobar area from another armed vehicle. A local Saudi Arabian faction of Al Qaeda claimed responsibility, stating that non-Muslims were in Saudi to steal its oil and resources. Not surprisingly after this many expat families left Al Khobar, as they no longer felt it was safe for them to stay.

Putting thoughts of previous terrorist attacks aside I realised we would soon cross the border of Saudi, to enjoy a long weekend away as Alan drove us over the King Fahd causeway. It was an amazingly grand approach to Bahrain, with watchtowers looming over us, giving the impression that Big Brother was watching every single move we made. I was left with no doubt whatsoever that he was. The causeway was opened in 1986, linking Saudi and Bahrain and is twenty-five kilometres long and one of the most expensive bridges in the world. It traverses Umm Nassan Island, a wildlife sanctuary. Halfway across the causeway is a facilities area with a restaurant and observation tower. Once over the causeway the road took us to Manama, the capital of Bahrain. It was amazing to see huge towering office and banking skyscraper developments under construction on reclaimed land off the peninsula, and advertising for new housing development projects on massive billboards bombarding images of what the finished projects' towers would look like.

Our long weekend to Bahrain, despite rainstorms, lightning and a sandstorm during the night, was a weekend to remember for many reasons.

On the first night, Alan had booked us a babysitter at the hotel, and we fed the boys, read them stories and settled them down for the night. Andrew was nearly asleep, and Calum was reading in bed when we left them with the babysitter, a local student, making some money to help her through her course by working at the hotel for a few nights a week. We had plans to go out for a meal, but decided to go for a walk first. I thought it was a good idea to check on the boys about three quarters of an hour later as we were walking past.

When we opened the door to our room we couldn't believe our eyes… Andrew was jumping up and down on his bed, and Calum was sitting on his bed with the biggest plate full of sandwiches and chips I had ever seen, with his mouth stuffed full of food, wearing the guiltiest look ever, having been caught in the act. It emerged that he had told the student babysitter he was hungry and she had suggested he phone and order some food from the room menu, which he did, and put it on our bill. To my knowledge, he had never even dialled a telephone number before in his life, so we were absolutely gobsmacked when we discovered what had happened. The babysitter's services were quickly dispensed with, and Alan and I had sandwiches and chips that night, although I think they were the most expensive sandwiches and chips we have ever had. It was just as well we didn't end up going out that night, however, as no sooner had we finished eating there was the biggest thunder and lightning storm I have ever witnessed, and I wouldn't have wanted the boys going through that in a strange place without us.

While in Bahrain, we did many things we were unable to do in Riyadh - we went to the pictures, we drank wine, we ate pork and we even had a tour of Al Fateh Mosque, the grand mosque (only Muslims can enter mosques in Saudi), as well as visiting Arad fort, the tree of life, and the shops. I was able to walk round without wearing my *abaya*, which seemed very strange in an Arab country, having become used to wearing it whenever I was out and about in Riyadh. The only thing I didn't do was drive, as I didn't have my licence with me. In comparison to Riyadh, the roads were orderly and driving styles relatively civilised and laid-back.

We were shown round the grand mosque by a woman, and discovered that the carpet in the mosque prayer hall was woven in Scotland. (If you are wondering, she only had her hair covered as women do not wear veils in Bahrain generally). We were shown where the imam would chant the call to prayer, and Andrew stood there. I had to move him away very quickly, as he had been listening intently and had a mischievous look which was spreading rapidly over his face which I knew meant trouble. When his mouth started to open, I was convinced he was about to mimic the start of the call to prayer, if I had left him standing there a second longer.

It was extremely informative talking to the Islamic staff in the mosque, who made the point of making sure that we understood that the form of Islam (wahabi-ism) practised in Saudi Arabia was a much stricter form than in other countries, and that true Islam is a peaceful religion and bore no relation to what was being depicted by much of the media at the time. The tour gave us a real insight into Islam. I came away with a considerable amount of reading material and pamphlets, which I had chosen on topics I wanted to find out more about, and was to keep me busy reading for some time. I had previously wondered why pork was prohibited in Islam, and I was particularly interested in a woman's role within Islam, as well as finding out more about the religion itself.

A Muslim's abstention from eating pork is based on hygiene and the purity of character through what is eaten. Pork is recognised as having the greatest germs and parasites content among all meats, together with the highest fat percentage. Pigs are considered lazy and unclean and were the biggest carriers of disease to mankind in a hot climate historically. Muslims do not eat the flesh of animals of prey either, as food is absorbed into the blood system and circulated round the human body. As the brain also absorbs food through the blood then it is believed that this would also have an impact on man's nature.

All animals require to be slaughtered in accordance with halal methods to allow them to be suitable to eat in Muslim countries. The animal must be in good health, and before slaughter, the butcher must say some words of dedication to Allah. The method of killing is immediate by a single swipe through its throat, allowing the blood to drain away. Meat sold in supermarkets is labelled as 'halal', the Arabic for 'lawful', which refers to things which are eaten. I later learned that it also applies to the way that money is earned. Corruption, deception, exploitation or any indecent way of procuring money are also considered 'haram'.

Alan and I did not venture out on our second night in Bahrain; instead we had a few glasses of wine on the balcony, while the boys were in the hotel room within our sight and earshot. The use of the telephone was banned and ordering of any form of room-service was most definitely off-limits. Our glasses of wine were a treat, although Alan had driven round for ages trying to find a corkscrew as the booze shop only sold alcohol. He had been gone for a good while, asking people in corner shops and small stores who didn't drink where he could find one, which was somewhat bizarre. When I think about it I couldn't help but admire his perseverance, as explaining what it was he was looking for by way of simple English and sign language to people who didn't drink and didn't know what a corkscrew was made little sense to me. To be able to buy corked bottles of wine, but not find a corkscrew would have been ridiculous, so he eventually succeeded. He had gone somewhat overboard when buying wine and had bought red, white and rosé and we had been unable to consume all of it during our short stay. Alan was most unhappy at having to tip out what was left from several different bottles, as unfortunately we couldn't take it with us.

Due to the weather, there was to be no time spent lounging by the pool soaking up some early morning or late afternoon sun that weekend. It had rapidly become clear to me that although we were not in Saudi, I would not have felt comfortable sunbathing at a hotel in this part of the world. From what I had seen, Arab families who spent time round the pool did so with their women and female children totally covered up in their usual black, loose-fitting attire, and the men staring at any other women who happened to be there. The women round the pool at the time were not wearing bikinis or swimsuits, but revealing short sundresses and it was starting to make me feel uneasy, just watching the extremes in both dress and behaviour side by side, as it was noticeably apparent that in this instance both parties were uncomfortable being right next to each other.

It was only later on, when I was back in Saudi reading through the information I had picked up from the Grand Mosque, that I realised some of the literature I had taken away with me was written by Yusuf Islam, formerly known as Cat Stevens. Given that I had his Tea for the Tillerman CD amongst my music collection, I had known that he had converted to Islam some time afterwards and decided to find out a bit more. Cat Stevens was born in London in 1947 as Steven Georgion and had hits with Morning has Broken, Wild World, Moonshadow etc. In 1977 he nearly drowned off the coast of California, and it was then that he converted to Islam. Ever since, as a devout Muslim and humanitarian, he has released Islamic albums of drum and vocals to help build links between Islam and the West.

We were stopped and had our 4x4 searched at customs before leaving Bahrain. I had purchased a number of books about Saudi Arabia which were of particular interest, while browsing in bookstores, and I had a horrible feeling only then that it was likely that some of the books in the car were banned publications in Saudi. I had no idea what books were on the banned list or where to find this information out, and hadn't even considered this while making my purchases. Alan was asked to accompany one of the customs officials to a building next to where the car was being searched, and he was gone for at least half an hour. I was beginning to wonder what had happened and whether one of my books was responsible for the delay. Although Alan had joked about taking some pork back in the car, I knew he wasn't serious and wouldn't dream of doing something like that in any case, particularly with us in the car with him. Eventually he re-appeared and I was able to ascertain that there wasn't a problem, he had just been in a queue waiting for a customs official to ask him questions relating to our visas, and that was what had taken so long.

On our journey back to Riyadh in the car, there were a large number of badly smashed-up and written-off cars at the sides of the road. There were also a high number of high spec 4x4s and sports cars that sped past us at speeds I had never witnessed before, frighteningly all over the road. At one point, a Porsche and a Lamborghini were clearly racing each other along the dual carriageway, but in the same lane as they overtook us. Most of them were driven by relatively young-looking Saudis in sunglasses and Western clothes, who were obviously returning from a wild weekend in Bahrain. We drove past a sports car that had crashed at the side of the road, and I was shocked to see that the driver was still in the car, and even more horrified when my husband didn't stop as we drove past.

It was then that Alan decided to tell me that if we witnessed, or came across a road accident whilst in Saudi, then we had to drive past and not offer any help. Pressing him further on this, I learned that there is a blood law here which effectively means that if anyone goes to the aid of a victim, and that victim subsequently dies, they and their family are held directly responsible and are required to pay compensation to the deceased's family. In reality, this means only those from an extremely wealthy family are in any position to give aid at the scene of an accident, as compensation pay-outs can be huge, due to a man having several wives and many children who require to be supported in the event of his death or injury. It felt very wrong driving past, but reassuringly a red-crescent ambulance was visible behind us, so at least someone had previously phoned for help.

Interestingly, my husband told me that trying to get any of his Arab colleagues to enrol on any first aid courses at work was practically impossible, as they would not want the responsibility of delivering first aid. Somehow, having just learnt what I had done, I was not in the least bit surprised. The few Arabs who were eventually persuaded to do so would only consent to this when given a letter beforehand absolving them from any liabilities arising from blood law claims, authorising them to administer first aid if required without any personal liability as the company would cover them.

We found out later that the day we drove back from Bahrain, which was Friday 25 February, terrorists attacked the oil processing refinery in Abqaiq, detonating two car bombs, but thankfully the Saudi oil plant's production was not affected as the attack had been thwarted by Saudi officials, stopping them in their tracks. A suicide bomber exploded his vehicle at the closed gates to the oil facility, having been unable to get through, creating access for a second vehicle. Police opened fire and detonated the explosives in this car. The Saudi branch of Al Qaeda claimed responsibility for the attack, which was the first of its kind aimed at a major energy facility.

We had actually seen some smoke when driving back, coming from the direction of the oil plant and had remarked on it at the time. We had naively assumed that it must have been a by-product from the oil refinery, although we had remarked that the smoke was a bit dark in colour. It was yet another reminder of where we were, and the threats of the times, not directly against Westerners this time, but by targeting oil production, it was still an indirect attempt at causing severe disruption to oil supplies in an attempt to drive a wedge between the West and Saudi Arabia. Given that Saudi Arabia is home to a quarter of the world's oil reserves and ten percent of the world's oil production, it was just as well the refinery's production was not affected. The Abaiq oil plant is the largest facility of its kind in the world and produces sixty percent of Saudi Arabia's oil.

I recall waking with a start to what I thought sounded like gunfire one morning a few days later, towards the end of February. It was shortly after dawn prayers, as I remember them waking me as usual, and then rolling back over to sleep. If you wanted to get up early, the first call to prayer was a very effective alarm clock. The gunfire continued, and it sounded extremely close. I shook Alan and he woke with a jolt... he could hear it too. He told me not to worry, but that it was only fireworks. (Fireworks were often set off but I had only ever heard them in the evening and they didn't sound like the gunshots I knew I was hearing). Somehow Alan was far from convincing.

I went through to check on the boys in their bedrooms and suggested that they come through with us for a story. Being upstairs in our villa, the steel security door had been bolted as usual on my way up to bed the night before, but at that moment a steel blast door on the stairs, shatterproof film and bomb-blast curtains on our villa windows did not feel like much protection. Not knowing what was going on, if our compound was under attack, was extremely frightening and it was just as well we had to keep up appearances for the sake of the children. Several of the families on the compound and some of the nannies had given me their first-hand accounts of surviving compound attacks several years previously in Riyadh and Al Khobar, and these recollections started playing havoc inside my head.

Our villa was on the edge of our compound with only a patch of ground and a footpath outside our garden before the inner compound wall. The compound warning system hadn't gone off, (there were differing siren sounds for different warnings) so I was hopeful that whatever was going on wasn't inside our compound, unless for whatever reason the warning system had not been activated. However, I did have a very quick glance through some of the windows, although I should have stayed well away from them for personal safety reasons. My imagination began to get the better of me when I started to think about potential terrorists tunnelling their way through from a tent I had seen on waste ground outside the compound and forced myself to stop conjuring up any further thoughts from my overactive imagination then and there. The gunfire seemed to go on for far longer than it actually did, and not knowing how close it was to us was particularly unnerving.

The first of many security text messages started coming through on my phone, advising us to stay in our villa and not to venture outside or leave the compound. Bit by bit, more messages started to come through, and we were soon able to ascertain that there had been a shootout nearby and that we were not in any imminent danger.

Eventually, it was decided that it was safe for the school bus to run the children into school, albeit much later than usual that morning. It was only later in the afternoon that day, when the incident was reported on the Reuters website that we had the briefest of facts to hand. The shootout made Sky News later, so I took the decision to phone home that night as it was likely the story would be reported by the BBC and I didn't want family back in Scotland worrying. The story had indeed been reported on the news at home, but I didn't reveal how close the shootout had been to our compound.

It was only a few days afterwards when I managed to obtain the full details. Shortly after dawn, on Monday 27 February, Saudi security forces had stormed a building in East Riyadh that was housing terrorists. The villa itself was just down the road from our compound in a residential district, so it had felt relatively close because it was. The gunshots we had heard were an intense exchange of fire, during which five terrorists were shot, two of whom were on Saudi Arabia's top fifteen wanted extremists list. Apparently a large amount of explosives were also seized. The dawn raid took place days after Al Qaeda suicide bombers had tried to storm the Abqaiq oil facility. Saudi police tracked down the militants as a result of intelligence gathered on two vehicles seen on the surveillance cameras at the oil facility before the attack, and through internet monitoring. One further extremist was arrested elsewhere in connection with this incident.

Early evening was a great time to spend outside on the compound. We would usually go for a family walk, with the boys either on their bikes, or walking. During the week, many couples would sit outside while their children played nearby or at the play-park. We had a table and chairs in our small back garden, together with a double sun lounger, but nowhere to sit in the front garden. I persuaded Alan that we should look at some covered swing seats in the shops to see what was available, as it would be good to have somewhere to sit, rather than on the doorstep. We eventually found a rather nice triple swing seat from Sacco, a garden centre, which was big enough for the whole family to sit on at the same time, and it became very well used.

In March, Prince Charles and Camilla visited Riyadh and spent some time on the compound next to ours, which was accessed from the same front security gate. For the duration of their visit, the compounds went into lockdown and no-one was granted access in or out. Everything had been kept quiet, and only a privileged few knew in advance what was going on - the majority of the residents only found out about it after the event. Their visit was covered in the *Arab News*, where Prince Charles had been quoted as speaking out against the publications of the cartoons, emphasising the similarities of the children of Abraham, and that the problems had arisen out of a failure to respect what is sacred and precious to others. Prince Charles was certainly raising a topical issue head-on and talking sense as an excellent ambassador for Britain.

Alan told me that he had had a number of detailed religious discussions with Saudis he had come to know well and that they were all surprised to learn that many of the bible stories we had been brought up with were more or less the same. It was good that they were able to talk and through this find common ground in their upbringings, despite their differences. This topic has been a cause of ancient conflict and misunderstanding, and evidently still is, even today. Jews and Christians are considered to be descended from Isaac, Abraham and Sarah's son, and Muslims are considered to be descended from Ishmael, Abraham and Hagar (his wife's Egyptian maid), so effectively we are all related. I found it surprising that in a country that took its religion so seriously to the extent of banning all others, some Saudis were quite comfortable to have such open conversations with my husband.

At the end of March, our next door neighbours moved out. Prior to then, for a couple of weeks there was lots of to-ing and fro-ing, things being sold and lots of boxes. The wife and children returned home, just before the school term came to an end, while the husband remained in Riyadh to work, but moved to alternative accommodation on another compound shortly afterwards. They were a quiet family who kept themselves very much to themselves, a British expat who had married a Filipino woman and they had three children. I established several months later from one of the maids on our compound that they had previously lived in Al Khobar and had survived the terrorist attacks there two years previously. Understandably, because of their previous experience, the recent shootout nearby had caused them to reconsider family life in Riyadh. They decided it was better for the family to return home leaving the husband in Riyadh to work to the end of his current employment contract on bachelor status. I also established that the maid I was speaking to had lost her dearest friend during the course of this attack as she had admitted to being a Christian, so goodness knows what they had all been through. Although it was a very matter of fact conversation, devoid of emotion, many things were left unsaid, as she had brought the subject up and I felt it was up to her to decide how much she told me, and it would have been inappropriate for me to ask questions. It left me feeling extremely uncomfortable.

I ascertained that following the terrorist attacks in Riyadh in May 2003, many of the families who were on the compound with us who had been there at that time returned to the UK shortly afterwards. In some instances the women and children only returned home, and in other families the whole family returned home - some men had managed to secure a temporary transfer with the company to offices in the UK. There were also families who returned home whose decision it was to secure alternative employment and stay in the UK. Some families whose children had previously been out with them in Saudi and were old enough, decided to send them to boarding schools in the UK. When we went out in 2005 I established that many of the families on our compound had returned to Riyadh after having spent anywhere between a year and a year and a half away when the perceived terrorist threats were very much still imminent.

CHAPTER 7

Return to the Land of Sand (April '06)

Returning to the land of sand following a couple of weeks in Scotland, we were starting to feel like we were coming home to our other home, if that makes any sense.

There are no seasons in Saudi Arabia as we know them, which made the passing of time seem timeless in a way. During April, we endured lots of sandstorms and rain, which apparently is normal for the time of year, but on the first day of the month, it rained all day without stopping. Some of the trees had lost most of their leaves, which I put down to the weather, but following discussions with people who had lived in Riyadh for several years, some trees lose their leaves at this time of year whether there are sandstorms or not. It was particularly strange having just come back from Scotland, where spring is starting, to return to Saudi, where there were trees that had shed their leaves. My mind kept telling me that trees' leaves change colour and lose their leaves in autumn, but I had to keep reminding myself that it was the beginning of spring.

In the last week of April there was a particularly ferocious sandstorm which we could hear beating against the villa's walls all night. We heard several loud crashes, and knew that there would be damage to inspect in the morning. We woke to discover that our garden furniture, although strewn all over the front garden and back yard, was intact and undamaged, and we only had a few ceramic plant pots that needed replaced. Compared to other residents on the compound, we had come off lightly. Trees had been uprooted across the city blocking the chaotic roads, resulting in numerous traffic jams all over Riyadh.

Most Saudis continue to eat the traditional foods they have eaten for centuries as their staple diet - camel, goat, beans, wheat, rice, yoghurt, *lassi* (a yoghurt drink), flat breads cooked on a curved metal pan and *kimaje*, similar to pita bread. Today Saudi Arabia consumes the greatest numbers of chickens per head in the world. Being a strict Islamic country, in accordance with Islamic law they do not eat pork or drink alcohol. Lamb is served as a treat to honoured guests and at religious feasts and celebrations. All animals are slaughtered in accordance with Islamic law and require to be blessed before they are eaten.

Traditional recipes include *Kapsa* - chicken and rice with onions, cardamom, garlic, lemons, oranges, cinnamon, tomatoes, salt and raisins, which is absolutely delicious; *fatir* or *kimaje* flat bread; *laban* drink; *saliq*, a rice breakfast dish cooked in milk flavoured with cardamom, raisins, almonds and gum Arabic; *Kubbat maraq* - balls of rice containing turmeric, pepper, cumin and dried lime round a meat and tomato dish.

Saudi food isn't available as a takeaway and is eaten at home, cooked by the women. However, bread and foul is a traditional breakfast here and we regularly had it at the weekend. It was a cheap, nutritious and tasty meal which was ideal to have first thing on a Thursday before going out as it would fill us up until much later in the day. The rounds of flat bread are huge… my favourite kind had sesame seeds through it and tasted as though it had been sweetened with honey. You would break up the bread into hand sized portions and scoop the foul onto it before popping it into your mouth. There were different kinds of foul, all made from mashed beans, with various ingredients through it, such as onion, garlic, feta cheese and tomato being the ones I could identify within it. You could also add sauces to it for additional flavour. The closest thing to it at home would be an extremely thick lentil soup, only with cheese through it. Other popular dishes in Saudi include hummus, couscous and many lamb, chicken, aubergine, parsley and olive dishes which originate from all round the Middle East - Syria, Lebanon, Egypt, Turkey, Greece and Arabia.

Traditionally, meals are not eaten by the family at the same time at home. The men eat first, with the women having the leftovers later. Saudi meals are eaten sitting cross-legged on the floor or on pillows around a rug or low table, eating out of the same shared dishes. Food is eaten by hand, using the fingers or with a piece of bread. Only the right hand is used for eating, as the left hand is considered unclean, as it is used for personal hygiene. Ritual hand-washing is undertaken before and after eating. Some

Saudis accustomed to Western ways of living do eat as we do at the table, but they are in the minority.

Coffee is a central part of Saudi culture, and there is an intricate ceremony to prepare and serve it in the home, involving four pots in which coffee, water, and spices are combined and brewed before the coffee is served in small cups. My son had an Arabic lesson at school devoted to this topic, and the children had their own ceremony in class. Saudi men spend a considerable amount of time in coffee houses, drinking coffee or tea while talking and conducting business and it is a huge part of the culture.

Married expat women in Saudi Arabia can only work if they have their husband's permission to do so. Generally from speaking to women on our compound and at coffee mornings I established they could find jobs in nursing, teaching, office work at the schools, nurseries or teaching English privately as a tutor. Occasionally, there were vacancies at the embassy. I found it incredulous when I established that if a woman was working in Saudi before she got married, then once married, her salary was substantially reduced afterwards if she continued to work in the Kingdom.

Single women do come out to Saudi Arabia to work, predominantly as nurses or teachers or secretarial workers for large Western oil companies, and there are separate compounds for single women, or company compounds with differing zones of accommodation to cater for families, bachelors and single women. Before we came out to join my husband, he was on a bachelor contract, and was in bachelor accommodation within a compound that also contained family villas in another area.

On our compound, everyone's husbands worked for the same company, or one of its main subcontractors. This made things interesting socially, as living in a community made up of people that your husband works with and their families can present unique challenges at times. This was equally true for the women and children on the compound as it was for the men, although the challenges were different. Your children could be friendly with children from another family, or you could mix socially and you might notice a slight atmosphere from time to time between the men. If there was a difference of opinion at work, or if there were items related to work still to be resolved between management and staff, then inevitably this could sometimes become apparent on the compound and find its way into life outside work.

Most women tended to mix with their husband's close work colleagues' families, who were at an equivalent level within the company, so things didn't get too tricky, and I noticed very quickly that there was an unspoken order to the social circles on the compound. My policy was to always plead ignorance to anything that was going on in the workplace, as regardless of whatever was going on, I was not party to It, and had no intention whatsoever of becoming embroiled in work related matters. Some of the women on the compound had deliberately tried to glean information out of me initially, in terms of entitlements, benefits and salaries, as they were aware that Alan worked in personnel. One of them even asked me why my husband had been given a promotion and theirs hadn't, but I would always remark that Alan did not discuss these matters with me, and feigned a deliberate lack of knowledge and disinterest, in an attempt to deflect their questions.

Of the women on our compound who worked, a handful were teachers or teaching assistants, a couple had administration jobs in schools, several were nurses, a few worked in nurseries and one had found private English tuition students. The expats we shared a compound with were a mixed bunch, as people everywhere are, but the one thing we all had in common was that they were in Saudi to work and make money. Salaries could be anything up to two or three times what they are in the UK, and whilst living abroad as an expat it is tax-free. For some, it was about the luxurious lifestyle in Riyadh, for others it was a new start after a failed marriage or two, getting away from the area they lived in at home, leaving behind family pressures at home, paying off debts, experiencing life and the culture of another country, working in Saudi Arabia for the work experience and to add to the CV, or even about taking a job abroad as they couldn't secure one at home. Each individual or family had their own unique reasons for spending time in Riyadh, and it was often interesting to listen to their take on what it was that had brought them out to the country in the first place, how long they had been here, how long they intended to stay, and what their long term goals and ambitions were once they left Saudi.

The first compounds in Saudi provided sleeping accommodation for the workforce of a company, which over time evolved to dormitory accommodation with a pool for company employees. It is common now for expat workers to take their families out with them to live, and compounds have become a lucrative business venture for their Saudi owners. Some compounds offer the facilities and luxuries of hotel living to attract top-end company chief executives, presidents, managerial staff and consultants who have huge housing allowances included within their job packages. Most of the larger compounds have saunas, Jacuzzis, multi-gyms, tennis courts, badminton courts, football pitches, squash courts, function halls, restaurants, coffee shops, supermarkets, beauty salons and a few shops on site. Some even have their own golf courses, or pools with wave machines and water slides. The majority of compounds have sufficient amenities to allow expats staying there the opportunity to socialise with others in a similar position. It is common practice for large companies to rent out a compound, or several different compounds appropriate for differing levels of their employees, to house all of their workers and their families.

A few of the compound residents on our compound kept pets, although personally I felt that with the temperatures being so hot outside for so much of the year, most of them were confined indoors for long periods of time, which wasn't ideal. Early in the morning and later in the evenings dogs would be walked round the compound on a lead. Some residents kept rabbits, fish or cats, although there were a large number of stray cats that would hang round the compound, especially round dustbins and barbeques and you would hear their caterwauling at night.

Calum looked after a couple of rabbits that belonged to some friends of ours while they were away for his Beavers Pet lover's Badge. In actual fact that meant that Calum and I looked after the rabbits for a couple of weeks as is the case in these situations. The rabbits were house rabbits as it was too hot outside. Their owners let them out from their hutch frequently inside in the living room for some exercise, but we found that catching these long legged, hopping, floppy-eared, cute-looking, clever bunnies was an art in itself. We ended up having to move furniture and create a trap for them to hop into, which was sufficiently tall enough for them to be unable to jump over in order to transfer them back into their hutch. This could take some time, as no sooner had we come up with a strategy that worked, we found it didn't work the next time we attempted it. I actually came to the conclusion that these rabbits jumped over higher obstacles each time we let them out and that our attempts to corner or coax them into their cage had become a game in which we had inadvertently become the players. It was incredible how many rabbit droppings you needed to clear up after two rabbits had been hopping round their living room for an hour.

Several of the residents on the compound owned bikes and would cycle round it for exercise. One man in particular used to cycle round the small compound's road at speed. Each corner of the compound had a centrally planted area that he would cycle round several times like a demented hamster on its wheel in its cage. At least walking round twice pushing a buggy took a bit longer, but I still felt hemmed in while doing so. Although I was getting some exercise, at times on my own and more often with other buggy-pushers, walking round within the confines of the compound, lovely as it was, did not equate to my idea of a proper walk.

One of the weekends we went along to our compound clubhouse in the evening to find that it was even busier than normal. There were women, men and children there I had never seen before. It emerged that there was a seller of Saudi diamond jewellery there that night. Having never heard of Saudi diamonds before, I was interested to establish exactly what they were.

I found out that they are natural semi-precious stones that have the same appearance as carbon based diamonds. Saudi diamonds are from the same crystalline family as citrine, topaz and amethysts and do not discolour or break up with age. They are heavier than carbon stones and are found in the central desert plains of Saudi Arabia around Riyadh. The jewellery that was being sold was at a fraction of the cost of real diamonds, and looked the part, although I decided not to purchase any at the time, as I didn't wear jewellery in the heat. I was certain I would have another chance to look at Saudi diamond jewellery at a coffee morning or another sale in the future, when it wasn't quite so busy and would have the opportunity to have a proper look in better light than inside our dimly lit compound's clubhouse.

Some of the families that we knew with older children would go scuba-diving or snorkelling at the coral reefs in the Red Sea and the Arabian Gulf at weekends. Other pastimes included windsurfing, sailing and water-skiing along the coastal waters off hotel or private beaches. Alan's company had a private beach and a compound on the coast, but as his job did not require him to visit that particular part of Saudi we never got the opportunity to go.

A few of Alan's friends were into flying and talked at length about the Saudi Aviation Club, where it was possible to participate in activities such as paragliding, para-motoring, model aircraft flying, sky diving and light aircraft flying. We got to know a few pilots - some of them were in Saudi as training instructors and one of them used to fly for the Red Arrows. Saudi Arabia have an equivalent, known as the Hawks, known for the green smoke trails they leave in the sky behind them,(as opposed to the red, white and blue for the Red Arrows), but unfortunately they were also known for their risk taking and accident record at the time. There is a fantastic Aviation Museum in Riyadh, Saqur Al Jazeera, which we found out about through another family and was well worth a visit. The museum covers the history of Saudi aviation, and has been a project between the Saudi Royal Air Force and BAE Systems. There are model planes, real planes, displays and videos in English and Arabic, as well as a space simulator.

The red desert sands around Riyadh provide an amazing playground to explore. In many areas, quad bikes, trikes and sand-boards are hired out and which are popular activities at the weekends. There were several four wheel drive clubs in Riyadh, which provided a great opportunity to learn techniques for driving in the sand, which is an art in itself. Dune bashing is a regular pastime among the Arabs. Venturing out into the desert alone is not advisable in the event that the vehicle you are in breaks down or becomes stuck in the sand or you run into some other difficulty. There were stories in the papers where this had happened, and the occupants of the vehicle were not found until it was too late, having died of dehydration in the desert heat. When driving in the desert, it is always advisable to go out in a convoy of vehicles, stay with your group and your vehicle, as it is too easy to get lost and dehydrated rapidly in the dry desert heat, regardless of how experienced you are in the local area and conditions.

Some of the men on our compound had motorbikes and a group of them would regularly venture out for early morning drives at the weekend when the roads were deserted, and occasionally go out on planned excursions for several days.

A few families we knew who had older children than ours loved going out into the desert and exploring the landscape at weekends, camping in groups. There are off-road clubs made up of people from differing nationalities that meet up regularly and show slideshows of their weekly camping excursions. Camping is rough and ready. It is advisable to sleep off the ground, or in a tent sealed against scorpions and snakes. Walking in desert or rocky areas should not be undertaken in sandals or flip-flops as the horned viper can lurk very close to the surface, and it is important to watch where you put your hands and feet. Children need to be closely supervised at all times.

Desert trekking is popular, and there are many spectacular treks with sights to see en-route including graffiti rocks depicting carvings and drawings of life in the Neolithic period, wadis (dry river beds) and wadi-beds with acacia trees (avoid these during the rainy season due to flash flooding), sand dunes, old camel caravan routes through the escarpment which traders and pilgrims would have taken, standing stones and stone circles, old forts, dams, hidden valleys, Neolithic and bronze age circular tombs, mountains, rock pools and even caves and extinct volcanoes if you ventured far enough.

Before we went out to Riyadh, my husband owned an old jeep, and he drove it out dune bashing with some friends a few times. The video footage he took was extremely bumpy and hair-raising to say the least, even though his tyres had been deflated and the driving was extremely slow over the uneven and bumpy dessert terrain. He had also taken part in a trip to the Edge of the World, where a group of them drove to an area at the top of the rocky escarpment that Riyadh stands on, from where they looked down through the rocks to the jagged cliffs that stretched as far as the eye could see either side of them to the gorges and the Acacia Valley below.

Another pursuit was hunting for sharks teeth at Khurais. Around fifteen to twenty million years ago the eastern part of the Kingdom was an ocean, and this is evident today when you look along the escarpments outside Riyadh, as you can see the rippled lines left by the sea on the limestone rock. There are many coral and marine fossils to be found in the valley below amidst the sand and rock. Sharks' teeth remain as fossils and at least four families of shark species have been identified as living there around fifty million years ago. The area is littered with sharks teeth, which are relatively easy to find.

I had got to know a couple of the Filipino maids on the compound quite well, as the children they looked after were friendly with Andrew, and very often we would talk while supervising the children at the play-park. I was saddened when one of them opened up to me one morning and told me how she came to be in Saudi to work as a maid and nanny in order that she could afford to support her family, who were bringing up her children at home in the Philippines. She told me how she had cried at night to begin with when she came out, as she missed her youngest baby, and how the toddler she was looking after now was around the same age as her smallest child. She considered herself to be lucky as she worked for a good family who treated her well, paid for her holidays and flights home every two years, in addition to taking her on holiday with them when they went away. She treated the child she was looking after as she would have done her own, and had a live-in position at the family's villa. My eldest son was the same age as her oldest, and she told me that whenever she saw Calum she couldn't help but wonder if her son was now the same size as mine. She had last seen her own son eighteen months previously when she was home on leave. I couldn't imagine not seeing my children for two years between holidays, let alone being away from them whilst looking after other peoples' children of a similar age.

Listening to her tale made me appreciate how lucky I was to be in a position to take some time out to spend with my own children, even if there were times when it drove me to distraction. There were plenty of stories in the papers about maids who had been badly treated by their employers, or whose embassies took them in after being made destitute, and I was certain that the full facts were not always printed in these cases. Whenever I felt hemmed in by the constraints of compound life and my life in Riyadh, I reminded myself that in comparison to many other women in the country, the things that frustrated me and caused me considerable angst at times paled into insignificance.

Before we had gone out to join my husband in Riyadh, he had played golf on occasion with work colleagues, as a pastime. He had taken a few lessons, only to find it taken very seriously and competitively. There are numerous golf competitions and company golf outings here, with one of the standard topics of conversation on the compound being the latest golf tournament. There are several golf courses in Riyadh, and as the courses are not busy while the men are at work in the morning, many women have taken up the sport, although it is best avoided during the hottest parts of the day if sunstroke and sunburn are to be avoided. Golf is most popular in the cooler dark evenings, as the courses are floodlit and the temperatures more comfortable. There is even a desert golf course, where the sport is played on the sand on 'browns' instead of 'greens' and players take a piece of astro-turf with them to place their ball on when teeing off.

The Intercontinental Hotel had its own golf club within the hotel grounds in the city, which had the government offices of the Ministry of the Interior overlooking it. This reminded me of Big Brother in George Orwell's book *1984*. One of the executive housing compounds, the Arizona Compound had its own golf course and offered private and corporate membership packages. The most established golf course is at Dirab, outside Riyadh and is renowned for the fact that there is no signage for it. Another golf course to the north of Riyadh is the Reef Golf and Country Club.

Alan would sometimes take us on drives which enabled us to see the rocky escarpment that Riyadh has been built on from below, in an area that would originally have been the sea-bed. The drive down is along an incredibly steep dual carriageway road through a gorge, blasted through the high rock faces on either side, giving you an amazing view of hangman's bridge and the steep rocky valleys. Heavily laden lorries were unable to stop on this road and would very often shed their loads, so Alan would always get past slow overloaded trucks as quickly as he could.

Dirab is also known for its Equestrian Centre, where many children would attend horse riding lessons. Horse racing events are also held there. Saudi is well-known for its pure lineage Arabian horses, its horse shows, races and competitions and the King Abdul Aziz Arabian Horse Centre is the official stud of the Kingdom and the authority for registering purebred Arabian horses in the country. The Arabian Horse Association have a wealth of data on Arabian horses and the history of the Arabian horse.

North of Riyadh is the King Khalid Wildlife Park, where it is possible to see Oryx, desert rheem, idmi, gazelle, zebra and ostriches. There are also desert foxes, hares, sand cats and rock hyraxes. Prior permission required to be granted from the National Commission for Wildlife Conservation and Development in order to gain access to the visitor centre. South of Riyadh there is an Ibex reserve, for which permission is required beforehand to visit also. It was great to find out about all these potential places to see whilst in Kingdom. However, it was frustrating that due to the times we were living in, we were strongly advised not to make arrangements to go.

Occasionally, my mobile phone would ring in the evening and I would listen to a male Arabic voice on the other end. I had assumed that someone had dialled a wrong digit by mistake and would confirm they had dialled the number in error. However, one evening I received a call from an Arabic gentleman who spoke impeccable English. He advised me that he had seen me whilst I was out shopping earlier in the day and had obtained my number using Bluetooth as he would very much like to get to know me. I advised him that I was married and I asked him very politely not to call me again. I was absolutely mortified... on one level it was flattering, but on another I couldn't help but wonder what some Arabs perceived ideas of Western women were.

There was a fantastic cartoon in a local paper which illustrated two misconceived understandings between Saudi men and Western women. It showed a Western woman in an *abaya* looking at an Arab with pound signs coming out of her head, and the Arab gazing lustfully at the Western woman. Clearly although stereotypes do exist, it is not the norm, and perceptions can easily stem from ignorance and misunderstanding of the extreme ends of each other's cultures. Both societies have misconceptions about the other - from a Western perspective the misunderstandings relate mainly around religion and women, whereas from the Saudi perspective they wrongly perceive Western culture being all about sex and immoral behaviour.

At this time I was surprised to learn that the older generation of Saudi women had not been brought up to wear the *abaya* as it is known today. Saudi women used to cover their hair, but they wore an off the shoulder garment which was open on both sides, which through attitudes and religious interpretation evolved into the *abaya* that is now worn. The article I read even went so far as to advise Saudi women of the behaviour that was expected of them when wearing it. This included the fact that a woman cannot be seen with, or talk to a man who is not her husband or relation, avert their gaze, look straight ahead, and walk slowly and gracefully. In addition the article from the Islam in Perspective page of the paper stated that women are not to laugh loudly or address any remarks to anyone. Behaving correctly would bring them honour and respect.

On one of our previous trips to Batha, we had come across Al Musmak Fort, regarded as the birthplace of modern Saudi Arabia, but as it wasn't open for families to visit, we had been unable to go inside. I had made a note of when it was open for families, and we went back one Thursday morning. It was originally built around 1865, and it was restored into a museum in the 1980s. It tells the story of how Saudi Arabia came into existence when in 1902 Abdul Aziz and around forty of his followers captured Riyadh by taking Musmak. By noon of the same day they had the allegiance of the people of Riyadh. The tip of the spearhead which was thrown by Abdullah bin Jamin at Governor Ajlan was buried so deeply into the entrance gate that if you look closely you can still see it there. King Abdul Aziz lived in Al Musmak Fort until 1938, when he moved to the Murabba Palace.

The fort has been reconstructed, with its triangular windows, vents and handmade decorated wooden doors throughout, each one unique. Four crenelated towers are at the corners of the square fort. Palm branches form the ceilings, while hay mixed with mud form the adobe walls. Videos, models, and information boards tell the story of the fort's capture and many artefacts from the time of Abdul Aziz are displayed. The building is made up of three residential units containing apartments for the ruler, the treasury and guests. There is a traditional sitting room with an open courtyard and a working well.

I had spoken nicely to the museum staff on my way in and was advised that I had permission to take photographs of the building, from inside and out, even though there was a sign which had a red line through a picture of a camera. A paved square had been created in front of the fort as part of the phased redevelopment of Qasr Al Hokm, the central core of old Riyadh, which allows the space to be used in festivals and cultural events, but it also enabled me to take some great external shots of the fort.

School was off for the last week in April, so we decided to have a trip away to Egypt. My husband's company provided us with funds for a number of first class fares back home in travel expenses a year whilst we were all staying in Riyadh. We had all travelled economy, apart from our first flight out, when the tickets were purchased for us. However I couldn't help noticing that when travelling alone, or on business Alan would always fly first or business class, which he insisted helped to earn additional air miles. As a canny Scotsman the difference to date together with air miles paid for most of our holiday, which took in the pyramids at Giza, the Sphinx, the Egyptian Museum, the Papyrus Centre, the Egyptian Oils Centre and a boat trip on the Nile. It was an unforgettable week.

On the first of May, King Abdullah ordered petrol prices to be slashed by thirty percent throughout the Kingdom. The very thought of that ever happening in the UK was incredulous, especially when I read that simultaneously at home, prices had risen to a record high. The new price of petrol in Saudi Arabia was lower than water, their most precious resource, and a tenth of the price of petrol in the UK. At the time my husband had a 5.7 L V8 Dodge Durango 4X4 SUV which we wouldn't have even been able to afford to buy in the UK, let alone fill up with fuel there. Although it seemed like an extravagance, having such a big 4x4 to drive in Riyadh was necessary. The majority of cars in Saudi were large and American, and given the high rate of accidents on the road it was far safer to travel at an elevated level. The height of the kerbs, bollards and numerous concrete blocks here are enormous and if we needed to get away from a potentially dangerous situation we needed a vehicle that would reliably do so quickly and safely.

As previously stated, water is the most precious resource, and in Saudi Arabia was more expensive than oil and petrol while we lived there. I was intrigued to find out that Saudi is the largest country in the world, with no permanent rivers or freshwater lakes. The Kingdom is a desert with dried up river-beds from a couple of million years ago called wadis, but contrary to myths that Saudi has no water, massive reservoirs of water are stored in water-bearing layers of sedimentary rock making up the majority of the Kingdom's water-supply. Many deep wells have been drilled in the desert to supply the Bedouin and agriculture and hundreds of dams have been built to reduce the consequences of flash flooding and to provide irrigation water.

Saudi Arabia is the world's largest producer of desalinated water, meeting seventy percent of its demand for drinking water from the sea. In Riyadh a recycling plant has been set up to provide recycled treated wastewater. With the population increasing rapidly, and urban life, industry and agriculture consuming more water than traditional life in the desert and villages, a National Water Plan was set up to economise, conserve and control the use of water to ensure better supply and distribution in the future. I found it incredible to read in the paper that towing icebergs from Antarctica to provide water had been calculated to be less expensive than desalination, and that this option had previously been given serious consideration.

Following any period of heavy rain, due to the lack of drainage it was common for water to lie for several days, rapidly forming mosquito-breeding pools. I can remember being in the car while it was filled up at the petrol station, watching in awe at a huge, sand-moving machine being hosed down, the water just cascading to the ground below, with nowhere for it to go.

From time to time, although I could get out and about to the shops and there were things to do on the compound, I would feel claustrophobic and restricted. One weekend, on a Friday morning when it was quiet, my husband drove us outside Riyadh and into the desert to lift my spirits, which was a truly awesome experience. The sand dunes were beautiful, a terracotta red, rippled by the wind and seemed to be constantly on the move. In some areas, it reminded me of being in the Highlands of Scotland, but instead of mountains with mist blowing over the peaks, there was sand, sunshine and mirages. We drove past dunes where local children had left abandoned go-karts and sand surfing boards, past small villages, past abandoned villages where all that remained was ruins of old adobe rammed earth buildings, fertile farmland and oasis, and past Bedouin camps. The contrast with life in the city was incredible.

I remember distinctly seeing piles of shoes abandoned outside a lone mosque at the side of a road and what seemed like hundreds of vehicles parked haphazardly in the vicinity. It was eerie not seeing a single car on the road because it was prayer-time. I couldn't help but contrast this with Riyadh during saalat, when traffic appeared to me to be even busier than usual.

Whilst out and about I ensured I carried four things on me - a water bottle, my mobile phone, my iquama and my ID card. It was interesting to read in the paper that personal identity cards, although optional for Saudi women, had been causing somewhat of a stir in recent months. Some of the banks had threatened to freeze women's personal accounts until photo IDs were produced, which did not go down well with women or their husbands. Women ideally required their husband's permission to obtain their own photo ID cards and many men had objected to a photograph exposing their wives' faces. Many women had not applied, choosing instead to continue to use the family card. As a result of this, a solution had just been implemented which was utterly incredulous to me - women would each be issued with two photo identity cards from the Ministry of Civil Affairs, one of which would show their face, and the other which would show a photograph of them wearing their veil. It seemed blatantly obvious to me that the women's veiled identity cards fulfilled absolutely no identity requirements whatsoever if their faces were covered. The solution covered all eventualities, and seemed to please everyone, but I just didn't get the point of issuing ID cards without faces.

Islamic banks do not operate as ours do, as interest is seen as excessive profit, which is un-Islamic. Profiteering is defined as making excessive profit out of people's needs, especially in hard times. A charge is agreed beforehand for the service provided, and business is conducted in a manner which abides by Islamic principles which forbid exploitation, monopoly and cheating. Maybe our bankers would be more popular if they looked into adapting more Islamic banking practices back home.

One morning I had been over at the gym as usual and was on my way back to the villa before collecting Andrew from nursery. George was standing outside the villa, and was completely still and silent, so much so that I instantly knew something was amiss. Looking closer, one finger was over his lips letting me know he needed me to be quiet, whilst the other was pointing down to his feet. When my eyes looked down to where he was indicating, there was a huge black desert snake lying directly over his feet. I had never before seen a snake this size before, and quietly turned on my heels, walking quickly and then breaking into a run, making towards the maintenance office for the compound. Bursting in, I described what I had seen, and a team of four men swiftly sprang into action, collecting a net and lots of long sticks. I decided not to watch the events that followed and instead made for the coffee shop and read the paper.

When I returned to the villa, everything was as normal. George gave me an account of what had happened - he had been out watering the plants at the front doorstep when he saw a shadow that seemed to be moving and felt something on his feet. The snake had been inside our central heating box, located on our front wall, and slithered out quickly onto his feet. By the time the maintenance men came the snake had quietly and smoothly moved to undergrowth beside one of the date palm trees in our garden. Thankfully he was fine, and the snake was found, captured and taken away by pest control. I did, however, have recurring dreams for a while afterwards about snakes that had found their way into the villa through the central heating system via the ducts and gaps around the pipework. Unconsciously I must have been pontificating over how the snake had got into the central heating box in the first place, as although it was off the ground and totally covered, it found its way in through our villa somehow, which was a somewhat disconcerting conclusion to come to.

Although Saudi Arabia has a rapidly growing population, it employs around seven million expatriate workers, which equates to around two thirds of their workforce. The majority of expat workers come to undertake jobs which Saudis consider to be beneath them, or jobs which they do not have the necessary skills, training or expertise to do. With more than half of the increasing population under sixteen and unemployment at around thirty percent the government found itself under pressure to find jobs to accommodate school and university graduates in particular. In an attempt to remedy the situation, a policy was in the process of being implemented called 'Saudisation'.

Under new laws, three quarters of the total workforce in any company must be Saudi nationals. However the proportion may be temporarily reduced if no competent nationals are available. With Saudi Arabia having recently joined the World Trade Organisation, human resources were being developed and a huge programme of learning commenced in the Kingdom. Achieving the Saudisation targets will take time, and the workforce will require extensive training, as the required expertise is not readily available. In addition, many Saudis are not used to being punctual, starting work early in the morning, or understand the concept of overtime, due to the way things have been operating traditionally and culturally.

The policy affected us, as Alan was advised that his job was to be 'Saudised' - that is to say that a Saudi national was to be employed to eventually take over the role that he was currently undertaking. Alan was to train the Saudi up to do his job, let him shadow him and gradually pass all responsibilities to him. In a few years my husband's position was to be 'Saudised' and he would then find himself paid off. I found myself wondering whether there were expats who would deliberately not make good mentors, and eke their jobs out for as long as possible, if the payoff on offer didn't meet with their expectations, and how legislation would get round this issue. Saudisation had huge ramifications on expat family life particularly for families with older children, as families had to take decisions whether to stay for another school year as the timescale for most Saudised positions was unclear, which was difficult if their children had important exams on the horizon.

Alan and I were amazed at how many couples had children attending boarding schools in the UK whilst living in Riyadh. The company Alan worked for would fund a certain number of children to board from each family, and the children would sometimes come out to visit or meet up during school breaks at various holiday destinations. From time to time visits home would require to be organised at short notice to see them. After the terrorist bombings more families chose to school their children back home, which cannot have been an easy decision.

Calum had become particularly friendly with an Arabic boy in his class - they had a lot of things in common, and one day his teacher told me that his friend's mother had approached her to ask me whether I would be amenable to the two of them getting together outside school. I made the necessary arrangements for him to come over and play at our villa, and notified our security guards at the compound gate. When they arrived, the boy's mother gave instructions to her driver to wait. I must admit I was relieved to see that she had jeans on under her *abaya*, and that she was only covering her hair, not her face, and she was wearing sunglasses. The boys immediately went off to play and we didn't see much of them for the next hour or so.

It felt very strange meeting someone for the first time and within the first five minutes listen to her apologise for the monstrosities of the Saudi terrorists who were responsible for 9/11. She took great lengths to clarify that Saudis as a nation are peaceful and that they are truly sorry and embarrassed for what happened, and also that behaviour of that nature has nothing whatsoever to do with Islam. It turned out that the Saudi family had lived in America for the past ten years, and that they had returned to Saudi because they had felt uncomfortable in America after the events of September the eleventh. She spoke about how her husband was a doctor, and how they were finding things as a family being back in Saudi, with their families nearby. They were struggling adjusting back to life in Riyadh, which was somewhat restrictive after having lived in America, and having brought their children up there for so long. They were staying on one of the more exclusive compounds in Riyadh, which she and her husband felt had more benefits for their children, but neither of their families approved. She was also a professional woman, who had worked while in America. She was genuinely interested in how I found Riyadh as a Western woman living there, and we found we had a great deal to talk about, and a great many things in common. The children had a great afternoon, and I must admit our conversation was informative and interesting, albeit that we had both found it somewhat awkward at first. I wasn't surprised to learn later, at the start of the next school year, that the family had moved to Europe.

On the compound there was a small office block housing the mailboxes, a general office and facilities for the maintenance workers. Most evenings we would check our mailbox for post when passing, as we walked by the office when we went for a stroll round the compound during sundown after our evening meal. It always was a nice surprise if there was post from friends or family and when we got back to the villa any post of this kind would be read and reread several times over.

I found out that there was a post office museum in the main Saudi Post building on the second floor. The museum covers the history of the postal service in Saudi and displays stamps from around the world, franking machines, post boxes, telephones, a few Saudi stamps and a Saudi postman's uniform and bicycle. When I visited with a couple of friends, I had to ask one of the staff if it was possible to see inside and to request whether the door could be unlocked for us.

I would usually go over to the general office on our compound and pay our telephone bill during the day, the day after we received it each month. On one occasion when I did so, the men in the office had the television on, and seemed to be fixated by the programme they were gathered round watching - so much so they couldn't take their eyes off it. The sound was turned down deliberately when I went in, but the television remained on. Being curious, my eyes naturally were drawn to the screen when I was waiting for my change, having handed over the invoice and some Riyal notes. I wished I hadn't given the screen a single glance, even though I looked away as soon as I realised what they were watching... to this day I don't know whether what they were watching was live, or was part of a dramatized Arabian soap, but it involved a punishment being administered of severing part of a limb in public in front of a mass of onlookers. I must admit I scurried out of the office having tried my best not to throw up before I was given my change, horrified at what I'd seen, but also aghast at how such a spectacle seemed to be acceptable prime-time viewing for the workers on the compound.

I was particularly glad that we did not have that channel on our television (I made a mental note of the channel at the time), but I did deliberately flick through every single channel on our television to double check, just to be sure when I got back, as I did not want the remotest possibility of seeing anything like that on a television screen ever again, and definitely not in our living room. I also wanted to be absolutely sure that the boys could not flick the channels of the television to that particular channel, even although they were only allowed the television on when either my husband or I were in the room with them. After having been privy to what I had just seen, I was adamant that this rule made a great deal of sense.

Although we had a couple of educational channels on the television, the children's favourites were *Nickelodeon* and *Cartoon Network*. Most of the cartoons were American, but there were a couple that I ended up watching from time to time that I rather liked - *Samurai Jack* was amazing because of the incredible graphics and fast-paced artwork that was crammed into each episode, with no narrative, and there was another one about Ninjas which I found rather amusing to watch in Saudi, because of their obvious similarities to veiled Saudi women. I found out later that the cartoons I had enjoyed were anime and were Japanese.

Saudi parents commonly give their teenage boys high specification cars and four wheel drives, and as a result many young Saudis speed, race and drive recklessly to show off, prove their abilities or to get a kick from doing so. There is also a trend for young Arab men in Riyadh to get their thrills out of car surfing or drifting. Car surfing has to be seen to be believed - young Arabs hanging out of moving cars, clinging on to open doors or the side of the car, leaning over in precarious positions whilst sparks fly from their sandals skating on the tarmac road surface as they do so. There have been many young men who have been run over and killed or badly injured while participating in this crazy pastime, but this sadly only seems to have increased its popularity. Groups of young men also meet up to watch and participate in car drifting, where competitions are held for the best manoeuvres and longest skids or two wheel car slides.

At this time we came across a new Cantonese restaurant which had recently opened in the shopping mall which was not far away from our compound and decided to give it a go. The layout was impressive, consisting of a central circular kitchen, with a circulation space around it. Directly round this, a circular screen of separate curtains led you to your own private eating space. The food was delicious and relatively healthy, with the added bonus of plenty of fresh vegetables in each dish and the setting contemporary. We became frequent visitors to the establishment, as there was something the whole family liked on the menu, the staff and service were great, and the ambience of the place made it a lovely place for a family meal out.

The temperature during the day was starting to hot up, and on one of my trips to Sacco I noticed some garden thermometers. I bought one and we put it up outside, as I thought it would be interesting to be able to see what the temperature was. The first time I looked, I noticed that the temperature gauge went up as far as fifty degrees, but that the needle was pointing past it and couldn't go any further. Alan advised me that he had heard that if the temperature goes above fifty degrees officially, then it is deemed too hot to work by the Saudi ministries. I couldn't help but recall that all of the thermometers I had seen in Riyadh did not have a dial that went above fifty degrees. I had heard that it was not unusual for temperatures to reach fifty-five degrees during the hottest part of the summer.

At this time of year you had to be careful what you wore on your feet to make sure that the soles stood up to the heat, and that you didn't wear sandals with metal buckles or decoration, as they could burn your feet if you were out and about for any length of time. Also, you would burn the soles of your feet it you attempted to go barefoot - even going from the pool to a shaded sun-lounger I would ensure I had footwear readily available, or someone who could pass it to me. You also learned quickly to keep your footwear in the shade whenever you had taken it off to go in the pool or lie on a sun-lounger. Any jewellery you chose to wear had to be suitable to wear in the heat, as well as with whatever you were wearing. It was far simpler not to wear necklaces and ear-rings or bracelets during the day, and that way they didn't annoy you, burn you, colour your clothes or skin, or give you a rash in the high temperatures.

During the extreme heat in the months of the year when I spent most of my time in an air-conditioned environment, I suffered from a permanently blocked up nose, and had a large number of nosebleeds. However, after having come out of an air-conditioned environment to the outdoors, my stuffed up nose would magically disappear within five or ten minutes, only to reappear as soon as I went back inside.

A couple of weeks before we went home for the summer there was a gun battle in the Al Nakheel district of Riyadh. Saudi security forces pursued seven members of a militant group to their hideout. Six militants were shot dead by Saudi forces, one policeman was killed and a seventh suspect was injured and arrested. Apparently they were in the final stages of planning to launch terrorist attacks in the city. It was a relief to know that Saudi intelligence services and security forces had worked closely together and taken swift action to stop things from progressing further.

I was particularly glad to be packing to go home, as the weather was becoming unbearably hot. We didn't have much to pack, and the thought of a summer spent at home, with plenty of long walks and fresh air was extremely appealing. At least it was guaranteed that we wouldn't be inside for most of the time because it was too hot and the sun too strong, even if we knew that at some point there would be some rain.

While Alan drove us to the airport, it felt strange knowing that we would have most of the summer at home without him. Once parked, it was a military operation in itself just getting through the chaos to find the check-in desk queue. People were everywhere, standing, sitting, lying, chatting, whispering, shouting, grumbling, talking and baggage and cardboard boxes of all sizes were all around which seemed to contain all manner of household items and personal possessions, parcelled up to fly to another country.

As we waited in the departure lounge at King Khalid Airport, which was becoming busier by the minute, I wondered what the plans for the expansions of the Kingdom's airports would be like, as I had heard that there were to be big changes ahead which would include duty-free shopping (without the alcohol obviously) and some new terminals. Thankfully I didn't have too long to wait with the boys as families with young children were always invited to board onto the plane first. When the announcement was made for families to board, absolutely everyone got up and tried to jostle their way to the front of the queue, but thankfully those without young children were told to go and sit back down.

I was flying back home with the boys myself, as my husband would join us for his holiday at home later in the summer. I was sure he would make the most of the time he had to himself with us gone and he would have some fun with the lads. He told me later that every summer the Dads and husbands would send their wives and family back home and have a wild summer of play-stations, gaming, films, golf, football, tennis, pool, home-brew and the like. They were all in the same boat, finding themselves with spare time on their hands for a while and I knew for a fact that whatever else went on, I was probably far better off not knowing. Alan found himself mixing with blokes he hadn't seen since he lived in Riyadh on single status, as his life was so different when we were out with him. In fact he told me later that he only discovered the city properly once the boys and I had joined him in Riyadh, as prior to that his life there had revolved around work, socials at the embassies, parties and shopping at the malls. I hadn't realised that whilst he was in Riyadh on single status, there were many places he was not allowed to go as an unaccompanied single male, which was something I hadn't appreciated.

CHAPTER 8

One More School Year (September '06)

As I sat on the plane on our flight back to Riyadh I thought about how I had felt arriving back home in Scotland for the summer. It had been like viewing everything that used to be so familiar to me through a new pair of eyes. Wherever you looked the colours seemed so vibrant, the grass, fields and leaves on the trees so many shades of green, the sky so blue and crisp. The colour of everything seemed so vivid it was almost overwhelming in comparison to the paler surroundings we had become accustomed to, viewing everything through the dry and sandy heat during the day.

I found myself going over a bizarre conversation I had when having my annual dental check-up whilst back in Scotland during the summer. My dentist had asked me how I was finding living in Riyadh, and I had spoken about having to wear an *abaya* when I was outside the compound. He thought I was having him on and couldn't quite get his head round the fact that this was something that women had to do in this day and age and asked what would happen if women didn't comply. It seemed very strange explaining the situation to him, as his mind-set was so fixed and typically Western. I'm not sure whether the concept of covering up to such an extent was so alien to his way of thinking, or whether he found it difficult to envisage Western women having to comply. Given that my dentist has known me since my teenage, more rebellious years, it was highly likely that he was struggling to imagine me adhering to such strict rules. When I started talking about religious police and deportation, from the completely puzzled look of incomprehension on his face I'm not sure whether he thought I was just exaggerating or whether I had seriously lost the plot. I decided to make a joke of it and subtly changed the topic of conversation before I sat back in the dentist's chair and left the rest of the conversation to him, which was much more within his comfort zone.

Having had a wonderful couple of months at home catching up with friends and family, on landing back at King Khalid Airport, we found ourselves looking forward to catching up with friends in Riyadh and getting back to our home from home. A friend of my husband's, Matt, met us all at the airport, and being close friends, gave me a brief peck on the cheek and a hug when we came through to where he was waiting for us. It was lovely to have a good friend to meet us and pick us up at the airport, but whilst our behaviour at the time was second nature, immediately afterwards we realised that our actions weren't appropriate for our surroundings, finding ourselves being stared at disapprovingly by numerous Saudi men. Goodness knows what some of them were thinking - imagine a family being met at the airport and a man giving another man's wife a kiss on the cheek and a hug in front of him (and in front of everyone at the airport). It was just as well that a Muttawa wasn't about, or we could have found ourselves in serious trouble.

Once back in Riyadh, we quickly adapted to the time difference and slotted back into our routines round prayer-times, school, nursery and Alan's work. Before the end of last year's school term there had been talk of new buses for the compound residents for school and shopping excursions that would meet new security requirements. However, the same buses were being used as before, driven by the same crazy Arab drivers, renowned for their erratic stop-start and breaking at the last minute driving. (To be fair in certain traffic conditions and heading into the centre of the city, that was the only way to drive). It subsequently emerged that the new armour-plated buses had been commissioned and manufactured, but when they were put through a test drive, they were considered too dangerous due to the time and distance they took to break effectively because of their weight.

Some of the women on the compound had heard that there was a new water park that had just opened in Riyadh, not that far away from our compound, and were interested in finding out more about it. Once it was established that women would be required to cover up, and would need to purchase some kind of outfit that would cover them from their neck to their knees (including their arms) that didn't show off their natural curves, it was unanimously decided that it wasn't worth pursuing further. When I thought about what on earth women would need to wear I ended up in stitches, but maybe this challenge would be of interest to a fashion designer somewhere, who could end up making a fortune. The vision of baggy wetsuits that hid a woman's figure that entered my head was ridiculously funny. I wondered what women and girls who go to the water park and venture into the water wear, but was saddened by the probability that it was likely they would end up watching from the side-lines in their *abayas*, as they do at the hotel pools. Maybe in the future the water park could open to women and girls only at certain times with female life-guards on duty.

One weekend Alan drove us over to the Diplomatic Quarter, as we had heard that we could walk round it. The Diplomatic Quarter, or DQ as it is commonly referred to, is an area that was built to house foreign embassies, international organisations, diplomats' residences and residences. The concept for a diplomatic village came about in 1975 when it was decided to relocate the foreign embassies to Riyadh from Jeddah. The central area of the DQ houses the embassy buildings (of which there were more than ninety embassy buildings representing their country), central facilities and businesses. The architecture is amazing with embassies having been constructed as a showcase for their country's design talents. Many of the buildings have won coveted architectural awards. The area is surrounded by five neighbourhoods, each containing schools, nurseries, shops and mosques.

We discovered wonderful gardens, with children's play equipment, water gardens, standing stone gardens, shaded walkways, bicycle paths and exercise circuits. There were seating areas, picnic places, water features, sculptures and a perimeter path landscaped out of the rock from the escarpment, landscaped with shrubs, plants and trees. It was lovely to be able to go for a quiet walk, with the fragrance from the flowering jasmine plants filtering through the air. I didn't think about it at the time and wandered round wearing my *abaya*, but established later that the wearing of an *abaya* was not a requirement whilst within the DQ. There were hardly any other people about as we walked round so it wasn't something I picked up on. We only came across a few gardeners on our walk and a couple of Filipino nannies, one pushing a buggy with a young child in it and another with a toddler at one of the play parks. Both nannies had an *abaya* loosely draped round their shoulders, and it was only afterwards I realised that they had been wearing them as you might do an unbuttoned coat at home. The views from the Western side of the DQ looked towards the palm trees and farms of Waddi Hanifah and were a pleasant surprise.

From one of the parks in the North-west corner we were able to see Tuwaiq Palace, designed by the architect Frei Otto and Buro Happold Engineers. It was built in 1985 to serve as a cultural facility for diplomats, but now hosts government functions, state receptions, conferences and festivals too. From a distance it appears like a ruined fort, with an encampment, and was designed to respect its natural setting on the edge of the wadi. It comprises a series of long terraced walls, with a roof-top garden, from which three tent-like structures project, made from Teflon coated fibre-glass fabric. One of the tents has three internal levels within it. The tents reflect the Bedouin culture and the walls the settled cities. The building won the Aga Khan Award for Architecture in 1998.

My closest friend on the compound, Grace, was heavily pregnant, and was given a call from her consultant's clinic on the day of her confirmed first appointment, first thing in the morning. She and her husband had made the appointment six weeks in advance, to fit round the consultant's holidays. It was an important meeting for them as they had arranged to meet him for the first time to discuss an elected date for a C-section and to go through the choices available to them.

On arrival at the clinic, it transpired that two other women were waiting who had earlier appointments scheduled with the same consultant. Whilst checking in, it became apparent that one of the receptionists was phoning round trying to locate him. Eventually she reached his wife on her mobile and established that the doctor was still on holiday in France. Grace and her husband were then told that all appointments were now cancelled and that at present the hospital did not know if and when the consultant was returning. The only useful piece of advice they were able to ascertain from the receptionist was that in an emergency they should go straight to hospital.

As you can imagine Grace and her husband Matt couldn't believe that they had received a phone call confirming their appointment earlier that day, only to learn once they turned up at the clinic that the consultant wasn't even in the country. They were understandably furious and upset at the ridiculous situation they found themselves in, and Matt spent ages phoning round in an attempt to find another consultant. They were extremely lucky, and managed to find one who could fit them in four days later, but the first consultant they approached was unable to see them until a week before the baby was due. Thankfully all the upset and trauma of this situation did not result in a premature birth, but this stress was the last thing Grace needed in a foreign country at this time in her pregnancy.

In September, there was an article in the Islam in Perspective Page headlines that asked the question 'Is the veil obligatory?' a question which had often found itself circling round my head since I had arrived in Riyadh, as things seemed so contradictory. Although most Saudi women were veiled, there were a few Saudi women who went out and about unveiled, and a select few Saudi women even had their photographs in the paper without a veil. I had noticed that some women wore gloves, and some didn't. The full question that was posed was that if Muslim women are permitted to go out with their faces and hands uncovered do the women in Saudi wear the veil covering their faces and gloves covering their hands on the basis of tradition?

Islamic scholars take two opposing views regarding the covering of the face which is confusing, but most scholars in the Muslim world maintain that the hands and face are not included in the parts of her body that a woman must cover. For an Islamic ruling, everything is deemed permissible unless there is clear evidence to the contrary in the Quran and the Sunnah.

I decided to buy a copy of the Quran so I could have a look through it for myself and read the verses that are referred to on this issue. I bought one from *Jarir's Bookstore* and scoured through the pages from the Kingdom's authorised edition. There would appear to be no specific statement which refers to the veil itself or to a woman's requirement to cover her face in public, but there is clear evidence that a woman should cover all her body with the exception of her face and hands when she goes out or is in the presence of men whom she can marry.

I kept the Quran in the living room on top of a coffee-table for all to see. Somewhere subconsciously at the back of my mind, I had stored what I had learned about the attacks on the compounds at Al Khobar, where Christians had been killed, but Muslims had not. It sounds a bit of a strange thing to do but by having a copy of the Quran on display, I suppose I felt that in difficult circumstances there was a remote chance it could possibly save our lives.

In Saudi, both tradition and cultural beliefs dictate the conviction that it is a religious requirement, but in other countries it is left to the woman to take the decision as to whether she covers up as an expression of her faith and Islamic identity or not. Some more liberal Muslim women in more developed or Western societies object to it, on the grounds that women have fought long and hard to shake off restrictions that are in their view outdated and originally imposed by men.

Five years on from the terrorist attacks on 9/11, I was interested to see how it would be portrayed in the local paper. Saudis were interviewed expressing sorrow for the lives lost, whilst at the same time voicing their opinions on Western and American policy in the Middle East, particularly in regard to the attacks, the invasion and the occupation of Iraq and Afghanistan. Since then, many Saudis have spent a considerable time reflecting on the events, and new policies have been implemented criticising religious extremism. It was widespread knowledge that most of the Saudi extremists had left for Iraq, Afghanistan and Pakistan, but there was concern and speculation as to what would happen when these extremists returned to Saudi, particularly during the latter part of our time in the Kingdom.

The Saudi government implemented a highly visible no-tolerance approach to terrorist activity and had evidently been working extremely hard to crack down on terrorism within its own borders, with regular spot road checks being carried out and many arrests being made. Whenever we went out in the evening we always seemed to come across congestion which was usually caused by spot checks, which we would just be waved straight through, as they weren't looking for terrorists or criminals who were Westerners. The spot checks were never in the same place or at the same time and there was never any warning of them, so you always encountered them at the last minute on the road, unexpectedly, but because there was no warning given to slow down on approach, swift breaking and lane changing at the last minute was a necessity which caused several accidents that we witnessed.

Later on in September I read in the *Arab News* that there was a growing call to ban the use of cell phones whilst driving here. If it was implemented I was sure it would make a huge difference in reducing the large numbers of accidents on the roads.

Being dictated by calculations of the Earth's movements and the moon, I was somewhat surprised when Ramadan was brought forward a day early in Saudi to 13 September. Given that future prayer-times are meticulously worked out many months before, I couldn't and still can't get my head round why this change was announced at the last minute.

I found out that Spazzios restaurant at Al Mamlaka did a buffet lunch at the weekend for families, and they also provided face painting and entertainment for children. I had promised to take the boys to the Sky Bridge, and persuaded Alan that it was something we should do. We had a fantastic buffet lunch with a milk chocolate fountain, a magician doing lots of tricks, and ended up with two children with brightly coloured tiger faces holding balloons accompanying us over the Sky Bridge afterwards. It had been a successful afternoon, but I wondered what the boys would remember - walking over the bridge and the spectacular views or the magician and the chocolate fountain. Given that one of them came out in a rash to the face-paints and the other made a complete fuss about having it taken off his face, my most vivid memory was the aftermath of a great day.

It is a long-standing joke that women in Saudi spend their time shopping and having babies. Grace gave birth to a beautiful baby girl during Ramadan (six weeks after the initial hospital consultant was supposed to have seen her) at the Kingdom Hospital, and we made arrangements to go in to visit a few days later. I felt she was incredibly brave deciding to have her child so far away from home, with no extended family around her, and knew that although it was a very happy time, it would be far from easy (not that having a new baby ever is), although the women on the compound would rally round when she got back to her villa. This baby was her third, although her other children were considerably older from a previous marriage. The entrance to the hospital was akin to a hotel, with seating and a reception desk set within a huge atrium paved in marble flooring. We arrived around six thirty in the evening, as during Ramadan there were no day visits permitted. It was remarkably quiet, as most Arabs would have been breaking their fast at that time.

It was incredibly special to have been asked to go in and see my friend and her husband and their new baby, and they were pleased to see us. As the baby had been born during Ramadan, Grace had not been allowed water to drink until after dusk, even though she had had a caesarean section. She told me that when she ordered her breakfast she chose cornflakes, but when they came they appeared with cheese. The next morning they came with boiled eggs, and it was only on the third morning that she was told that she was now allowed milk.

She complained to me that she was extremely tired, but that this was not due to the baby, but as a result of the hospital staff, who came in every hour during the night to check on her and her baby, continually asking if she would like them to take the baby to the nursery for a while. This did nothing to reassure her, as she and her husband had specifically instructed that the baby was to stay by her side at all times. If anything, the frequency of the nightly checks made her petrified that they would take the baby from her room, so as a result she got very little sleep. The hospital was very noisy at night and it seemed like everyone was visiting with lots of children playing and making noise in the corridors.

The care Grace received was excellent, although she was in a private room. In the end she was kept in for five days, but was desperate to get out of hospital by the time she saw us. Despite her experiences of pregnancy whilst in Riyadh, and vowing at the time that she had no intentions of becoming pregnant again, she went on to have another healthy baby in the Kingdom, this time a boy, a couple of years later.

In Saudi it is common practice for the baby to be looked after by others straight after birth. When a baby is born to Saudis, the first thing the baby hears isn't his mothers or fathers voice, but sections of the Quran being recited. Matt and Grace made sure that when their children were born their own wishes were adhered to instead.

A few days later, my son came home from school somewhat shaken and visibly upset. It appeared that an Arabic girl he knew from school had been killed when she was thrown through the windscreen of the school bus she was on, when the bus had to brake suddenly earlier that day. I spoke to the bus monitors for my son's bus, and established that what my son had told me was true. I was extremely relieved that I had always made such a fuss over seatbelts, and that our children's bus had monitors who were sticklers on this issue, and also that my son hadn't witnessed this incident. I felt sorry for the family concerned, and for the children who had been on the bus when this dreadful accident occurred and the children that knew her. It turned out that she was one of the best friends of a girl Calum was good friends with at school and he knew her to talk to.

I was astounded to hear from my son that the siblings of the deceased girl were all at school as normal the next day. The girl was from a large Arabic family, and they had just carried on with their usual routine, Anshallah. To this day, Calum gets particularly upset if children misbehave, don't sit properly or don't have their seatbelts fastened the way they should be when travelling in a bus or car, as he is only too aware of the possible consequences.

One morning, my driver drove a friend and I into the centre of Riyadh, as we wanted to hit the shops. The traffic was unbelievably busy, which it always is around the Al Faisalia shopping centre, which was where we intended on going. However, all the roads around it and entrances to it were blocked off and we were unable to get anywhere near it. Thinking that something must have happened or there must be some kind of terrorist threat or incident taking place, I checked my mobile for any current security alerts I needed to make myself aware of in the area. I had no text alerts, so I phoned the duty officer to double check, and to see if there were other places in Riyadh which we should avoid, just to be on the safe side. However, as he had no information available at the time as to what was going on, he advised us to make our way back to the compound straight away.

We found out later that some of the King's wives and their entourage had gone shopping, so the centre had been closed off to the public. Trust us to want to go shopping on the same day and in the same place as Saudi royalty. We ended up spending the morning that we had planned to go shopping in the car, stuck in the chaotic traffic jam that surrounded all of the roads around the Al Faisalia Centre, only just making it back in time to collect my youngest son from nursery.

From time to time main roads would occasionally be completely shut down to allow various members of the Royal family swift and secure access to wherever they were going. No notice would ever be given to the public and we found ourselves caught up in traffic on the side-roads when this happened. Once when a road was shut, and we were stopped by the police, but had a clear view of the road, it looked as though a huge palace's possessions together with its staff was being transported across the city, perhaps to a new palace - the number of vehicles was incredible, loaded with oversized furniture, rugs and household belongings.

All schools in Saudi were closed for Saudi National Day, and the King declared an additional week's holiday for the Eid period, so government workers and the Arabic schools had an extra week off. We went to a shopping mall on Saudi National Day for something to eat, and it was very busy with lots of proud Saudis celebrating and waving their flags. Both of our boys were given flags, which they loved waving about. The Saudi flag is green with Arabic writing in white, which is the Muslim Statement of Faith, translated as 'There is no God but Allah, and Mohammed is his prophet.' Underneath the writing is a white sword pointing from right to left, symbolising justice and Abdul-Aziz. Green represents Islam and also honours the wahabbi sect, and is believed to have been the prophet Mohammed's favourite colour. Green also represents fertility or prosperity. The current flag was adopted in 1973.

The Kingdom of Saudi Arabia came into existence in 1932 when Abdul Aziz consolidated tribes and land to form the country. The tribal name of Abdul-Aziz was Al-Saud, which is where the name Saudi Arabia originated from. Although Saudi is ruled by a King, the Kingdom is not a monarchy as we know it. In Saudi the King is both a religious and a secular leader of faith and government, as well as being Prime Minister, Commander in Chief of the Armed Forces and Custodian of the Two Holy Mosques. In addition he appoints the Crown Prince, whose role is First Deputy Prime Minister. The Al Saud family decide who is best suited to be Crown Prince and then King. Historically, all of the Kings to date have been sons of Abdul-Aziz.

The emblem for the government is the palm tree over two crossed swords, and this symbol is also used by members of the Royal Family. The swords represent strength and justice, while the palm symbolises vitality, growth and prosperity.

The King and his officials receive petitions from his subjects in the Royal Diwan, which houses the offices of the King and his principal advisors and some government departments. Ordinary citizens can air their grievances within the Arab tradition of the majlis. The council of ministers deals with government business, and the King approves any decisions before they can be implemented. The consultative council is the advisory body, advising the King on policy and planning, politics, economics, education and matters of national concern, with its members being selected every four years. Saudi Arabia is made up of five provinces with thirteen regions, with each one having an Amir and regional officers, local advisory councils and sub-committees.

The central province Nadj contains the capital city and government centre of Riyadh, together with Buraidan and Hail, centres for agriculture and livestock. The Western province Hejaz houses the commercial and seaport capital of Jeddah, Taif, the summertime seat of government and Makkah and Medina, which is strictly out of bounds to non-Muslims. Al Kasa, the Eastern province has the major city of Dammam, with its seaport and industrial centre, Al Khobar with its residential and commercial centre and Dhahran the headquarters for the provinces oil-fields. The northern province of Tabuk is of strategic importance due to its location and also its agriculture. Finally, the southern province of Asir includes the main city of Abha, near Khamis Mushayt.

Reports from the councils go to the Ministry of the Interior, who pass them to the relevant government department for action. Departments include the National Guard, the Ministry of Defence and Aviation, the Ministry of the Interior, Foreign Affairs, Petroleum and Mineral Resources, Finance and National Economy, Municipalities and Rural Affairs, Housing and Public Works, Higher Education, Education, Women's' Education, Haaj, Islamic Affairs, Labour and Social Affairs, Communication, Justice, Culture and Information, Posts Telegraphs and Telephones, Industry and Electricity, Commerce, Health, Agriculture, Planning and Youth Welfare.

In the centre of Riyadh, we would often drive past what seemed to us to be a government building, which was surrounded by a garden of palm trees. We had no idea what the building was, but we nick-named it the Ministry of Palm Trees. I made the assumption that it was probably related to agriculture, but given that the emblem for the government was also used by the Royal Family I am still none the wiser and was most probably way off the mark.

The Ministry of the Interior building has the appearance of a flying saucer or spaceship when seen lit up at night, looking as though it has just touched down on earth. It is built in the shape of a reversed pyramid, with its narrower base supporting the upper floors on a structure of steel interconnected beams, looking over and watching the movements and actions of the inhabitants of the city. Given that the ministry is responsible for the security forces and the smooth functioning of health, courts, police and municipality within the Kingdom, its 'Big Brother' appearance is remarkably apt.

The police security forces are responsible for maintaining law and order, dealing with crime and matters of internal security. In remote tribal areas the tribal leaders undertake this role, reporting to the security forces within each province. Millions of visitors visit Saudi Arabia to perform the Hajj every year and this is administered and managed through the Ministry of the Interior. Police security forces are made up of the Public Security Directorate who are in charge of the regular police and the General Directorate of Investigation who are responsible for the special investigation police, known as the mubahith, or secret police. Records are kept at a centralised database within the ministry on identity, passports, residence and work permits, visas, vehicle registration, criminal records and intelligence. The ministry also houses the Special Security Force, a national special weapons and tactics team who are experts in dealing in matters such as hijacking, terrorism and protection and support to the Royal Family.

Patrolling of the Kingdom's borders, stopping smuggling and infiltration and custom inspections are undertaken by the Frontier Force. The National Guard keeps the army in check to reinforce internal security and guard the borders of the country. The National Guards personnel are from Bedouin tribes known for their loyalty to King and country. We were lucky enough to have been assigned some of them to guard our compound's front gate. The Coast Guard patrols territorial waters and is based at Asisam. The religious police or Muttawa are an intelligence gathering organisation, in addition to their role ensuring public compliance with the Kingdom's religious requirements. The Directorate of Intelligence reports directly to the King and is responsible for external and internal intelligence, gathering, co-ordinating and analysing information from intelligence agencies. The college for the training of the security forces is the King Fahd Security Academy.

It seemed somewhat bizarre getting a letter home from our son's school confirming that although the school would remain open, members of the school community observing Ramadan could absent themselves from school for Eid, if they chose to do so in accordance with the King's wishes. Another strange piece of correspondence we received from the school at this time was a form to fill in, to confirm whether our child would be fasting over Ramadan, whether he would take part in PE and swimming at this time, and if so, confirming that a letter would be required from us if he wanted to opt back into activities. Apparently for Muslim children who opt out because they are fasting, they become bored and want to join back in again, after watching and not participating for a few days, despite being tired, hungry and thirsty.

The previous year around Ramadan I had noticed that many tents sprang up on vacant plots of land all over the city and remained there for several weeks. Once again this year the tents appeared, as if by magic, and I established that throughout Ramadan food was cooked and distributed to those who were in need of it from these tents late in the evening, once the fast had been broken.

Alan loved going to work during Ramadan. As an official lunch hour was not recognised, he would usually eat and drink cups of tea while working at his desk as there was no canteen. However, during Ramadan, non-Muslims would congregate in an office which was set aside specifically, out of sight from their Muslim colleagues. This meant he would get together with colleagues for lunch and tea-breaks and have a bit of chit-chat whilst at work, away from his desk, which made a change. The tea-boy got a break too, as he could not make cups of tea and coffee for the workforce to drink while they were working. As Ramadan was a relatively quiet time at work, Alan found he was not bothered by numerous requests from customers and senior management, so he could achieve a great deal without interruptions. Many Arabs would come into work later than usual and work reduced hours, as they were up late at night and fasting during the day.

Alan told me that he had taken a while to get used to the all-male working environment, as the workplace differed in many ways from what he had previously been accustomed to in Scotland. There could be a great deal of aggression which would raise its head, and sometimes the language and behaviour from the Western men surprised him. Equally, he told me about one of the first meetings he went into with a Saudi, who had his foot up on the desk, and who proceeded to take calls on his mobile throughout the meeting. At first Alan considered this to be rude, but rapidly realised that this was just the way some busy influential Saudis behave, and they do not mean to cause offence. He had to get used to the fact that he could not be late for a meeting, but it was to be expected that some Saudis would be and that he couldn't just get straight down to business after a few pleasantries in a meeting. However, there was a great deal of respect from the Saudis, who were effectively hiring Westerners for their expertise, providing many amazing career opportunities in the process. The workforce was made up primarily of Westerners who were mainly focussed on getting the job done, and Saudis, who wanted the job done, but simultaneously had a focus on who's who, accountability and respect for elder colleagues. Alan quickly established that it was important to build relationships and develop networks amongst the Saudi nationals in the workplace, as in that working environment, Westerners could be given their cards very easily if they upset the wrong person or said the wrong thing at the wrong time and did not have a Saudi with the right connections and influence who would be prepared to back their corner, if and when required.

Whilst at home over the summer I had bought Calum a children's history book of Scotland, as the history he was being taught at school in Saudi for the last year had been purely English history. He had taken the book back out to Riyadh with him as he hadn't finished reading it and found it interesting.

At school he was doing well academically, but there seemed to be a few problems in the playground with some larger boys. I tried not to get too involved, and had just mentioned some of my concerns to the school so they could keep an eye on things. Some of the children in his year were several years older, and therefore were considerably bigger, as many children were bilingual, or hadn't started to learn English as a second language until they were a bit older. One Arabic boy in particular who was older and in his year was particularly rough in the playground and had been giving him hassle.

Calum came home from school one day and told me not to be cross, but that he had finally sorted things out with this boy, and he didn't think that he would have any more bother in the future. Imagining all sorts, and noting that he didn't appear to have a scratch, cut or graze on him that was visible, I asked him what he meant. He told me that he had had enough, and had taken things into his own hands, spoken with Mohammed, advising him that he was a Stewart, and that the Stewarts were the Royal family in Scotland. This was sufficient warning for the Saudi boy to back off, as the Saudi Royal family are numerous due to the number of princes and wives and children, and not to be messed with, but revered. Some of the Saudi Princes were feared both by expats and locals as they were renowned for using their position in Saudi society to obtain their own way or obtain favours. Presumably, this boy now thought the same of the Stewarts. My son did not have any further trouble in the playground from anyone, but I found the whole tale hilarious. The Collins' history book of Scotland for children had a lot to answer for. I found out later that some of the girls in the class had even been making him crowns, when speaking to one of the parents at a school event later in the year.

The number of birthday parties my children had attended since living in Riyadh was incredible. Most weeks there was a children's party, if not on our compound, then on another, and I seemed to buy birthday presents on a weekly basis. The parties our children attended ranged from magic shows, discos or games and food in clubhouses on different compounds, to parties held in the funfairs at shopping centres, pool or bowling parties, most of which were good fun but with far more children and adults than parties at home would entail. The boys had never been to so many parties before, and I had to consent and allow them to have the occasional *McDonalds*, although they had to agree to choose something other than chicken nuggets.

My eldest son attended a party of a Lebanese friend in one of the malls, while I went round the shops yet again. When I went to collect him the birthday cake was being cut, and parting gifts handed to each child from a table at the back of the room as they left. On close inspection, we had been handed a polystyrene cup, which had a balloon attached to it. Opening the lid, I was disgusted to find a tiny plastic bag with hardly any water in it and a small fish flapping about, together with a small pouch of fish-food. The fish had been in these tiny cups throughout the duration of the party and several of the children received a dead fish to take home, or a fish that only lasted for a day or so after the trauma it had gone through. Calum called his fish Fin.

Fin turned out to be a party bag I hadn't counted on, and when we got him home we made a temporary home for him in a glass vase. Against the odds, he survived the next week, so George drove me to a pet shop, where I purchased a fish tank and some fish food. The shop was in an area of town I hadn't been to before and was a visit I would not forget. On my way to the fish tanks, I had to walk past a number of very brightly coloured parrots, what looked like a couple of falcons, some caged monkeys and some fluorescent pink and green rabbits. There were even fluorescent goldfish. The shop assistant had been very keen to sell me fish food that would make Fin even more colourful than he was, but I did manage to convince him to let me purchase fish food that would not change his colour, but he did take some persuading. I was glad to get out of the pet shop and back into the car, the fluorescent animals having embedded themselves a bit too brightly on my mind. I had definitely made the right decision not to take the children with me on this occasion.

My husband and I were invited to an evening out which was to be held in the garden of one of his company's vice-president's villas in the Diplomatic Quarter. Everyone who was invited was sent out personal invitations. The security to get into the DQ (Diplomatic Quarter) was always particularly tight, and as there were several events going on that night, we seemed to spend ages sitting in the car waiting to go through the various checkpoints on the way in. It always seemed strange dressing up to go out, and then having to cloak yourself in your *abaya* while travelling to get there. It was a great evening, with various awards of achievement being handed out, speeches made, good food, and interesting conversation. It was particularly informative to glean information on the many clubs, events and activities which were held within the confines of the DQ and which women could attend which I had previously no knowledge of their existence. Unfortunately for me, although some of these were of interest, the timings did not work round pick-up and drop-off for school and nursery and the time it would take me to get to and from the DQ from our compound, which was some way away. It was extremely nice to be asked though.

I read an article in the *Arab News* about a book a Saudi woman had written called *Girls of Riyadh* which was an extremely controversial book, written about the love lives of several fictitious young, wealthy Saudi women, whose characters and stories unfold throughout the pages. The narrator wrote the book as a series of e-mails, sent out on a Friday after prayer, receiving praise and criticism in reply as part of her book. The book's content defies accepted behaviour in Saudi's reserved conservative society.

The newspaper article I read had been written as the Saudi Court of Grievances was about to decide whether the book should be officially banned in the country and the author fined. The author was attending university in the United States at the time and was an advocate for open dialogue on social issues in Saudi, despite its strictly conservative society. The author was convinced that social change will happen in Saudi and that there will be an acknowledgement in the future of many social issues that are currently not only disregarded but not accepted as taking place within the Kingdom. I made a mental note of the book, as I thought it sounded intriguing, and decided that it was a book I would like to get my hands on. I didn't manage to obtain a copy of it until we had returned home for good, and I must say that the book bore absolutely no resemblance to the Saudi that I had known, but then I was mixing in entirely different circles than the fictitious young wealthy Saudi women in the book, even if I had been to several of the buildings and locations within its pages.

It was blatantly obvious that there was a pecking order within society in Saudi, which was totally alien to my way of thinking, as it was something I wasn't used to. In Scotland, there are numerous nationalities and everyone has the right to be considered as an equal. However, whilst in Riyadh, as a white Western expat you quickly established where you fitted in, which could sometimes be disquieting. It was particularly uncomfortable for Western Asians, as assumptions would often be made which could be acutely embarrassing at times. One woman I knew was regularly taken to be her husband's maid when they were out with the children, as she had a different skin colour from her husband. My husband told me that one of his colleagues went to a business meeting with his boss, who was driving. On arrival at the designated meeting place, the Saudi who met them spoke directly to Alan's colleague, ignoring his boss, making the assumption that he was his driver. He told Alan's colleague where his driver should go and park. Apparently this kind of thing would happen all the time. As a woman I had to quickly adapt to being addressed as ma'am, or madam, which I didn't like, but which was the standard means of address when out and about, particularly by Asians working in shops or restaurants. I never did get used to the fact that Alan would often be referred to as Mr Alan, as here your first name is used, never your surname, and to me it would always sound comical, especially as it was always said so earnestly. Amongst his friends he was known as Al, which was a good nickname, as in Arabic 'Al' is the common prefix for 'the' before a proper or a place name.

Saudi names at first appear to be quite complicated, as they are long with reference to family members within their name. The personal name used by family and close friends is at the beginning, followed by *ibn* or *bin*, meaning 'son of', or *bint*, meaning 'daughter of'. It is not unusual for three or more generations to be used, but it varies from family to family. The family surname is at the end, preceded with the word *Al*, meaning 'house of'. For example Fatimah bint Tariq bin Khalid al-Fulan would translate as Fatimah, daughter of Tariq, son of Khalid of the family al Fulan. Saleh ibn Tariq ibn Khalid al-Fulan can be translated in the same way, with Tariq being Saleh's father's name and Khalid his grandfather's name. Although children take on the family name of their father, their mothers keep their original family names.

As I needed to buy some new underwear, I got my driver to drive me to the Granada Centre which had a large *Debenhams* store, where I thought I would be able to find what I was looking for. I spent ages browsing in the lingerie department, and there did not appear to be anything available in my size. I moved on to look at the swim and beach wear, which was directly behind the payment till. Men staffed the shops throughout the Kingdom at that time, and *Debenhams* was no exception.

However whilst looking at the swimwear, I couldn't help myself become completely distracted by the unusual behaviour of a male shop assistant next to the cash desk. I ended up watching his bizarre antics for a couple of minutes in complete disbelief, unable to stop myself watching what was going on, whilst I was obscured behind a concrete column. There was a cardboard box containing women's lacy briefs, and he had clearly been given the task of putting them on hangers. However, it was the way that he was doing it that caught my attention. He would pick up a pair, slowly and carefully attach them to a hanger and adjust them, and then hold the hanger up in the air and survey it, all the time gazing at the briefs with a look of complete adoration on his face, clearly imagining a woman wearing them. It was entertaining in itself just watching him from behind the swimsuits. I had never seen anything like it and it was all I could do not to burst out laughing. I was relieved I hadn't found anything my size and taken it to the till, as knowing my luck he would probably have dealt with my purchase. I must say I vowed then and there that I would not buy any underwear whilst in Saudi, as the thought of taking underwear to the till was just too much.

When shopping out and about, if you ventured from one shopping mall into another, it was common practice to have your bags searched for security purposes. Once when I went on the shopping bus, a couple of friends and I did some shopping at one mall before walking into the one next door, as some of the shopping malls are literally right next to one another. The security guard was particularly thorough, and took every single item out of the bags to inspect, deliberately holding each item up in the air for anyone who was walking past to see, (every Saudi Arab walking past at the time was able to have a very good look and took the opportunity of doing so, to our utter embarrassment), before putting them back in the bags. Unfortunately for one of my friends, she had bought some underwear from *Debenhams* on the top shopping floor of Kingdom Tower, which is exclusively accessible to women only. The shops on this floor are staffed only by women, so she had felt comfortable enough to have bought some matching bras and pants, without thinking that a security guard would later take them out of her bag and wave them about for everyone to see. I wished I had gone out fully veiled so I could have been anonymous while I was standing next to her as the security guard showed off her purchases, and the everyday undergarments weren't even mine. It was just as well she hadn't bought anything special. It seemed particularly ironic to be standing there modestly cloaked in our *abayas* whilst garments that are usually hidden under our Western clothes were on show. This incident gave me yet another reason not to even consider buying underwear in Saudi.

I was not surprised to learn shortly afterwards that the council of ministers in Saudi had recently decided that it would be a good idea to launch an initiative encouraging more women into the workplace, with the ultimate aim being to replace salesmen with saleswomen across retail lingerie departments. This would definitely boost sales, as I was certain I was not the only woman that had decided that buying underwear here would only be something to be undertaken as a last resort. I had images of Saudi and expat women persuading their husbands to take them for a weekend away outside the Kingdom, in order that they could buy their underwear on a hassle-free shopping expedition.

I lost count of the times young children tugged on my *abaya* when I was out shopping. On each occasion when I turned round and the child saw my face, there were the biggest looks of surprise on little brown eyes I have ever seen. I was never sure which would have been the biggest surprise, the fact that I was unveiled, a blue-eyed foreigner, or whether I was not the child's mother. I always smiled as I did not want to frighten a child and would immediately look round about me in search of the child's mother, aunt or grannie. I would say a small hello or greeting in Arabic, usually 'As-Salaam alaykum,' or 'Murahuba." Each time this event took place, thankfully the child always smiled back at me and jabbered away in Arabic before running off to his or her family, or before his or her mother came over to me.

It must be a common occurrence for a child to tug on a stranger's *abaya*, and each time it happened, apart from when I was wheeling Andrew in his buggy at the time, I expected it to be him tugging on my clothes. I couldn't help thinking that it couldn't be easy for children to recognise their mother's eyes and *abaya*-clad shape. For Saudi children whose mothers completely veil their faces I felt they must have to develop a heightened awareness of their senses in order that they can still identity their mother and not lose her or go off with a strange woman. This would apply to going out anywhere where there would be large numbers of women, who would all be cloaked in black *abayas*. Whilst *abayas* obviously come in differing sizes, most Arabic women wear plain black ones and, as a result, unless you look closely it can be hard to tell one woman from another when a group of women are veiled in the same manner, if they are of a similar height and size.

In October I watched the issue of the veil flare up in the UK courtesy of Sky News. Jack Straw had been asking his Blackburn female constituents from Islamic backgrounds who wore the veil to remove it during their meetings. He had suggested that women wearing veils which covered the face made community relations more difficult and represented a physical barrier, separating them from the rest of the community. Whilst I did understand that for some, the veil can seem intimidating or too concealing for a two-way dialogue to take place, especially if the veil covers the eyes, I was sure he was completely unaware of the controversy he was to cause on the subject at the time. His request was understandable, as with a face to face meeting both parties must be better able to communicate, and of course there are no security issues. I was most interested to read in the *Arab News* at the time that the debate was on-going, that even in Saudi, female lawyers are required to remove their veil in court when addressing the judge, in order that the judge is not misled by an imposter. (It was a shame that it took him so long to acknowledge his shortcomings but rather coincidentally, just prior to the 2010 election in Blackburn, Jack Straw made a public apology to his Blackburn constituents for his controversial remarks in 2006).

It seemed surreal to be watching the debate unfold in the UK while I was living in the strictest Muslim country in the world, where I required to wear an *abaya* and to cover my hair at times. I couldn't help but consider that in the UK, Muslims have freedoms that are unavailable to them in many Muslim countries. As a non-Muslim in Saudi, it would have been against the law to practice our religion in public, or to bring a Bible into the country, or possess religious emblems here. I had gone to Riyadh with the knowledge that out of respect for another countries beliefs and culture, religious laws and traditions, I would require to ensure I dressed appropriately when outside the compound while I was living there. Wearing the *abaya* was strange at first, as it seemed wrong to be putting on an extra layer of clothing to go out when it was so hot. Once I had stopped tripping over the hem and got used to it, it was just like putting on a long coat. Of course, it wasn't as tailored as a coat, but I didn't have to think about what I was wearing, as I would just put my *abaya* on over my clothes when going out, and although it was shapeless, it hid all of my lumps and bumps.

Personally I had no problem wearing an *abaya* whilst outside the compound and just accepted that it was something I had to do to conform to what was expected of me. Some of the women I knew hated wearing an *abaya* with a vengeance - some felt it took away their identity, their ability to express themselves in what they chose to wear, or that it just wasn't them. I suspect that the underlying reason was that going from complete freedom of expression and personal choice with what you choose to wear and to what extent you flaunt your natural assets is a form of personal identity, so having to conform in public to wearing a black relatively shapeless cloak which all women wear makes the wearer the same as all other women. One woman I knew told me she felt invisible when she put on her *abaya*, which in my opinion was a bit of an exaggeration, as no matter what she wore she was still whoever she was on the inside. Her point was that what you wear changes how others perceive you to be.

Britain was usually known for its liberal stance and attitude and respecting the rights and individual beliefs of an individual, but I couldn't help but feel that the underlying issues of the times - terrorism and security lay behind it. Certainly in Saudi, it was being purported that it wasn't only women who wore the veil, but on occasion men would do so to gain access to places and events that would normally be denied to them, or to conceal their true identities. I wondered how this worked in terms of high security events, and hoped that veiled women's identity cards were not accepted in the current climate.

The veil represents a huge part of Islamic culture and tradition. For many Muslim women it is a statement of cultural identity, social modesty and religious adherence. To them, wearing the veil is a public statement in which they proclaim their faith. The Quran instructs women to dress modestly, as stated in verse 31 surah 24: "faithful women are to lower their gaze, guard their private parts and not display their beauty except what is apparent of it, and to extend their scarf to cover their bosom." Hijab is common among Muslim women, a scarf covering their hair and neck. Niqab consists of covering up completely including gloves and a veil for the face, incorporating a slit for the eyes, or the veil made out of transparent material that affords the woman a certain degree of vision whilst hiding her face. Religions and cultural traditions vary across the Muslim world and in Saudi the majority of women wear the niqab, gloves and veil.

Male modesty covers above the navel to below the knee according to the Quran, and in Saudi Arabia, Western men must dress conservatively when out and about outside the compounds. Long trousers and short sleeved shirts that do not expose the shoulders are deemed acceptable. I do remember shopping in Carrefour on one occasion, being somewhat taken aback at the sight of a Westerner in shorts which exposed his knees, as it was a sight you just would not normally see. Absolutely everyone, including other Westerners avoided looking at him, and I presumed because of his extremely pale skin, he was a Westerner who was new to Riyadh and its ways. I couldn't help but notice how Arabs who were shopping with their wives seemed to instruct them to change the direction they were walking or managed to divert their attention somehow in order that their eyes would not see him. Even my boys picked up on it and couldn't help but point out to me that there was a man wearing shorts outside his compound wandering round the supermarket.

School had a half-term holiday in October, and yet again we were able to use our air miles and flight allowance to pay towards the majority of the costs of a trip away. We flew Saudair to Cyprus and had an excellent holiday, exploring the ruins, the temples, the mosaics and the coast.

The boys both had a fantastic evening at the Halloween party on the compound. This year they knew all the children and were happily joining in the activities. Andrew cavorted about scaring anyone in sight in his dinosaur costume with accompanying vocals and Calum was in an inspired homemade outfit as Harry Potter. I had bought him a girl's black *abaya* to which I attached a printed Hogwarts badge I had downloaded and printed from the computer. With school uniform underneath, his glasses and a zigzag over his right eyebrow on his forehead he looked the part.

Alan succeeded in obtaining the necessary paperwork for my Mum and stepfather to come out and have a holiday with us. They flew out via Dubai, and spent a couple of days there en-route, before landing in Riyadh at the beginning of November. They had crammed a day of sightseeing in Dubai first and had even gone on a trip into the desert, making the most of their time there to take in the sights. Mum had had her hands painted with henna in a very intricate pattern, which was beautiful. It was lovely to have them out staying with us, and the boys were remarkably well-behaved sharing a room for the duration of their stay.

We crammed a lot into their two-week visit - we managed a coffee-morning on another compound, lots of swimming and lazing by the pool, games of football with the boys, some lovely meals out, drives into surrounding areas to see the red sands and escarpment round Riyadh, drives round Riyadh to see the sights and trips to the shops. During their time out with us, Calum rode his bike in one afternoon after some help from Grandad with no stabilisers, which was the highlight of their stay.

We even took them up Kingdom Tower one evening without the boys, and I was amazed that Mum walked over the Sky Bridge, as she's not good with heights. I made sure I had photographic evidence to prove it. We managed to fit in some culture and heritage and took them to visit Al Musmak Fort and experience Batha. At the weekend we walked round Palm Tree Square, which is a square made up of one hundred palm trees built in

2002 to celebrate one hundred years since the capture of Riyadh. We could see the striped water tower on Wazir Street built in the 1970s which together with the TV tower built in the early 1980s, now inside the Ministry of Information were the symbols of new Riyadh at the time. We walked round some of the parks nearby in the morning, which were deserted and being tended to by gardeners. These parks are open to families only and are a lovely place to visit for a relaxing stroll, although they are mobbed in the evenings when the Saudis go out. We then walked around the buildings and courtyards in the King Abdul-Aziz Historical Area, and spent time in the water garden. Unfortunately at the time we chose to go, we couldn't all get in at the same time, due to segregation, but it was worth the effort just taking in the area and its architecture. Mum loved the signs for the toilets, which were signs showing the heads and shoulders of Arabic men and women, the main difference being the veil. We saw the fortified wall and the old water well which used to supply Murabba Palace. Time went by too quickly, and it didn't seem long before the boys and I were waving goodbye to them from the villa, when Alan drove them to the airport.

On some of the main approach roads to the city, very young boys would be selling water at the traffic lights, walking out through the traffic and knocking on car windows to sell water. It was an incredibly dangerous thing to do. The authorities would move them on if they were seen, and they would then move onto another road. You would see Asians and Arabs crossing the road from time to time, but whenever they did so, I would be holding my breath, as the traffic around them was moving so quickly - thankfully I never witnessed anyone being run over, but I had to shut my eyes on numerous occasions as there were so many near misses. Our local row of shops in the area housed the bread and foul shop, a *Baskin Robbin's* ice cream shop, a *Dunkin' Doughnuts* store, a pharmacy, a tailors, a dry cleaners, and some take-away food shops. It was saddening to see a woman covered from head to toe with only her hands visible, sitting on the pavement in a shady corner outside one of the general stores, grasping a bottle of water in one hand and outstretching her other hand for money. I wondered what her personal circumstances were and how she had ended up in that predicament. Giving her my change and a few more riyal notes, I noted that she was the only woman I had seen begging since I had been in Riyadh. I speculated whether her husband had divorced her and she had returned to her family only to find they would not or were unable to support her.

In Saudi, a man can divorce his wife by saying "I divorce you" three times in front of two witnesses and then instruct for the divorce document to be compiled. Women however, must take the matter to court to legalise the marriage dissolution. A divorce can only proceed if a mediator fails to help them to sort out their differences. A husband and wife can divorce three times, and the couple can re-marry after each divorce. However if they have done so three times they are not permitted to marry each other again unless the wife has married and divorced someone else first. Within their marriage contract a woman can divorce her husband if there has been abuse or her husband has failed to support her financially.

After divorce children will usually stay with their mother until around the age of five, when the father will take custody of male children. Female children will normally remain with their mother, and the divorced woman is expected to return to her family.

One of the women on the compound and her husband were asked to attend the marriage of one of the National Guards who worked at the front gate of the compound. It was interesting to hear how she and her husband were separated when they arrived, and remained separated for the time they were there. The women ate separately, once the men had finished, but the men had first pickings of the food. The bride wore a Western-style wedding dress in white with a veil, but her new husband was the only man to see her face.

Marriages are arranged by female family members or match-makers and are marriages which lead to love. Suitable grooms and potential brides require financial security and standing within the community. In any match the husband must keep his wife in the manner to which she is accustomed, and their social and economic status is acceptable if similar. The ideal marriage was considered to be between first cousins, but it has recently become acceptable for men and women to marry outside their family circle. Muslims may only marry other Muslims. A Muslim man may marry a non-Muslim woman, provided their children are brought up as Muslims. Muslim men can have up to four wives at one time, as long as they are all treated equally, although there are clear exceptions to this rule.

Divorcees can choose their husbands and negotiate their marriage contract. It is considered commendable for a Muslim man to marry a widow, although a widow would usually be a second wife. For a Muslim woman, a first marriage to a widower or a divorced man who already has children is not acceptable.

Several of the women on the compound who had lived in Saudi for several years longer than we had approached me, as it emerged that their husbands had not been successful in arranging for close family to come over for a holiday. They wanted to know why it was that my husband could manage to get both sets of parents out within the last year and theirs hadn't been able to arrange for any family to come out. Not wanting to get embroiled in personal or company matters, I feigned no knowledge of the situation and suggested that their husbands ask my husband directly on the subject, as he would be able to confirm who to contact in order to get things moving for them on this matter. I couldn't help but wonder whether their husbands actually wanted their in-laws and families to come out, their husbands didn't know who to approach, or whether they just couldn't face all the paperwork and to-ing and fro-ing involved in the process. I did find it odd that they couldn't just have spoken to their husbands and asked them to ask my husband in the first place.

Calum had appeared back from school several times during the last term with a stuffed toy teddy-bear called Max. On each occasion, he had to write a diary about what Max got up to when he came home with him during the week or for a weekend, as part of a British National Curriculum Course. I was astounded when I watched Sky News one night in November to find that a British schoolteacher in Sudan, an Islamic country, had been arrested by the authorities there, as she had let the pupils in her class call their bear Mohammed. Although Mohammed is a common name, and twenty out of the twenty-three children in the class had voted for the bear to be called Mohammed, in doing so, in some peoples' eyes they had made an image of the prophet, which is seen as idolatry and insults Islam's prophet. I had to think about it and I supposed that in our country, you wouldn't call a toy Jesus, but then I haven't met anyone named Jesus back home either. When I asked my son why his class bear was called Max, he told me that their teacher had chosen the name - a wise move indeed, given that Mohammed is also a very popular name in Saudi.

The debate on the veil continued to take up space in the news broadcasts and the papers, with the Archbishop of Canterbury writing a report on the matter which concluded that politicians should not interfere with the right to wear the veil or the cross.

In December we attended the British Embassy to participate in a concert. Nights out at the embassy were always good fun and it was great to meet a variety of interesting people and enjoy stimulating conversation afterwards. There were drinks in the lit up garden and plenty of people who did not work for my husband's company to talk to, which made a refreshing change. I became aware of some strange noises behind us in the shadows, and realised that all round the garden were a number of tethered falcons, who no doubt had been disturbed by all the chit-chat. They must have been given as presents to the Embassy, as Arabs are very much into their falconry. In some of the souqs, you would see groups of men gathered with falcons on their arm in deep discussion and debate about their birds.

Packing to go home for Christmas hardly took any time at all, as it had now become routine, and we didn't need to take much back with us that we would require in Scotland. It was only once we had flown from Riyadh to

Dubai that we felt 'we were on holiday. On arrival at Dubai airport we managed to grab a few hours' sleep at the airport hotel before getting up incredibly early for our flight to Glasgow. On the flight from Dubai to Glasgow, Alan bought some duty free alcohol – a bottle of brandy for his Mum for Christmas, and a bottle of twenty year old whisky for himself. Once the plane had landed and we gathered together all of our hand baggage, he turned round to discover that his duty free purchases had disappeared. Unfortunately, although the cabin crew and the staff at the airport were helpful, his purchases were not recovered, and with Christmas on our mind we didn't report the matter to the police, as we wanted to get home and time was of the essence. Theft in Riyadh is rare, and it brought home to us the fact that there is far more petty crime in the UK than in Saudi. I had to listen to Alan go on and on about it for the whole of our holiday, as it had clouded his view of the passengers who had been sitting in the section of the plane where we had been, as they were all from the UK. He kept repeating that a thing like that wouldn't happen in Saudi, but then on thinking about it, it couldn't have done anyway.

CHAPTER 9

Move to a New Compound (January '07)

We had spent a couple of rushed weeks at home in Scotland for Christmas, doing the rounds of seeing close family, friends and relations. It had been lovely to be home for Christmas and New Year, but although we had succeeded in seeing everyone, it had gone past too quickly and too franticly. We hardly seemed to have had any time to ourselves between packing in Riyadh and packing in Scotland, the only difference being that our cases were considerably lighter going back than they had been coming out, as they had previously been full of Christmas presents. We were all pleased to get back to Riyadh as our trip home for the holidays had worn us out.

Putting on my *abaya* over my clothes, whilst still sitting on the plane was a struggle. I had left it too late to do so in the toilets, as there was an increasingly long queue of women standing in the aisle holding tightly onto black garments just before the plane started making its descent into Riyadh. Many of the women were Arabian, donned in the most up to date, expensive designer clothes, who seemed to be travelling without male companions or husbands. The contrast between the women entering the toilets done up to the nines in the latest fashions, heels and jewellery and the veiled women in *abayas* that then miraculously walked out a few minutes later was unbelievable. My jeans and kaftan had become heavily crumpled and creased on the journey, and an Arab who was sitting directly behind me on the plane took great pleasure in telling me that I looked much better in my *abaya*, much to the obvious embarrassment of his wives who were with

151

him. On that particular occasion, I had to agree.

We were all pleased to get back after the holidays, as although our visit home had left us all shattered, we were keen to get back to life in Riyadh. As soon as I had unpacked and the boys were back at school and nursery, I had to start packing again. This time it wasn't cases for a holiday, we were moving to a larger brand new compound further away from the city centre and the school, but which had more facilities and amenities. As I looked round the villa, I was amazed at how much stuff we had accumulated in such a short period of time. In particular it was toys, books and games for the boys that had taken over, as by this time they had acquired a keyboard, bicycles, a paddling pool and a green machine go-cart. I had also obtained rather a number of plants and containers which brightened up the garden, together with candles and lanterns from *IKEA*. Over the last sixteen months we had bought a double sun lounger, a shaded swing-seat and a table and chairs for the garden, as we spent a considerable amount of time outside when it wasn't too hot and all of these items would require to be moved to our new villa.

Having spent the past year and a half on a relatively small compound had its advantages and disadvantages. It had meant that we had got to know most people and families on the compound very quickly, but equally everyone knew everyone else's business, whether you wanted them to or not. Work life and circles permeated into home life in many ways, and even personal life, as the company was responsible for the welfare of its employees and their families. There was an element of snobbery among the expat community as to the compound that you lived on, with most senior managers living on one compound, managers living on another and so on, but there were some of us who had based our decisions purely around family life. Alan told me afterwards that a few eyebrows had been raised when we had moved into the first compound we chose, as it was not the compound that we had been expected to choose, but then we have always done our own thing.

Given that my husband worked in Human Resources, this sometimes made things very interesting, as HR had to deal with many additional things that ordinarily would fall out of the scope of the workplace in the UK because here many domestic matters could become company responsibilities - arranging for a wife and children to return home in the event of a separation or divorce, or becoming involved if an affair was discovered, or helping to organise and arrange marriage ceremonies at the Embassy at short notice (because of strict laws here, if an unmarried woman becomes pregnant then she requires to return home or get married as quickly as possible - a pregnant woman could be severely punished if found out, and her punishment could include lashings as well as deportation), informing next of kin and making the necessary arrangements for a dead body to be returned home to the UK after having dealt with the necessary Saudi authorities, dealing with employees and their families' health care whilst in Kingdom - illnesses, health issues, suicides or car accidents are only a few of the things I had been aware of. Although *EastEnders* was broadcast on one of the television channels we had, it was behind the broadcasts in the UK and I never watched it. To be honest, I found compound life in Riyadh to be far more interesting due to the fact that it was real and had a unique cultural slant due to where we were.

At this time we started watching the series *Lost*, and became seriously hooked, watching back to back episodes whenever we could, as soon as the children were settled down for the night. The frustrating thing was that the more you watched the more questions you wanted answers to, and it became infuriating when you had to wait for the next series to become available. The boys liked watching *Cartoon Network* and *Nickelodeon* once homework was finished, although their time staring at the screen was strictly limited.

I had become adept at becoming engrossed in reading books by the side of the pool and being selective at the conversations I would enter into. Talk amongst the women at the poolside varied considerably depending upon who was there, and subjects discussed included who on the compound had had what plastic surgery undertaken, and the best places or surgeons to have the work done, celebrity gossip from the latest *Hello* magazine if someone had managed to get hold of a copy, holidays, recipes, fitness, clubs and societies, property, children, school life, family life, social events and shopping.

One of the strangest conversations I have ever been party to involved one of the women telling me that she couldn't understand why her husband hadn't received the promoted post he had been interviewed for the year before. After a lot more talking on her part, and very little from me, it rapidly became apparent that she was talking about the job that my husband had been promoted to before we came out to Riyadh to join him. What was even more bizarre was that she knew that it was my husband who had been given the job her husband had applied for unsuccessfully. I pretended I had no knowledge of what she was talking about and merely stated that I was sure that the best candidate was given the job and I was certain there would be other opportunities for her husband in the future within the company. The prospect of moving to a larger compound where at least to begin with everyone wouldn't know everything about everyone else definitely had its benefits.

Packing and organising our move didn't take as long as I thought it would, as we had a removals company and packers to help us in addition to

George. Obviously there were things I wanted to pack myself, which I wouldn't have been happy for anyone else to do for me. I was glad we had opted for a furnished residence, as we didn't have the prospect of moving furniture to our new villa on top of everything else.

The day of the move was exciting. Calum left on the school bus first thing in the morning from our old compound, and returned from school on another bus which took him to our new compound. Getting settled took a bit of time. Because it was new, most of the facilities were not quite finished, so I made a start on the unpacking and had a walk to familiarise myself with my new surroundings. Once all the amenities were completed and up and running and the plants taken root it would definitely make a difference and soften the harsh manmade finishes everywhere that stood out so much as they were all new.

The villas were even more spacious than on our last compound and everything inside was in pristine condition. I still had a strange cooker, although it did work, which was the main thing. The only problem was that the smoke alarm would go off every time I used the cooker or boiled the kettle (and that was when I didn't burn anything).The washing machine used to dance round the floor and move out of its designated position as far as it could towards the middle of the kitchen as far as its attached hose would let it go, until workmen came to bolt it to the floor. The microwave was a joke - it played music that drove me to distraction when you used it - versions of songs like 'Auld Lang Syne' and 'Polly Put The Kettle On', sung in English by foreigners in accents and in a manner which totally murdered the original, so the microwave was often used by the boys in an attempt to try and wind me up, make me laugh or annoy me, depending on their mood and mine. Despite my numerous attempts, the infuriating soundtracks persisted as we needed it.

Clusters of villas were grouped round communal pool areas forming individual residential blocks, the gates around which were still taped up as the work hadn't quite finished. As soon as the tape was off, and the pools filled with water, Andrew learned how to unlock the back door when my back was turned, escape through the back garden, open the back gate and open the gate into the pool area. I called maintenance in quickly to sort this out, and childproof locks were fitted throughout the compound on my insistence. There was a central swimming pool indoors for serious swimming next to a large gym, tennis courts and we even had a couple of restaurants and a supermarket. The compound was much bigger than our last one and even had a bus to take you from the supermarket back to your villa. Although the walk wasn't long, in the heat it was necessary if you didn't want your shopping to have gone off before you put it in the fridge or freezer.

On my first trip to the compound supermarket, it was immediately obvious that it had been stocked with food by people who had no idea what staple foods Westerners had in their kitchens. There were rows upon rows of multi-coloured cocktail cherries, and numerous other food items that I had never seen before, as well as aisles stocked with soaps, washing powders, dishwasher powders and hand-washes. I came away from my first shopping trip to the compound supermarket somewhat disgruntled, as I hadn't even managed to find enough ingredients to make the family a meal, and they didn't even sell a newspaper. I purchased some bottles of water and cans of diet 7-Up, which when I returned to the villa erupted all over the kitchen floor and worktop and my clothes when I opened one, reflecting precisely how I felt at that moment. No more going on a bumpy bus with fizzy drinks if I didn't want a repeat performance of making myself hotter and stickier than I already was.

Our first couple of weekends on the compound started unforgettably when we were woken at six in the morning by the sound of a lawnmower. Given that during the week we were all up before six as the working day and school day starts so early, the weekend is a lie-in in comparison, even though you are still up relatively early. As the workers on the compound work six days a week, it hadn't even entered their heads that this was not what the residents of the compound would want to wake up to at the weekend, but there must have been a significant number of complaints to the compound manager, as this only happened on the first two Thursday mornings we were there, and didn't happen again.

About a week after the supermarket opened there was the most awful stench, as you walked in, which we later established was rancid fish that had gone off. At least they were now stocking meat and fish and edible bread rolls, but still no cheese or pasta. A few days later, the women on the compound had had enough and took matters into their own hands. One of them used to be a manager of a supermarket and she approached the compound management with a list of suggested foods. It still took time before the shop stocked a decent range of staple foodstuffs, but her relentless efforts on this front eventually paid off.

At this time, a takeaway facility opened on the compound, which had a few reasonably decent choices on the menu that were a real treat on a Wednesday night at the end of the week. We would find ourselves eating out more frequently until the supermarket shop improved, because although we went out of the compound and did a large supermarket shop once a week, you would rarely be able to purchase everything on your list.

Alan had informed me about a fantastic Thai restaurant he used to go to before we came out, and I finally managed to persuade him to take me with another couple we were good friends with. He hadn't been keen on taking me as the setting and surroundings weren't great. The restaurant's ambiance and décor were shabby, but the food more than made up for that, and we returned several times afterwards with the boys.

The new nursery was not operational on the compound to begin with, and the building was not fully completed, but it was a relief to learn that the manager from the nursery Andrew had been attending was going to run it. Most of her staff from the previous nursery would be coming with her, so I was pleased to hear that, even if it meant that my son had no nursery for a while. At least I knew some of the other women and children on the compound, so he had some friends to play with until the nursery was operational. I managed to get a sneak preview of the building whilst the staff set up the new facility, and I helped the manager compile a snagging list.

One weekend Alan took us for another drive early in the morning which is the best time to venture out and about. We had previously followed both the blue and the brown signs which direct you to Dirr'iyyah at the north-west of the city on several occasions without finding Addir'yyah. It was normal practice to spend a long time looking for somewhere you hadn't been to before, due to the lack of road signage and directions. This Friday morning we found ourselves driving along a wadi in this area purely by accident and we could see the ruined walled city right next to us. Addir'yyah was the Saudi dynasty's first capital in Wadi Hanaf and was formed in 1446. Just outside the city walls we could see an old well which had been restored and appeared to still be used in the traditional way, with donkeys harnessed up to pull up the water from the well. We saw brightly painted traditional doorways set into the walls along the properties that bordered the wadi, and I was glad we had stumbled through this area as it was in such a beautiful setting - the contrast of the ruined city against the sky and the oasis was unforgettable.

Having driven round in circles a few times, frustrated, we eventually worked out how to reach Addir'yyah by car and parked a short distance away from the entrance gate. We walked through one half of the main gate, which had been left ajar and past the caretakers office which was locked. There was a sign which had a map of the site on it, with the various buildings and palaces shown. We wandered round the deserted ruins of the one, two and three storey palaces, through narrow old streets and ruined dwellings constructed of mud bricks and adobe plaster on limestone foundations, exploring the uninhabited old walled city. Most of the windows at ground level were triangular, reducing the requirement for lintels to be used. Rainwater outlets were formed from hollowed out pieces of wood, which projected out over the walls at a slight gradient, channelling the water away from the buildings' outer walls, and some of these were still intact.

We were the only people there, although it was evident that surveying work was in progress as there were numerous levelling marks at various locations throughout the site. Strolling round the peaceful ruined streets, imagining how different and full of life it would have been when it was inhabited wasn't difficult, as the place was steeped in history, and there were little clues everywhere as to how life had previously been when you looked closely.

Walking round the old city walls along the ramparts, the views back towards Riyadh from the corner watchtowers over date palms, rocks and sand were unforgettable. From one side there was a fantastic view of the Diplomatic Quarter. Amazingly we could see the unmistakable landmark of Al Mamlaka in the distance from the other side, and get our bearings on where we were relative to the centre of the now modern capital city Riyadh. It was incredible to be standing in the beautiful antiquated ruins of the old capital and yet to be able to see such modern and contrasting architecture of the new capital at the same time. Standing there and taking my surroundings in, it summed up to me the very essence of Riyadh - a thoroughly modern city that is intrinsically linked to its roots and historical past, not just through its buildings but its culture and traditions.

As we had left to just go out for a drive that morning and hadn't intended on visiting Addir'yyah I hadn't brought my camera with me, so wasn't able to take any pictures that morning. It wouldn't have made any difference if I had, I would still have gone back. Addir'yyah had left its mark on me as my favourite place in Riyadh.

As the compound's inhabitants started to increase, social events started being organised, and clubs and societies formed, and a DVD library opened up. I started going to a keep-fit class at the gym, which was taken by a friend who had previously been denied permission to take classes on our last compound, even though she was a qualified fitness instructor. The restaurants opened, and we decided to live dangerously and try a Chinese sweet and sour. Unfortunately the food was completely unpalatable, tasting like chicken in a tomato and vinegar sauce, which is exactly what it must have been. In retrospect, we should have known better and stuck with the wonderful curries that the Indian catering staff were renowned for.

For a complete treat one day, or probably because I wanted a break from cooking (again), I bought *Birds Eye* Potato Waffles and fish fingers, which, being Western foods were at least three times the price back home. In Scotland, we would hardly ever have a meal like this, but it was something I would keep in the freezer as a standby for children coming round. We were all looking forward to our meal and I had even bought tomato ketchup to go with it, but when we put the food in our mouths, we all spat it out straight away as it tasted of soap. Unfortunately it must have been stored next to detergent at some stage in its journey - I didn't purchase any other frozen food again from the compound supermarket. So much for having an easy meal to put in the oven for a change... I ended up having to make us all something else to eat from scratch.

In hindsight, whilst I like cooking, I did not cook as much when we lived in Riyadh. I found that because of the heat, I was usually more thirsty than hungry and as a result did not like cooking as much. Many foods I would make at home frequently to warm us up in Scotland were just not the kind of foods you would cook or eat when it was so hot. In addition, although I found I could source most ingredients, the end result never tasted quite the same as it did at home as the ingredients were slightly different.

The compound had lots of open areas and pedestrian walkways, which, together with the courtyard areas, had all been planted up with varied plants and lots of climbers around trellised walkways and garden structures. There were also plenty of grassed areas. Walking Andrew to the new nursery on the compound in the morning coincided with the timing for the water sprinklers giving out sprays of water. As the water used was recycled, it always gave off an unmistakable odour that smelt off and left a pungent, rancid smell in the air. Walks to and from the new nursery on the compound were spent dodging the sprinklers, or in Andrew's case, making a beeline for them, and making as many wet footprints on the way as he could. Meeting up with play-mates en-route made for even more distractions, with the children running ahead, making a beeline for newly planted areas to explore on the way, or the play areas in each cluster that had been installed with no sun canopies or shading overhead, and the Mums and nannies doing their best to catch up behind them.

Andrew's best friend at the time Daniel was just as full of mischief as Andrew and when the two of them got together you never knew what would happen. Getting the two of them to and from nursery if they came across each other en-route was always interesting and would guarantee to give Daniel's Mum, Sarah, and I a workout on the way in the heat. On one occasion when I went to collect him after he had been playing at Daniel's, the pair of them had locked themselves in the bathroom and were having great fun playing with cotton buds, oblivious to the fact that we were outside and had had to work out a means of unlocking the door from the outside, as they had been in there for so long.

George drove me to the Kuwaiti Souq one morning, so I could choose some brightly coloured tapestry wall hangings and cushions to brighten up our new villa. There were several shops and stalls that were selling exactly what I wanted, so I haggled with the shopkeepers to obtain a good price. I had developed my bartering techniques during my time in Riyadh and had fun doing so, as it was an art in itself which could involve gesturing, pauses, huffs and even walking out of the shop. Feigning shock or horror at prices quoted is common practice, as is laughing at the initial reduction in price offered. Shopkeepers in the souqs expect to haggle and as a general rule, it was possible to obtain what you were after for three quarters of the original price quoted, but sometimes you could do even better. The best result occurred when both parties successfully negotiated a sale, where both the buyer and the seller were happy with the outcome, the buyer having made a sale at a good price and the seller thinking they had obtained a bargain.

The souq was full of Arabian women choosing items for their homes, and I felt perfectly safe wandering around looking at the goods on sale, taking in my surroundings and the people around me. I browsed stalls of home ware which sold everything you could think of, probably including the kitchen sink if I had looked persistently enough. Around me there were tailoring shops, furniture shops, carpet sellers, stalls with rolls of fabric and materials, carpet and rug stores, domestic stores, tapestry and cushion stores, a few gold selling outlets and spice stalls, where the aroma wafted through the air, enveloping you in its path as you walked past. There were beautiful patchwork quilts and bedcovers for a fraction of the price back home and I was sorely tempted, but I didn't buy them, as for us we would have found them too heavy and warm to use in Riyadh for most of the year.

George was very protective of me and on several occasions when I ventured out on lone shopping trips, although he was very discrete, he was never very far away. On the morning I frequented the Kuwaiti Souq I noticed that as soon as I had disappeared from his sight, he got out of the car and kept his eye on me, returning to the car before I did, giving the impression that he had been sitting in the car waiting for me all the while. Alan would have gone mad if he knew I sometimes ventured out on my own, but it was usually to a large shopping mall and not one of the open air souqs. Although with hindsight it perhaps wasn't an advisable thing to do as a Western woman at the time, I felt perfectly safe and I needed to get out of the compound on my own, as well as with friends from time to time, in order to keep my sanity. I wouldn't have gone out to the places that I did on my own if I didn't feel it was safe for me to do so.

I phoned the maintenance office on the compound to arrange for some men to come out to put up some picture hooks for the tapestries and pictures I wanted to hang on the walls. A few days later they appeared on the doorstep to do the work, having given me no warning. I showed them exactly where I wanted the items hung and uttered a few please (*minfadlak*) and thank-you's (*afwan*) in Arabic. Alan arrived home just as they were finishing, and as he was pleased with the standard of workmanship and the fact that they hadn't created too much mess, he expressed this in Arabic with a word I hadn't heard before - *'mumtaz'*, which means excellent. I think they were happier to receive a tip for their work than a compliment, but I think it's an excellent word.

There are some fantastic sounding words and phrases in Arabic, and one of my favourites has to be 'al-hum dil allah', which translated means 'thanks be to God'. It can be used as a response to 'how are you?' - *Kayf haalak?* (when addressing a male) or *Kayf haalik?* (when addressing a female), which translates as 'I am well thanks be to God'. It could also be used after burping, sneezing, waking up, narrowly missing crashing into another car, or one nearly crashing into you and obviously on numerous occasions. *Muta' assif* is another useful phrase, which means 'sorry'.

It was touching to learn that so many simple everyday phrases and greetings have deep meanings echoing Islamic beliefs, which reflect the extent that religion plays in daily life. Another example of this is *As-Salaam Alaikum*, which, although used as a standard greeting, means more to Muslims than a mere 'Hi' or 'Hello'. *As-Salaam* is one of the names of Allah, so the greeting means in the name of Allah may peace be upon you and may he protect you. *As-Salaam* also means submission or surrender, so when uttering the greeting it means that within the limits of Sharia Law we are submitting to what you want. An additional definition of *As-Salaam Alaikum* is protection or safety, and the greeting means that we will protect them from wrongdoing or evil, we will not do anything to cause harm to them physical, spiritually or cause grief through anything we say. To summarise, therefore when one Muslim greets another and uses this phrase, he or she is making the promise that Allah's laws will not be broken, reinforcing the peace of the Islamic religion.

We had been busy getting settled into our new villa on the compound, and Calum had decided that he didn't want a party, as his birthday fell during the school week and as he had Beavers after school, he had a busy day anyway. He specifically asked me to make him a cake and that we go out somewhere for a grown up meal out that evening as a family.

I had made the sponge for the cake earlier in the day and had left it to cool. When my youngest son went for a nap, I made some different coloured icing and decorated it and put the cake in the fridge for later. Once Alan was back from work, I waited till he had changed and went into the kitchen to put the candles on the cake. I could not believe my eyes when I opened the fridge door and saw the cake, as it bore no resemblance to the cake I had put there earlier - all round the top were immaculately placed curved chomp marks at regular intervals, where someone with a small mouth had taken small bites of cake and icing from the top edge, forming a perfect pattern all around the cake. Andrew started to cry as soon as I opened the fridge door, knowing he was in big trouble, but it was Calum I felt sorry for, as it was his birthday cake.

Andrew did not have a meal out that night, and neither did I. Purchasing an ice cream cake for us all to share at the last minute was out of the question on this birthday, as our compound was too far away from the nearest *Baskin Robbins*, and the ice cream would have melted by the time we got it home as we didn't have a cool-box. However, my husband and my eldest son had a great evening out just the two of them, which from the little information I gleaned afterwards included a visit to an amusement park at a local shopping mall and some ice cream.

On 4 February, seven Saudis and one foreign resident were arrested by Saudi security forces, suspected of fundraising for terrorists groups that operated outside the Kingdom. They were believed to have been collecting money and donations illegally in Saudi, and then passing the funds on outside the country.

Later in February, King Abdullah opened the Janadriyadh Festival, a celebration of the culture and traditions of Saudi Arabia, organised by the National Guard under the command of the Crown Prince. The festival was started a couple of years previously by the King to celebrate Saudi Arabia's culture and roots, amidst a country where the majority of its population has gone from nomadic desert life to modern city living within a few generations. The central reservations of the roads on the approach to the site of the festival were planted with brightly coloured flowers to mark the occasion. From what I had read in the press, the King and other Royal Princes had opened the festival, performing a traditional Nabatean sword dance known as the Al Ardah. Historically, this kind of dance would precede a march into battle, with swords and rifles thrown spinning into the air, before landing in the hands of the performers. Traditional drumming and music recitals featuring the Arabic oud, the Arabian lute, poetry readings and national dances performed by folklore troupes formed part of the celebrations. As part of the festival, on one day the Annual Kings Cup Camel Race is held, with more than two thousand riders taking part.

A women's day was publicised at the last minute, and an excursion to the festival was swiftly organised on the shopping bus. That morning, every single seat on the bus was taken. I went with my friend Grace, who had her three-month-old baby with her, and we were looking forward to having a wander round. The entrance to the festival was busy, and eventually we were all dropped off, having agreed a set time and location to return to the bus.

Walking round, we approached a courtyard set-up of traditional style buildings, with square corner towers, with white-painted, triangular-stepped castellations along the top. Tradesmen were demonstrating their traditional trades and crafts behind the covered open air walkways behind the white painted columns, with examples of their work on display and for sale - some were weaving, some making rope or pottery or traditional footwear or carving or woodworking or producing calligraphy. Numerous buildings were scattered over the site, reflecting differing building styles and traditions from across the Kingdom. There was a fort-like circular tower, which was built out of stone for the ground floor, and then adobe construction on the upper floors, with a thin layer of stone which projected over the outer face of the wall between courses, forming a horizontal stripe affect. Some buildings were clad entirely in stone, with stones of differing colour forming distinctively Arabic triangular and geometric patterns on the building's façade.

Every wooden doorway was beautiful, some hand-painted and decorated in bright colours with circular and triangular patterns, in the style of traditional doors at the historical sites I had previously visited in Riyadh and some painted plainly in one colour, but with geometric wooden decorations applied to the door faces, and some were not painted and were plain, whilst some were more intricately carved with patterns. One doorway in particular was unusual, as the opening itself was circular, with two semi-circular doors forming a perfect circle, adorned in symmetrical geometric brightly coloured patterns.

One area had been built to resemble an old city street, with meandering narrow pathways, along which you were able to browse through many items for sale from the numerous stallholders. Looking upwards, there were a number of beautifully crafted wooden vents, carved wooden screens, designed in such a way as to allow air to permeate through, but offering screening for privacy to the upper floor. There was also a mosque in this area, but we didn't attempt to go in as we knew that mosques in Saudi allow access to Muslims only.

I ventured onto an old dhow, an Arabic fishing boat, which had been set into the sand, with wooden access steps to allow you access on board. It was interesting to note that there was a wooden framework over the boat, over which material could be draped to provide well needed shade in the heat. Some buildings had rooms inside furnished with rugs and Arabic patterned cushions on which to sit, together with a few traditionally made lights which appeared to have been made out of goat or camel skin.

Women clad in *abayas* and veils over traditional brightly coloured clothing were selling woven goods made of goat or camel hair from a traditional Bedouin tent. At another location, slightly hidden away, a group of Arabic women were performing a dance which involved tossing their waist length hair from side to side and emitting loud shrieks and hopping from one side to another in time to the music. It seemed strange to have seen Arabic women fully veiled one minute and then to have moved on to see other Arabic women dancing unveiled and tossing their dark locks. This dance is known as *al-na-ish* or the hair toss. Traditional folk dances and songs are often performed at wedding parties by a folk band singing, dancing and playing for the guests.

Traditionally music forms an important part of life in the Middle East, with the call to prayer from the minarets five times a day from the mosques. Celebrations, national days, religious holidays and marriages provide an opportunity for family and friends to get together with music, dancing and singing. Historically music accompaniment would encourage people to work together to get the job done - whether it was pearl diving, camel or sheep herding, or making traditional craft items. The Bedouin have a large repertoire of chants and songs, the words of which reflect harsh desert life, memories or romance.

Musical instruments accompanying dancing and singing are percussion, string and wind. Some of them originate in neighbouring countries and travellers and traders passing through have left their influence. Drums are popular, with tensioned goat skin stretched and held in place with ropes fabricated from goat hair. For celebrations, various differing types of drums are laid round a fire. Rhythmic drumming very often announces the start of the festivities, with men in a circle or lines facing each other taking tiny steps, swaying to the music which usually increases in tempo towards the end. A mismah resembles an oboe and is a double reed wind instrument made of wood. A rabbah is a Bedouin fiddle, with a single string and bow. In towns and cities, the oud, the Arabian lute is popular. The oud is carved out of rosewood and resembles a guitar. Technically, music is seen as a frivolity in Saudi and the Muttawa discourage it, unless it forms part of a religious celebration.

It was lovely walking round with my friend Grace and her baby, as every single Arabic woman we encountered gave the baby attention, whether it was smiles, making faces, or singing. The Arabic women attending the festival were largely unveiled, deep in conversation, and were noticeably much more vocal and expressive, laughing and chattering away with their female companions, than I had seen them when comparing them elsewhere out and about. My friend and I took the opportunity to sit down when we found a quiet bench in the shade, and we took turns at feeding her baby her bottle.

Grace was just about to get up and put her baby in the pram when a group of unveiled young women approached us. One of them picked up the baby from my friends arms and started playing with her, holding her up and throwing her in the air, making faces and exaggerated facial expressions at her. Photographs were taken, and with our limited Arabic, we exchanged small talk before it was obvious that their English far surpassed our Arabic. I must admit my friend dealt with the situation calmly, taking everything in her stride, but I don't think I would have been quite so laid back if a stranger had attempted the same thing with one of my children at the same age. Having said that, at no time did we feel uneasy at what was going on.

One of the buildings housed information on Saudi's geology, minerals, the desert and sand dunes and protected areas. There were some truly amazing items on display and beautiful pictures showing sand formations and rock minerals. The desert roses were incredible to see - one of nature's amazing creations - crystalline formations of gypsum and barite creating petals and mineral flowers. In another was information on the development of women's involvement in society and at work in the Kingdom, together with lots of brochures and information on new policies and initiatives on the subject.

Another building was devoted to Saudi food products, and the development of agriculture and the farming industry which has happened so quickly and is already so advanced was most informative. There were pictures on the wall of the circular irrigation systems used in Saudi, resulting in the circles of crops which are visible from the air. Almarai and Al Safi, the two main dairy producers, had areas devoted to their industry, with data on their environmentally controlled sheds which house cattle or chicken. There were displays about date farming and lots of information on dates and date palms. I had never known there were so many differing varieties of date before. I left with a huge bag full of goodies which included dates, yoghurt, milk and fruit juice. I found the information available on hydroponics was particularly interesting, where plants were grown in plastic tubes with running water in which plant food is dissolved, and in some cases where only a very minute amount of water was involved, which has huge potential.

There was a fascinating exhibition of the history of the telephone and communications in Saudi Arabia, with examples of phones and communications equipment, demonstrating their development. The telecoms exhibition was staffed by two women who were unveiled, and not wearing *abayas*, but suits, and we spent some time with them eating dates, drinking coffee and making conversation with them. Their English was excellent. There was also another building displaying information from the governments finance ministry, and another about the armed forces. The Saudi Arabian Monetary Agency had a display of currency and its history which was informative.

Two camels were harnessed up and were drawing water up from an underground well through a structure using ropes and wooden pulleys, which was great to watch. Bottled Zamzam water was also available. Zamzam water is water from a well in Mecca. Millions of pilgrims visit the well and drink its water, as it is believed to have miraculous powers. Despite the amount of water that is consumed from the well, it has never gone dry. In Islamic history, Hagar, the wife of Abraham, was unable to find water for her baby son Ishmael around the year 2000 BC. According to one version of the story, Hagar was searching unsuccessfully between the hills of Safa and Marwah, when Ishmael scraped the sand with his feet and water sprang out. In another, God sent the angel Gabriel (Jibreel) who kicked the ground before the water appeared.

An ancient-looking cannon was strategically placed in front of a gated doorway to another inner courtyard area. There were so many things to see, we were unable to fit everything into the few hours we had available to us before we had to return to the bus. I was glad to have had the chance to attend the festival and it was obvious that both the Saudis who were taking part and the Saudis who were visiting were extremely proud of their heritage and culture and were only too happy to share the festivities and information on their country with foreigners. Some of the women from the bus stayed on, making arrangements for drivers or taxis to pick them up outside the main entrance later, but it was starting to heat up and the sun was becoming too strong to make wandering about outside between the pavilions feasible. Besides, I had a child to pick up from nursery on the compound as soon as the bus dropped us back.

A couple we were good friends with were going out to a social event we were also attending, so my husband and I managed to cadge a lift. The men sat in the front, obviously because one of them was driving, and I sat chatting in the back to my friend. The rear windows of the car were not fitted with tinted solar film, so as passengers we could be seen from outside the car. We couldn't believe it when a car drew up next to ours, flashing its lights at us, the driver driving at the same speed as the car we were in, bringing his car dangerously close to ours, with both hands off the steering wheel, making frantic hand gestures for us to cover our hair.

My friend Lisa had long blonde hair and had not been in Riyadh for long. Our husbands were livid as we had been approached directly and not them. The driver of our car put his foot down and drove us away at incredible speed, telling us that the Arab driver shouldn't have been looking at other men's wives and that whilst in his car we did not have to cover up our hair. Within the week, I couldn't help noticing that the car we had been passengers in had tinted solar film fitted to its rear windows. This had happened once before when I had been travelling in the front passenger seat with my husband driving, but on that occasion, the signing had been to my husband and not to me. My husband had done the same thing, putting his foot down on the accelerator, making his Dodge Durango's engine growl in the process, which he took immense pleasure in doing whenever he could get away with it, and was why he had nicknamed his car 'the beast'. I had a feeling that the beast growled somewhat more frequently in the Riyadh traffic when the boys and I were not passengers in the car.

In the early hours of the morning of 24 February, Alan shook me violently like he had never done before.

"Get up. Get up now, Nicky." He was yelling at me with an unmistakable urgency in his voice I had never heard before. I didn't want to get up at that moment and could easily have rolled back over again - I was tired and had been in a deep sleep, but my nose twitched with a tickling sensation, and as I struggled to open my sleep-filled eyes something didn't feel right. I couldn't see properly, everything seemed to be a mustardy yellow, and there was an acrid sulphuric smell. I found myself unable to breathe through my nose, and had to open my mouth to compensate for this. However, my throat contracted automatically and I started to cough and splutter as I took in some of the thickening yellow smoke through my mouth. Coming to and realising that the familiar surroundings around me were smoky and blurred, I instantly jumped out of bed.

We rushed out of our bedroom to open the boys' bedroom doors, our only thoughts being to get them out of there and out of the villa as quickly as possible. The smoke was even denser and it was hard to get my bearings. Alan carried Calum while I cradled Andrew into my arms, feeling our way cautiously but purposefully downstairs through the murky smoke and out through the hallway and the kitchen and out of the villa. By this time we were all coughing and choking badly, struggling for breath and gasping for air. The same thing was running through both our minds simultaneously, which was terrifying. We were both convinced there had been some kind of chemical attack on the compound.

Whilst attempting to catch our breath outside, it became obvious that whatever had happened had only affected our villa. Alan returned inside to the living room, which didn't seem to be so badly affected, and phoned for the compound fire engine even though we could see no fire. I had managed to grab a bottle of water on my way out through the kitchen and was making sure everyone was taking some sips in between coughs and that our breathing was slowly returning to normal. I then phoned my best friend on the compound, Grace, from my mobile, sitting on the swing seat in the garden in my nightie, to see if I could bring the boys over to sleep on her couch for the remainder of the night.

Having taken the boys over in the early hours of the morning, for the first few minutes or so, our conversation was at cross purposes and not making any sense. My friend had a very young baby at the time and another two children, and this was the third time she had been woken up that night, having been up earlier to feed her baby. She was still half asleep and had assumed that Alan and I were in the midst of a huge domestic argument.

Returning to the villa, having borrowed some of Grace's clothes, I could see the compound fire engine with its flashing lights on outside. We were given the all-clear to go back inside. There was a fine light grey powder that seemed to cover absolutely everything in sight. There was no way we could return to our villa to sleep that night, so I gathered together some bits and pieces that the boys would need while I was there. It emerged that the fire extinguisher fitted on the upstairs landing for our safety had exploded - the pressure had built up inside and caused the cap to be blown off, making a huge dent on the ceiling on the upper floor landing and releasing the ultra-fine powder contents all over every available surface throughout the villa, under extreme pressure. Thankfully the noise had woken Alan immediately.

The investigation that followed established that somewhere on its route from the factory to being fitted in our villa, the fire extinguisher must have been knocked or dropped and this is what caused the pressure to build up. Exploding fire extinguishers are a rare occurrence, but if our door hadn't been left only slightly ajar, or if one of us had been on the landing when it happened, the consequences could have been very different. We were all very lucky to have had such a narrow escape.

After experiencing this event and having had a huge fright, we were all ill for several weeks, having inhaled the contents of the dry chemical powder from the fire extinguisher. It took at least two weeks and a lot of washing and cleaning before we had the villa back to normal. Every single surface, toy, or household item needed cleaned. All of our clothes required to be taken to the dry-cleaners as the fitted cupboards were all open with no doors. George was a fantastic help - without him it would have taken at least a month's worth of cleaning and washing to get the place back to normal.

Alan and I were extremely relieved that the reality of what had happened wasn't as it had first appeared to us, but to this day (not surprisingly) we are all particularly wary of fire extinguishers.

My husband's company had its own medical centre for its employees and families, which was staffed by doctors and nurses and provided excellent care and facilities throughout the time we were in Riyadh. We were referred to local hospitals on a couple of occasions when we were in Riyadh and found the standard of medical care and treatment available to be excellent, although setting up appointments was tricky and could take time.

Unfortunately towards the end of February we learned of the shootings that had taken place when Westerners were returning from a visit to the historical site of Madain Saleh. Due to the fact that visitors to this archaeological site were required to apply in advance for permission to visit, they had become easy targets. The group had been travelling in three vehicles and had stopped for a rest when they were attacked. All four males in the group were shot, two of whom died at the scene, one on his way to hospital and a sixteen-year-old boy died the next day in hospital. I was relieved that we had paid heed to the advice given at the numerous security briefings we had attended, as there were various places that would have been wonderful to visit whilst we were in Riyadh that required advance permits or permissions, which we had been advised was a strict no-no at the time.

Our kitchen floor had started to show signs of movement cracks, which was not reassuring. Whilst on the phone reporting it to the compound manager I was horrified to see the front tyres of the compound bin lorry sink into the ground straight across the road from our villa, and nearly tip it over in the process. Thankfully no-one was hurt. That afternoon, the maintenance men made repairs to the paved road area, after the bin lorry had been towed out. I wondered what kind of foundations had been built under our villa, if they were adequate and whether the paved road areas were unable to take the weight of a laden bin lorry, or whether there was a fault line that ran through our villa and across the road. It emerged that many of the floors in the kitchens of the villas in our block had cracks that were appearing, and we were advised that the cracks were not as a result of the washing machines being bolted to the floor, but only minor settlement cracks. As the compound was built on sand, I suppose cracks were only to be expected.

The weekend after Mothers' Day, which had been Sunday 18 March in the UK, the boys announced on the Friday that they had planned a surprise for me, and we headed into the centre of town for something to eat. Alan parked next to the Al Faisalia Shopping Complex, and I presumed we were going to have something at the food court there. I was astounded when I was told that a reservation had been made for us to have high tea at the Globe, which I knew from the women who had been, cost a fortune. We spent a bit of time wandering round the shops first, as we had given ourselves plenty of time, as you never can tell with the traffic, and getting parked in this bustling part of the city can take a while. I hadn't been into Harvey Nicholls before, so I did that, although I didn't buy anything as the few things that caught my eye were incredibly expensive.

The Al Faisalia Centre is made up of the Al Faisalia Hotel, luxury apartments, thirty floors of office space, and a two storey shopping mall and a function suite. The banqueting and conference centre under the ground floor plaza is one of the world's largest single support column free spaces and can hold up to two thousand people for Islamic weddings or even more for conferences. The space has been designed to be flexible, to maximise its use and can be subdivided into as many as sixteen separate rooms.

At the base of the tower there is a five storey lobby and a huge piazza which links parts of the building together. In the lobby there is a glazed wall which houses the largest stained glass window to have ever been made. The window depicts natural, regional, environmental and desert images and was made by the artist Brian Clarke. The tower contains a restaurant within the glazed sphere which is known as the Globe, and there is a cigar lounge on the top floor. The elevators and stairs are within the central tower. It was designed by the British Architects Foster and Partners and Buro Happold Engineers and was completed in the year 2000, when it was Saudi Arabia's first skyscraper. It is two hundred and sixty-seven metres high and has a total of forty four floors, and at the time was the second tallest building in Saudi Arabia, the tallest being Al Mamlaka.

The conceptual design idea was that of a ballpoint pen. The tower is one of the two major landmarks in Riyadh, with four angled corner steel beams rising from the ground to join together at a central point above a sphere, topped by a bright lantern and a steel finial. The building is clad in anodised aluminium panels and has non-reflective energy efficient glass panels and cantilevered sun shading devices across it. Its K bracing within the structure transfers the loads from the building to the four external columns.

Having taken the elevator up to the observation deck, we were able to walk outside onto an observation platform, from which you could see the huge sphere that housed the restaurant directly above us, and we could see our distorted reflections through the glass. We walked three hundred and sixty degrees round the deck and viewed the city in all directions. There were benches to sit on, but I walked round slowly taking everything in. There was a slight breeze, which was pleasant, although I did have to hold onto my *abaya* and headscarf (which was round my neck as usual), to stop them flapping about and exposing more of me than was acceptable. I couldn't help but chuckle to myself as I found myself coming face to face with full size line drawings of people clad in Western clothes adorning screens, in the same style as those I had added to my architectural drawings to give them a sense of scale when I was a student many years previously. I wondered which one of the many graduates from Scott Sutherland School of Architecture was responsible, and whether our previous studio tutor Ian Ramsay knew the full extent of his influence in another part of the world. Those drawings definitely looked like 'Ramsayman' figures to me, as we used to call them.

Making our way up from the observation deck to the globe restaurant, we were guided to our seats, past the assortment of delicacies for us to help ourselves to. The boys were jumping up and down in excitement, not at their incredible surroundings, being inside a restaurant with curved glass walls, so high up, but at an enormous white chocolate fountain, with an assortment of fruits next to it that they could dip into the chocolate. We sat down, and I was told by the staff that I could remove my *abaya* if I wished, which I did instantly.

Filling up my plate from the assortment of sweetmeats, precisely cut miniature sandwiches and delicacies on offer, I watched city life unfold beneath me from an exclusive rooftop view. The weather was slightly dusty on the day we had come, but we were still able to get a good look at the traffic and the rooftops across Riyadh. As the building is in direct axis with the most famous landmark in Riyadh, the Kingdom Tower at Al Mamlaka, we were also able to gaze straight over to it. It was a Mothers' Day treat I will never forget, and was Calum's idea, who knows what I appreciate. My husband, being a typical Scotsman said he enjoyed the experience, but complained about the price and the small finger sized snacks on offer, and joked about wanting to buy a take-away on the way home afterwards. He didn't say so directly, but I think he was still hungry.

We were looking forward to our Easter holidays, which involved us having a break at home, but also flying to Wrocklaw in Poland to attend a friend's wedding, for a long weekend. Wrocklaw was a pleasant surprise, and well worth a visit, with lots to see and do. The main square's architecture was beautiful with styles ranging from Gothic to Art Nouveau. Much of it had been painstakingly rebuilt in the twentieth century after its devastation in World War Two.

CHAPTER 10

Making the Most of Our Time Left in the Magic Kingdom (April '07)

It seemed unreal flying out on Emirates from Glasgow to Dubai, and then flying Saudair to Riyadh, with the knowledge that these would be our last flights out. Andrew had been winding me up on our last few trips, deliberately advising me that he had a bomb in his rucksack he was taking on the plane. He would usually tell me this when we were standing in a queue at the airport, surrounded by plenty of Arabs who could hear every single word he uttered. His voice at that age seemed to have an on and off switch and would either come out very deeply and very loud, or would be so quiet you had to ask him to repeat whatever it was he had said to you. It was guaranteed to be loud and inappropriate if he repeated himself, after I didn't hear what he had initially said, so I couldn't win either way. Security had been markedly stepped up in the time since we started making our journeys back and forth and he had taken all of this in, knowing exactly how to rile me at the most inopportune moments.

On the past few flights we had taken, the security had been upped considerably, which had resulted in the boys taking an overactive interest in it and asking endless questions. They both wore belts to keep their trousers up, and their belts required to be taken off to go through security, but one of them ended up with his trousers at his ankles when walking through, which did not go down well and resulted in a huge tantrum. In addition, shoes now also required to be removed, which was a complete kerfuffle, and even if it was for a good reason, try explaining that to your children, who are refusing to take their shoes off when there is a long line of passengers behind you. I didn't tell them that there had previously been a failed bombing attempt by Al Qaeda in which someone had boarded a plane with bomb making equipment in their shoes a few years previously, and that recent intelligence now meant that everyone's shoes had to be checked as a precaution. I just told them they had to take their shoes off to go through the machine, or we wouldn't be allowed on the plane.

As I hadn't given them enough information, I found myself having a long chat with them as they had worked things out for themselves and had taken it personally that the airport staff thought they would be carrying a bomb in their shoes. Having to then explain that everyone had to be treated the same way, regardless of their age or who they were and that I was sure the airport staff didn't really think that they were child bombers just caused the boys to come up with even more questions. To their minds, no parent or adult would give children shoes to wear that could blow up a plane. Having these types of uncomfortable conversations with my children was tricky, but at a time when passengers had been thrown off planes for even mentioning the word bomb, and with people round you listening to every single word you said just before boarding a flight, travelling with boys who had enquiring minds was certainly not stress-free. At times like those, I found myself questioning why I had brought them up to ask questions, which was ridiculous, and it would usually end up with me telling them to be quiet and asking them to leave their questions till later, once our journey was over and we could talk properly in private. Sometimes with particularly difficult questions I hoped that they would forget what they had asked me, but one of them would always remember. At least with a bit of time to consider my answers, it meant that I could prepare my responses for later.

Not being allowed to take water through with you when it was hot, guaranteed that it would be difficult to find water to purchase once through the other side of security, and of course, it would be at an inflated price if you were lucky enough to find any. I hated it if I couldn't find any water, as we preferred to take sips from water bottles on take-off and landing to help our ears adjust to the altitude. I always purchased some sweets if I was unable to find any water, as on a particularly bad series of flights, you could end up with extremely sore ears for several days afterwards if you didn't have anything with you to suck or drink.

The boys had been given wonderful Saudair rucksacks when we flew with them the year before. The rucksacks were good quality and perfect hand baggage for them for the plane, but unfortunately as they had Saudair logos and graphics all over them, it meant that their bags were always given an extra search at Glasgow airport and again in Dubai. Given that our passports had Saudi multi-visit visas in them the customs officials always seemed to have an extra-specially good look at them, and at us, asking us questions about where we were going and what we were doing in Saudi Arabia. We had all become accustomed to the quick external body searches too, as a matter of routine - even the children had to go through this procedure. We had all too quickly adapted to all the flying backwards and forwards during the holidays, and having two places that we called home. It was sad to think that the next time we would be flying home to Scotland we would be leaving Riyadh for good.

On 19 April, the day we arrived back in Riyadh, the authorities announced that eight people had been arrested for aiding and abetting in the terrorist incident in Madain Saleh in February. I also learned that while we had been away there had been a gun battle with militants at a villa twenty kilometres outside Medinah and that Al Radadi, who had been on the country's most wanted terrorist list since 2005, had been killed in the shootout. It transpired he had been behind the French expat killings in February, and that the shootout had occurred during an investigation into the incident.

I was absolutely determined to re-visit some of my favourite haunts around and outside Riyadh during the few months we had left, and to make sure I had pictures of the places we had visited. There were also a number of places I hadn't yet visited that I wanted to see, and scoured my copy of Riyadh Today, that I had found in Carrefour in January, even though it was now out of date. It had been an incredibly useful purchase and was a good guide to Riyadh, with lots of useful information put together by the Chamber of Commerce and Industry. Inside this handy compact guide to Riyadh it contained information on everything from compounds, hotels, eating out, businesses, things to do and see, shopping information, lists of businesses and back ground and historical information on the country. It even had a map which you could pull out from its back cover, which had been invaluable.

I made sure I had a variety of pictures depicting places we had visited, receipts showing Arabic writing and some small Arabic riyals for the boys' scrapbooks. I had taken photographs of them at nursery and school when I had gone to attend charity fundraisers, sports days and plays, and they had pictures of their nursery and school classes, and these all were pasted into their scrapbooks over the next couple of months.

I took the boys to the National Museum which is a wonderful modern museum to visit and was completed as part of the centenary celebrations, a hundred years after the taking of Riyadh by King Abdul-Aziz in 1902. The architecture itself is splendid, with the building having been inspired by the red sand dunes that surround Riyadh. The museum has eight themed galleries of information and displays the history of the Kingdom. The first gallery depicts the creation of earth and man - Man and the Universe and the environmental conditions which led to the formation of the Kingdom's minerals and oil, while the second covers the Arabian Kingdoms - the civilisations in the Arabian peninsula from 600 BC to AD 400, including the development of trade and calligraphy. The third gallery is all about Jahilyyah, the period of ignorance before Islam. The next gallery is the Prophets Mission, which documents the life of the Prophet Mohammed. The fifth gallery, Islam and the Arabian Peninsula deals with the history from the hejira of the Arabian peninsula up to the early nineteenth century, when the first Saudi state was founded. The sixth gallery displays information on the first and second Saudi states, life in Dir'iyyah and the alliance between Imam Mohammed bin Abdul-Wahab and the Al Sauds, the expansion and conquest of the peninsula, the invasion of the Ottoman forces, the siege and destruction of Dir'iyyah, Imam Faisal bin Turki's return and the second state and the early life of King Abdul Aziz. The seventh gallery concerns the unification of Musmak and Riyadh and the conquest of the regions within the Kingdom. Typical architecture from each region is displayed in full size models, which are fantastic to explore. The background to the exploration and discovery of oil is also displayed. The final gallery, Hajj and the two Holy Mosques show the routes that pilgrims took in the past, and the history of the mosques and their role in the pilgrimage and the development programmes that have enabled millions of pilgrims to perform Hajj each year.

We also managed to pay a quick visit to the Al Murabba Palace where King Abdul Aziz set up court in the late 1930s. The two-storey building has been restored and is a tribute to him. It has a central courtyard, with the royal office upstairs. The King had a personal lift installed, as he suffered from arthritis, and it was the first ever lift in Saudi Arabia. From the second floor there is a walkway which leads to the King Abdul Aziz Memorial Hall which is full of personal belongings, clothes, jewellery, swords, glasses and photographs showing him meeting many statesmen from all over the world.

I could easily have spent much longer than I did going round the exhibits and displays, but as I had the children with me at the time, we did pretty well, even if I didn't get the chance to look at everything in as much detail as I would have liked.

It was reported that there was a vast quantity of explosives, ammunitions and firearms found buried in the desert. This led to the arrests of one hundred and seventy-two militants towards the end of April, after intelligence had been gathered following the raids of seven terrorist cells over the past few months. Watching this on sky news, we couldn't help but scour the screen, trying to establish if we could work out where the pictures had been taken, but aside from the colour of the sand, there were no landmarks or distinctive features in the shots that gave any clues to the location. Five million US dollars had been recovered in the operation, which seemed incredible. Most of those arrested were Saudi nationals, some of whom had trained as pilots, and there was evidence to prove attacks were being planned on military and oil installations together with plans to assassinate high profile individuals. The scale of this was hard to comprehend, but it was evident that there was a huge amount of work going on to stop terrorism in the country.

Around this time, there were some very large spiders on the compound. I had seen many spiders since I had been in Riyadh, but I had familiarised myself with those to be avoided. On the same cluster of villas where we were staying, a black widow spider had been spotted, so it was advisable to be on the lookout. A few days later, a couple watched a small black widow spider encircle a tiny snake into the tubular web that it created to capture the snake in. It was incredible to think that the web that the spider spun was strong enough to capture a small snake. I did see one small black widow spider on the compound, but it wasn't anywhere near our villa. I never did see a tarantula in Riyadh but I did see some large spiders.

At short notice, Calum came home from school with a letter advising that he needed to come into school the next day wearing a green T-shirt, as they were being split into colour co-ordinated groups for the activities they were to undertake. As he did not possess a green coloured T-shirt, we needed to go out to the shops late that night when Alan could drive us, after tea and prayers. Going to one of the malls late at night with the boys was a totally different experience to going when it was quiet, early in the morning. It was so busy we had to wait to get parked, and the mall was bustling with groups of young Arabs, both men and women, immaculately dressed to impress. Many of the young women were just standing chatting in small groups, and were unveiled, with their heavily made-up faces on display. I didn't have to wait long to ascertain what was going on, as while we walked down the mall I witnessed a young man throw a young woman a mobile phone with a smile, and further on I couldn't help but notice another man slip a very pretty young girl a folded-up piece of paper which must have had his mobile number on it when he walked past. I wondered how many of the girls had managed to give their guardians the slip that evening, and whether we had stumbled across a typical evening at this mall, or whether this kind of thing only happened when organised at differing locations across the city on set dates and times. It goes without saying that there were no Muttawa present when we were there that night.

We had heard that whilst we had been in Riyadh there had been a marked increase in criminal behaviour, but this did not find itself reported in the papers. One of the managers in Alan's company had been out at a neighbouring mall at around the same time that evening, and we learned the next day that he had found his vehicle window smashed in on return to his car and his company laptop stolen, which was a major security risk for the company. He had never given a second thought to concealing his laptop if leaving it in the car before this, whilst out and about in Riyadh as the crime rate was so low. The laptop was never recovered. Alan's company briefed all employees that they could no longer leave items of any value on display in a vehicle when it was parked.

We paid one last visit to Addir'yyah, and I made sure I took my camera this time. The caretaker's office was open on this visit, and I picked up a brochure from the tiny information centre, which had a map of the walled city and more detailed information on the buildings contained within it. When we had walked round the last time, although there were wooden signs outside some of the buildings and palaces, going back again, with a map and some information on the buildings made our trip to such a memorable place particularly worthwhile.

I took photographs the whole time we were strolling round the site, as I wanted to try and capture the essence of the place and have a record of it. I was pleased to learn years later while I was writing this book that in 2010, Addir'yyah became a UNESCO archaeological heritage site, so its history and buildings are now protected for future generations. The whole area is currently being substantially reconstructed in a huge development programme of three phases, and a new visitor centre and facilities, together with new road networks are part of the proposals. Following one of our previous visits, I had found black and white pictures on the internet which had been taken initially when Addir'yyah was still a bustling, vibrant and inhabited capital. Everywhere we had walked was instantly recognisable, and the pictures I had seen brought the city to life.

The houses are of traditional Nadji design, with rooms that open off a central courtyard, and would have been partially open to the elements and partially covered by the women's quarters on the upper level, which were supported on limestone pillars. The men's majlis or sitting area is located to one side of the entrance on the ground floor. Athil wood, palm tree leaves and branches would have been used as roofing, while the doors and lintels and rainwater outlets were made from local palm, athil or tamarisk wood.

The highest part of the city houses the Saad Bin Saud Palace, which has an external courtyard which was used as a stable. Once inside the beautifully decorated floral blue red and black wooden entrance door you could see the traditional inner courtyard, which all of the rooms in the palace opened into. To the left of this palace there was a Turkish Steam Bath House, which was unusual to find in an Arabian city, which was waterproofed with a special type of plaster.

The mosque of Imam Mohammad Bin Saud was originally constructed during the first Saudi state and students used to travel to it from all parts of the Arabian peninsula, as it was a centre for religious education. There is another mosque on the site and many more palaces and houses, but my favourite, the oldest, largest and most picturesque has to be Salwa Palace which is right next to the entrance. This palace was the home of Al Saud Amirs and Imams during the first Saudi state from 1803 until 1814. There are five main parts to this palace, housing residential complexes, built at differing consecutive periods. Originally a bridge linked them to the mosque at the other side of the main entrance. I was glad to have remembered to take my camera and that I had managed to take so many pictures of such a special place.

Yet again my blonde, long-haired friend and I went on an excursion to the shops in the morning. We would usually purchase what we had gone in for, have a browse round and make our way to *Starbucks* for an iced coffee Frappuccino, which was particularly refreshing. We had gone to Kingdom mall, and decided to have a wander around the ladies only top floor. There was one lift that went all the way up to the top floor, although there were also escalators and stairs, all patrolled to ensure men could not gain access. On this occasion, we decided to take the glass lift and as we made our way towards it, a couple of veiled Arabic women came out from the lift, who I would guess were around the same age as us. We smiled at them as we walked towards them, and they smiled back with their eyes. Before we knew what was happening, both of the ladies had approached my friend and gently touched her hair, while continuing to smile at us as they chattered away in Arabic. We exchanged a few small limited pleasantries in Arabic and the women continued on their way. My friend and I were both gob-smacked, as the incident had taken us so much by surprise that we found ourselves unable to say a single word straight afterwards, but we both burst out laughing, before discussing what had just happened.

A formal ball was organised to take place on the compound, which was to be the first on the new compound. It was to be a tuxedo and ball-gown affair, with one of the large hotels in the city providing the cuisine and waiter service. There was a band and a disco and it was an unforgettable evening. We had managed to get seats at a good table made up of some close friends and others we knew which made a huge difference. Alan wore his kilt, although he must have been absolutely sweltering, but he was not alone, as there were a few Scots who donned kilts that night.

Sitting on our swing seat outside the villa one morning reading a book under its shaded canopy, something made me look downwards onto the ground. Marching diagonally forwards at top speed with its loaded tail curled high in the air heading towards my feet was the biggest scorpion I had ever seen. I quickly brought my feet up onto the swing seat and kept them there for a while. I'm not sure why I looked down when I did, but I think I had noticed something moving quickly out of the corner of my eye. If I hadn't looked closely I could have thought it was a large leaf getting blown across the paving, but its movement was too deliberate. As the compound was situated slightly out of town, it could get quite breezy, but a bit of a gentle wind was always welcome in the heat.

Driving in an area of Riyadh we hadn't been to before, we were amazed to find that along one long road were a series of outdoor amusement parks and funfairs. It was very strange driving along in daylight, because it felt as though you were driving along a road at a beach promenade, only instead of the sea at one side of you there was sand and amusement parks behind walls that were deserted during the day. They would have been packed in the evenings, when the Saudis go out. You could just about make out the tops of many of the rides over the walls.

On 27 and 28 March the Arab Summit was held in Riyadh. Due to the dignitaries who were attending, many of the roads were off-limits in the centre of Riyadh for the full two days, with access only being made available to those attending the summit. The Saudi Ministry of Education instructed that schools were to be closed on these days and companies in the area gave their employees a couple of days off work as their offices were closed.

At around this time there was a tremendous uproar on the compound. A fair-haired woman had been seen gallivanting with one of the house-boys early one morning apparently romping about on the grass behind one of the sloped grassed areas on the compound. Whether it was just a malicious rumour that was being spread around or not I had no idea, but every blonde on the compound was required to account for her actions on that day, if not by her friends then also by her husband. Not surprisingly, no-one owned up to being involved.

I had heard stories from several differing sources that one executive's wife had run off with her house-boy in the past, several years previously, never to return, and I subsequently established that this was true. I must admit I had to smile to myself at the thought of having a husband who would willingly undertake all domestic household duties and do them well. I also secretly admired the woman who had left her luxurious lifestyle and executive expat husband to live an entirely different lifestyle to that which she had become accustomed to, with a man she had obviously fallen deeply in love with.

There were a few execs of whom I had had the misfortune to encounter whilst in Riyadh who were despicable individuals who did not have much respect for women, and I presumed that her executive husband must have fallen into this category. Regrettably for their wives and families, and presumably not for them, it was not unknown for some executives and married bachelors to live double lives. I was horrified to discover that it was often common knowledge that some married men living in Riyadh whose wives and family were living back home, but had long-term live-in girlfriends in Saudi. The girlfriend would move out temporarily together with her belongings whenever the family came over for holidays.

Obviously the girlfriend would have her own accommodation elsewhere, as technically she would not be living with a married man (or indeed an unmarried man). Clearly, any live-in arrangements failed to comply with Saudi law and could have potentially severe repercussions for all involved. Some of these relationships went on for many years. I knew of several wives who only found out about their husbands' double lives when their contracts expired and they decided not to return home to their wife and family, or they decided it was time for a divorce, or they discovered evidence or found out that someone else was living with their husband in the villa.

Yet another new shopping mall had been completed, the Hyatt which was enormous. The supermarket within it was the Danube which was expensive but well stocked, with foods from around the world and plenty of foods and brand names that were recognisable. You still couldn't beat Tamimi for their meats, fish, cheese and bread selection though. This mall was particularly spacious, and had a fun zone within it, together with a very large food court.

On one occasion when I went to the Sahara mall where Tamimi is, I decided to have a look round the shops first, but couldn't get the mall doors to open at all. While I was trying to puzzle this out, an Arab who was sitting down inside watching my pathetic attempts got up and came over to the doors I was trying to open, and beckoned me to another set of doors, which he held open for me while I walked through. There was actually some kind of sign on the doors in Arabic, presumably advising customers to use the other doors, which I only noticed afterwards, as I couldn't read it. I said, "*Shukran*," to the *thobe* clad Arab, who had kindly come to my aid, and was stunned when he replied in an impeccable Cockney accent, "No problem, you're welcome," with a big grin. I gave him a big smile, but couldn't manage to contain myself, and burst out laughing, as the reply was so far removed from the "*Afwhan*" I had been expecting.

Around this time, my husband managed to obtain tickets through a friend for us to attend the Hash Ball at the British Embassy. We had a great night, after which I knew much more about the Hash Harriers than I had done previously. The Hash House Harriers have clubs worldwide where groups of people meet to participate in running and social events. In Riyadh there are several hash groups who meet up in the desert, usually at the weekend. Sometimes co-ordinates are given, or there is a designated meeting place, from where a caravan of SUVs set off together to their destination, as a lone vehicle should never venture into the desert. On arrival, everyone would take in their surroundings, before most people in the group would set off on the hash. The leaders on the run are called the hares and the rest of the group the hounds. If I had been in Riyadh before young children, I would definitely have joined. Perhaps I should now clarify that the term 'hash', although commonly used as a shortened word for 'hashish' has absolutely nothing to do with the Hash House Harriers. I must admit, I did wonder myself when I first heard about a group of people who went hashing at weekends, what on earth that actually meant. On further investigation, I established that the first club was formed in Kuala Lumpur, when British colonial officers and expats would meet up to undertake a Hare and Hounds paper-chase like run. They came up with the name Hash House Harriers after the hash house where they consumed notoriously monotonous food.

The table that we were sitting at was directly between two tables that had some occupants who decided to start a food fight when some of the speeches started to drag on, and we were stuck in the middle. I was sitting between a Swedish man who I came to the conclusion must have been a manager at *IKEA* from what he said (although he didn't say so directly) and my husband. I found myself pelted with grapes, strawberries and kumquats, and resisted the urge to fight back (only just). There were eight of us at the table, who had never met before, so it was an opportunity to find out about how other people lived and what they did while they were in Riyadh and share experiences and recommendations on places to go. It made a change speaking to people who had been in Kingdom for a shorter period of time than we had, providing them with information, rather than us trying to assimilate information from seasoned expats.

I found out later that the Embassy had a list of people who were the key players to gaining access to the evening social events that were held there. This list of people were each able to invite a pre-defined number of people, depending on their wasta (an Arabic word for who you know). Your name had to be on their list to get in, as it was the only way to get in, and the person whose list you were on was responsible for you when you were there. Not surprisingly people who were in a position to ask others were incredibly popular, and to be on good terms with someone who could include you in their list from time to time was a bonus. This was an interesting new take on social circles for me to comprehend, and although it was something I never spent any time mulling over, I knew women who would give their husbands a hard time if they were unable to find themselves on a list to an event which many of their friends and their friends' husbands were attending.

At the beginning of May there were the Scottish elections. I can recall being somewhat annoyed that there was only very brief, fleeting coverage on the television channels which we had available to us in Riyadh during the run-up to the election. Alan had bought two Scottish flags earlier in the year, one being the St. Andrews Saltire flag, and the other being the Lion Rampant, at Glasgow airport. We put the flags up outside the villa, the St Andrews one on the street-side and the Lion Rampant on the courtyard side. It was amazing the reaction we had from the other residents on the compound - no-one else apart from the other Scottish residents had known about the election, and most people had never seen the Lion Rampant before (it was amazing how many people mistook it for the Welsh flag, but we soon put them right on that). Shortly afterwards, a few more flags went up from other countries outside some of the villas, and we had set a trend, as one of the function areas on the compound later went on to sport flags from around the world as its theme on its walls.

There had been a mosquito problem on the south side of the compound, which had become increasingly worse. There were large evaporation ponds containing rejected water from the water treatment plant, but although fish were introduced to eat the mosquito larvae, the mosquito hatching continued, despite fogging taking place regularly. The temperature was due to rise quickly throughout May and I hoped the hotter weather would help to improve the situation. A new eco-friendly insecticide made from potent liquid garlic was introduced which was intended to eliminate the need for fogging. Apparently mosquitoes can stay away from areas that have been sprayed with this mosquito barrier for up to a month. All of the compound residents, particularly those in the worst affected areas near the treatment plant hoped it was going to work, as the smell was an improvement on weekly diesel fumes and better than the prospect of continual fogging.

There was a tailors shop on the compound, which was run by a Filipino woman, who would make and alter clothes. Previously she had had a stand at one of the first coffee mornings I had attended, and she had made me a lovely hooded black *abaya* with a lined hood and cuffs in turquoise. I had taken several things in to the tailors for her to alter and had found her polite and courteous and her work of an acceptable standard. I was astounded to hear one morning in May that the tailors had been temporarily shut down until a new seamstress could be found. I wondered what had happened, and within the day the compound wives telegraph had been working overtime filling everyone in. Our seamstress had apparently also been running a Filipino escort service to put it politely, and she had been found out and handed over to the authorities. I never did find out what happened to her, but it would not have been pleasant.

Flicking through the numerous television channels one evening, I was somewhat amazed to find that *The Passion of the Christ* was being broadcast on a satellite film channel. As the film had just started and I hadn't seen it before I decided to watch it. Whilst the gruesome events of the last day in the life of Jesus of Nazareth unfolded in the film, it seemed strange to be watching a film of this kind whilst in Saudi, as the story was obviously told from a Christian perspective.

Towards the end of May, school had another break, and we flew to Amman, Jordan for one of the most amazing holidays ever. Alan hired a 4x4 and drove us to Petra, somewhere I had always wanted to go. That night we took part in the candlelit procession along part of the spice trail, along a long narrow rocky gorge to the Treasury, where we were treated to Arabic coffee and a musical oud performance that was unforgettable. The next day we did the walk again, only this time in daylight but going much further - as far as the monastery, with the two boys on a donkey for the latter part. Alan drove us down to Waddi Rum the following day, where we spent a day in the footsteps of Lawrence of Arabia which was incredible. The sand, the rocks, the colours and the scenery was spectacular - it was like being on another planet. I wish we could have spent longer there, it was so beautiful, but we didn't have the time to see everything.

Alan then drove us over Mount Sinaii - we missed the turning to continue on the main roads, but I noticed another route signposted shortly afterwards, and being the designated map-reader, advised Alan to take it. Whilst driving over the mountain on the twisty back roads that slunk from side to side and seemed to go on for ever, we could see over the water to Israel. Eventually coming round yet another sharp bend at dusk, with the light beginning to fade, we approached a military checkpoint, and armed army personnel appeared out of nowhere, either side of the car. Not being convinced we were driving in the right direction, I panicked for a minute thinking we had inadvertently driven to the Israeli border and would be turned away to have to drive all the way back along the bending mountain road we had come from, in the dark (anyone who has a Saudi stamp in their passport cannot enter into Israel). Thankfully we showed our passports and were ushered on our way - we had just taken a back road that led down to the Dead Sea Resort area.

We visited the River Jordan the next day. I floated in the Dead Sea which was a strange experience, as the water was so salty, and my body kept trying to swim, but because of the natural buoyancy of the water, you just floated on the surface if you raised your legs and attempted to do that, making a complete spectacle of yourself in the process. It took a bit of getting used to.

We had a day in Jerash, an ancient Roman site to the north of Jordan's capital, which was something else - we arrived as an event in the Hippodrome was starting, and found we didn't have enough local currency to get us all in. Alan found a twenty pound Scottish bank note that he had been given for his birthday still in his wallet and we only managed to persuade one of the officials to take it after another official became involved. It turned out his daughter worked for the Royal Bank of Scotland, so a Scottish bank note was deemed to be fine, even though it wasn't officially recognised currency. The Roman gladiators and chariot racing was superb, and our youngest son kept putting his thumbs down and shouting, "Die, die," in his deepest, loudest voice whenever the gladiator fighting requested audience feedback. The chariot racing round the arena was amazing, and it was obvious that it took a great deal of skill. Both boys had their photographs taken with very fierce-looking Roman gladiators wielding swords and shields afterwards, and managed to stand inside one of the chariots. The ruined city was a feast for the eyes - taking in columns, amphitheatres and the surroundings was something I will never forget, not to mention Jordanians in traditional dress playing the bagpipes. The sheer scale of the ruins and the site itself was amazing, and imagining the city in the days of the Romans was not hard to envisage because of the extent of what was all round us on such a grand scale.

Flying back to Riyadh from Amman, I was convinced that the religious souvenirs in my husband's case he had bought as presents to take home when we returned to Scotland from the River Jordan would be confiscated, but thankfully we were just ushered straight through customs on arrival.

CHAPTER 11

Masalama Riyadh, A Fond Farewell (June '07)

Our tickets were booked for flying home to Scotland and the boys and I had secured our exit permits. It didn't seem real, going through the children's toys and sorting our possessions into piles to be sold or packed into a container to be shipped home, or to be given to George for him to distribute to people who would appreciate them. I could remember scouring through compound notice boards when I arrived in Riyadh scrutinising lists of items families were selling before leaving Saudi. We had picked up some bargains, and now it was our turn to sell on our stuff. Suddenly the fact that we were leaving had crept up on us, taking us all unawares. It must have been exceptionally hard for Alan, as most of the things that we had bought for the villa would now be shipped home. Once we were gone, Alan would move to a smaller apartment, devoid of children and family clutter, apart from a few photographs, letters and pictures, and he would no longer attend family barbeques, parties and school events, but would return to a bachelor style existence once more.

I found myself unable to tear myself away from the television watching *American Dad* one evening, as the central character Stan was posted to Saudi Arabia in the episode on the screen. A brief but stark glimpse of life here as an American was given, which had been crammed into a short cartoon. It focussed on the extreme differences between cultures and had obviously been compiled by someone who was knowledgeable about the Kingdom. Watching it whilst in our villa in Riyadh seemed unreal, the content crude, and although it was accurate, it was very much in your face.

The boys finished their scrapbooks with several weeks to spare before we flew home. It had been a challenge, as there were so many photographs and things we had collected to fit in. We decided to include photographs of some of our holiday destinations as well, so it had taken Calum an age to write where he was and what he was doing on each page. It had been well worth making a memoir of their time in Riyadh and I felt it was something they would be able to keep and look back on in years to come.

It was interesting to read in the papers that following the deaths of two people within two weeks who had been held in custody, the Department for the Protection and Prevention of Vice had come under severe pressure to ensure its members complied with the law. Department rules, regulations and requirements were to be implemented as a result. Previously in May 2007, the Government National Society for Human Rights had criticised the behaviour of the religious police in its first report since the society had been set up in 2004. In May 2006, reforms had been implemented which ceased the practice of the Muttawa interrogating those individuals whom they had arrested and detained. The Muttawa were now required to hand over the individuals to police once they had been arrested, who then had responsibility to decide whether to refer them to the public prosecutor. Things had come on a long way in the short time while we had been in Kingdom.

The first ever coffee morning had been arranged on our compound, and we trailed round the stalls in the heat. I managed to find a couple of T-shirts for the boys, one with Masalama Saudi written on it showing a laden camel, and another of a camel on a Harley Davidson motorbike for them to take home. There were all the usual stalls associated with the coffee mornings, and some of our compound's residents had their wares on sale too, mostly unwanted or un-needed items for the villa or garden, or clothes. I found some beautiful notecards showing Arabian women in an assortment of brightly coloured embroidered and decorated traditional Bedouin veils and clothing and purchased a pack to take back with me, together with a couple of bookmarks with an antique Bedouin silver coffee-pot on one, and a camel on the other. Unfortunately the only thing that had been overlooked was the most important part of a coffee-morning. There was nowhere to sit down and have something to drink. As the event was held in the main car park, the only shade was under stalls that had a canopy, so most people didn't stay very long apart from the stallholders.

Having sold, packed up and given away so many of our things, we had only a few things to pack to take home. Andrew's best friend's family took Fin the Fish off our hands, as they had a large fish tank in their villa and were happy to take him.

Our closest friends on the compound planned a small surprise leaving do for us which I didn't know anything about. Not being one for big celebrations or fuss, it was perfect, as a curry had been laid on (my favourite), and a few families we had become good friends with got together for our last night in Riyadh.

George drove us to the airport, and I was cross with myself afterwards, as I felt I should have said a proper goodbye to him in person before we left the villa, but even after all of the time I had spent in Saudi, things still managed to catch me unawares. I would have loved to give him a hug which I know he would have taken it in the manner it was meant, but I didn't get the opportunity or the time to do so when we were on the compound, which I regret. It was particularly difficult at the airport watching the boys give him a hug and say their goodbyes, when the best I could do at the last minute was to wish him all the best for the future and ask him to keep in touch. I hate goodbyes at the best of times, and we all had more than a few tears in our eyes.

I flew home at the end of June 2007 with mixed feelings. Our time in Riyadh had been an experience with extreme highs and lows along the way which most expats feel due to being in a foreign land so far away from home, friends and family. Life for the past twenty-two months had been full of the strange and unexpected on a daily basis which led me to question many things I had never thought about before. Despite the initial culture shock of living in a land so different from our own in so many ways and on so many levels, and having so many substantial cultural adjustments thrust at me, Saudi and many of its bizarre ways had grown on me. Being away from Scotland gave me very strong feelings towards home and my cultural identity. I also had a far deeper understanding and appreciation of the simple things and pleasures that are important in my life as a direct result of having lived in Riyadh that previously I took for granted.

I now have a huge fondness for Saudi Arabia and its people, who despite initial pre-conceived perceptions have so many things in common with us, and yet so many differences. That's what makes the tapestry of life so interesting… things may appear to be a certain way on the surface, but it is worth the effort to delve a little deeper to find out more. I feel I now have an awareness and respect for another culture and religion with its own traditions, which has not only given me an entirely different perspective on life in Saudi, but also on life in general.

Saudi - Arabia and Scotland both have large oil and gas industries and petrochemical plants, albeit on an entirely different scale from each other in terms of the countries' exports. Saudi has sand dunes, desert, rocks and mountains, whereas we have mountains and glens, and green countryside, but in both countries their people like to escape from their day to day life - either to the desert in tents remembering their roots and ancestry, or to the outdoors to take part in sporting activities or just to clear our heads and enjoy the scenery and get away from it all. Saudi has an amazing number of mud brick adobe forts, or fortified buildings, and Scotland has its stone castles and tower-houses which are sometimes coated in a lime-plaster finish. I was amazed how many of the Arabic adobe forts and walls would remind me of Scottish tower-houses or castles. Although they were very definitely Arabic in material, structure and character, with their triangular castellations and vertical slits, many of them were similar in scale and proportion and had a strong resemblance to Scottish Architecture, but set in very different surroundings and a different climate. Arabs and Scots are renowned for their inventions and enterprising spirits and both have made major contributions across mathematics, physics, engineering, medicine, art and architecture, science and technology. Football, shooting, horse-riding, racing and falconry are popular past-times in both countries. Scotland's Christians traditionally can generally be regarded as Protestants or Catholics, whereas in Saudi there are Sunni Muslims and Shia Muslims so there is an element of sectarianism history in both countries, albeit that the religions differ. At the time of writing this, education is free in Saudi and in Scotland (apart from private education) including tuition fees, which is a wonderful legacy for the future generation. Let's just hope it can continue.

A few people still think that Scotland is full of men in kilts chasing furry animals called haggises round the mountain glens, but thankfully they are very much in the minority. For people who know very little about Saudi, their perceptions are just as inaccurate, with the incorrect general dated assumption that Saudis live in tents in the desert, and live five centuries behind ours. It is true that the Islamic calendar is currently in the fifteenth century but that is only because their calendar starts from the Hijra, the date when the prophet Mohammed emigrated from Mecca to Medina.

There are many similarities between our cultures historically. Saudis are traditionally a tribal society, with importance being given to the family or tribe which is still evident today in many aspects of life and society. In Scotland society was tribal too, with the family clans. Many Scots surnames take their names from the father's first name (Anderson is 'son of Andrew'), occupation, places or nicknames. 'Mac' or 'Mc' is a common first part to a surname, which in Gaelic translates as 'son of'. In Saudi, *ibn* or *bin* is used within a name which translates as 'son of', but interestingly women do not change their surnames when they get married and the Arabic for 'daughter of' or 'mother of' is used within the name.

In Britain, we do not have to turn the calendar back long to see that in the past women here wore headscarves and covered their hair too. Prayer-times were more frequent, and religion played more of a pivotal role throughout the community. In the Highlands and Islands of Scotland there were whole communities who attended church five times a day. It has only been in recent years that ferries have been allowed to run on a Sunday, and many still do not hang out washing on the Sabbath day. Women were traditionally seen as being the homemakers, and it was the onslaught of war that took them into the workplace in large numbers in the UK, initially in the munitions factories. Of course there were some professional working women at this time, but they were generally from privileged backgrounds, as a career was not something that most women would traditionally aspire to. Folk songs and stories sung by women whilst undertaking work in groups is another thing the countries have in common, with the Bedouin being renowned for their songs and story-telling - in the North and Islands of Scotland, women would sing in Gaelic while they waulked the tweed, softening it by beating it. Throughout the UK, songs were sung to pass the time by women whilst undertaking activities such as spinning wool, milking or churning butter.

There is no doubt that Saudi Arabia is an extremely modern country - one of the fastest developing countries in the world in such a short span of time. To have gone from desert life to modern living over the past fifty years is an incredible feat in itself, which has brought about numerous challenges for the Kingdom.

Because of the terrorism threats that were in place whilst we were living in Saudi there were a number of things I would have loved to do, but due to security issues or restrictions at the time, or indeed not being aware of certain things to do or see, the opportunities did not always present themselves. When we were in Riyadh, the majority of information relating to what was going on, or social events were spread by word of mouth, so your knowledge was limited to that of your contacts and networking circles. Now there is a great deal more readily accessible information through the internet on expat sites and blogs which are regularly updated.

Many expats with young children were not interested in finding out more about the cultural and traditional side to Riyadh, as their lives centred purely round work and young children which at that time of your life is normal wherever you are living. However understandably, due to the perceived terrorist threats, and the advice and warnings given out by companies employing Westerners in the country, most of us were particularly cautious about where we would go and what we would do. All expats had some level of interest in the country they were living in and what went on outside the compound walls, whether it was culture, religion, traditions, heritage, the people, Saudi's history, wildlife, land, farming, plants, architecture, crafts, the country's legal system, education, shopping or if none of the above then terrorism and areas to be avoided, or places considered safe to visit in the city... the list is endless.

I was particularly aware that whilst I was living in Riyadh, I was living amidst a predominantly Western community on a Western compound. Whilst it could be argued that by doing so it meant we were isolated from the world outside the compound walls to some extent, it meant that on the compound women could dress normally without wearing an *abaya* and undertake activities such as swimming or sunbathing and men and women could mix socially and talk to each other as we could back home - all things which we were not permitted to do outside the walls of the compound. It was interesting to note that some Saudis too chose to live on compounds, and there were many affluent compounds inhabited by differing nationalities because of the lifestyle on offer.

Due to the extremely private and segregated nature of Saudi society in Riyadh, I did not feel detached from the culture which I was surrounded by whilst living on a compound. You heard the call to prayer five times a day whether you were out of the compound or not, together with the traffic, the birds and very often fireworks. For a woman in particular, whether she was a Westerner or a Saudi national, life in Riyadh was constrictive without doubt when compared to life in the West, and living in a villa surrounded by walls so high you cannot see beyond, in a society where you would not venture outside on your own would have been even more restrictive. In addition although several years previously some Westerners chose to live in villas in the Arab community, at the time we lived in Riyadh no Westerners were doing so, as it was considered far too dangerous, given that there had been instances of Westerners having been dragged out of their villas and kidnapped or shot only a few years before.

Although I had struggled to come to terms with such a different way of life initially, I eventually turned it to my advantage, learning about the country I was in and its people. I visited, photographed and sketched buildings or places that I found of particular interest, kept a journal and undertook a handful of architectural concept design proposals for friends. I also dealt with day to day matters that needed attention in Scotland and in Riyadh, whilst enjoying quality time with the children.

I would have loved to have seen Medain Saleh, the archaeological site recognised by UNESCO as a world heritage site with its rock-cut tombs and elaborately carved facades of the Nabataeans and the Hejaz Railway. The railway was built along the Haj route from Damascus to Medina by the Turks, but the section to Medina was never completed. However I hadn't pursued this, as a permit required to be obtained in advance, which went against the security advice we had been given at the time. Unfortunately I didn't go and see the desert irises opening up, as I only found out about them after I had left. Although I did meet up with and got to know a few Arabic women at social gatherings and through the children, I didn't meet with them in their homes. The only women I knew of who had done so, or who had been asked to do so taught English privately. I would also have liked a meal out at one of the restaurants inside a traditional adobe fortified building, where traditional Saudi meals of soup, camel, lamb or chicken kabsah, saleek and mandi are eaten on rugs on the floor at Najd village or Al Qalaa. However, again due to the fact that a booking had to be made at these establishments, I didn't get the chance. Part of the security advice we had been given at the time was not to make prior arrangements or appointments in certain situations and areas as this could make us vulnerable as terrorist targets so we didn't take the risk.

The Wabha Crater would have been an awesome sight to behold, but as it was seven hundred kilometres away from Riyadh, we decided against travelling with the boys for such a distance with other vehicles in a caravan in the heat, as not only was it was too risky but it would not have been feasible. Pictures I have seen of it are incredible, and the sheer size of it must be a sight to behold. There are two theories as to how the crater came about - the first is that it was caused by volcanic activity and an underground explosion, and the second is that a meteorite formed a three kilometre wide hole seven hundred feet below the surrounding ground level when it landed.

We had an extravagant few days holiday in Dubai on the way home, which was a real treat. We stayed at the Jumeirah Madinat Jumeirah, which was a great base to explore Dubai's heritage - highlights of our visit were the spice souq, the fish souq, the fruit and vegetable souq, the Dubai museum at Al Fahidi Fort, wind tower house, and the boys particularly loved the wild wadi water park and the beach. Being transported round the waterways within the hotel complex whilst sitting in a leisurely gondola was idyllic in the heat, allowing us to take in and appreciate our surroundings, although we did make use of the buggies too, taking pleasure in the welcome breeze as we were being driven along, feeling the sensation of comforting air rippling against your skin in the humid heat.

Sitting on the plane, going home with my boys next to me, it struck me that we had all grown in different ways whilst in Saudi Arabia. Andrew was no longer a toddler, and could say and understand a few Arabic words, Calum was far more worldly wise than I was at twice his age, could converse in simple Arabic, and had an appreciation of a different culture and religion first-hand. For me, my time in Saudi had given me a different perspective on life. I had grown particularly fond of Saudi and found myself going over memories in my head of our time spent in Riyadh - fierce sunshine, sundown, getting up early, prayer-time, the calls to prayer, family walks round the compound in the evening, ice-cream cakes, friends we had made, meringue palaces, waste-ground and rubble, fruit juices, air conditioning, dates, flip-flops, Saudi champagne, strong Arabic perfumes, prayer beads, coffee-mornings, time spent at the pool, sunbathing, burning hot sandals, bread and foul, schwarmas, souqs, shopping, iced coffee Frappuccinos, adobe Arabic architecture, modern Arabic Architecture, Islamic geometric patterns, ripped out pages from magazines and newspapers that had been censored, Ramadan, date palms, sandstorms, Muttawa, Arabic writing, the dreaded lurgae, blacked out images of women, the *abaya* and headscarf, the delicate blend of Arabic spices wafting through the air, Arabic doorways and gates, compound fever and the need to get out of the compound, mosques, children's parties, watching back to back episodes of Lost, the driving (and not being allowed to even on the compound),my driver and house-boy, camels, time spent at the play-parks, the desert, dust and dry heat, eating out and bottles and bottles of water. It made me feel sad to think that it really was goodbye, as the likelihood of obtaining a visit visa at some stage in the future was remotely unlikely.

The weekend after we arrived home, terrorism struck Glasgow airport - it was hard to believe that we had been standing where it happened only a few days before. It seemed particularly ironic, as the perceived threat in Riyadh towards Westerners was far greater than a terrorist attack happening back home in Scotland. What a welcome back!

For the first few months after we were back home permanently, I took great pleasure in being able to drive myself and the boys wherever I wanted to go, whenever we wanted to; something I had previously taken for granted without even thinking about it. However I was horrified at the price of diesel, which was shocking compared to the prices we had become accustomed to. I also more than made up for the pork and bacon which I had missed when in Riyadh - it's amazing how you can crave something you wouldn't often eat when you are denied it. Turkey rashers were a poor substitute, and something that I no longer buy, even though they used to always be on my shopping list in Riyadh.

Being able to go for walks and breathe fresh air was invigorating, although I did have to put a bit more thought into what I was wearing according to the weather and what I was doing, as previously I just had to throw on my everyday *abaya* over my clothes whenever I went out, or my more elaborately decorated and embroidered one for special occasions. No more headscarves for me. Despite the hang-ups some Western women have about wearing the *abaya*, I had grown somewhat attached to mine - it was just like putting on a long coat, only one that covered all of your lumps and bumps. My youngest son flatly refused to wear long sleeved tops, jumpers, cardigans, coats and trousers when we came home. He had lived in shorts and T-shirts for the time we were in Riyadh, and was not used to wearing layers of clothes. It took him around a year before he finally accepted that he needed to wear anything other than T-shirts and shorts without making a huge fuss.

As for being able to go shopping without a driver to get you there and back, or a husband in tow, you cannot believe how liberating that feels. For the first few supermarket trips I made with the children with me, anyone watching us would have thought we had never been in a British supermarket before. The boys would find things on the shelves we hadn't bought in a long time, and get excited about food they had forgotten existed. I do miss the luxury of having a house-boy - cleaning, ironing and watering the plants are now down to me and I often still think of George when ironing or doing the housework. I must admit I no longer have a wardrobe full of freshly pressed clothes ready to wear or an immaculate dust-free house like I had in Riyadh.

After spending a few weeks at home in Scotland with us in the summer, Alan returned to Riyadh for another year in order to complete his contract, before his job was Saudised. It seemed strange dropping him off at Glasgow airport, seeing protective concrete bollards in Scotland, when previously I had only ever seen them in Riyadh, around compounds, hotels, embassies and important buildings that were deemed to need additional security, and manned security checkpoints.

CHAPTER 12

Changing Times

The economy of the Kingdom of Saudi Arabia has been dominated by oil since its discovery, but steps have been taken to diversify into other markets to ensure the long term future prosperity of the country. Industrial products currently make up the majority of non-oil exports in petrochemicals, plastics, electrical appliances, construction materials and metal products. Industrial cities have been built and government incentives have allowed many private companies to establish their businesses.

The relatively recent discovery of precious and semi-precious metals within the Kingdom will lead to the mining and export of minerals from Saudi in the near future. Huge solar energy farms have and are being set up in desert areas, as the country receives some of the most intense sunlight in the world, making it an ideal place for solar power and photovoltaic generation projects. Solar energy is already being used in some remote areas as an energy source, and extensive funding has been allocated for research and business development in this area, as the possibilities and applications are endless. Renewable solar power could be utilised in lighting, cooling, water heating, crop and fruit drying, irrigation pumps, traffic lights, road signalling, road and tunnel lighting, all building types and structures and air conditioning, not to mention everyday electrical power requirements. Currently there are some solar signs on desert roads and manufacturing plants are now manufacturing solar panels. The Kingdom is also in the process of setting up a number of wind farms on coastal areas.

A number of sports cities have been built, located within large population centres and include stadiums, swimming pools, playgrounds, conference halls and sports clinics. Neighbourhood sports facilities, playgrounds and recreational areas have been developed, with the aim of providing facilities for youths. Historically, women have not been encouraged to take part in sporting activities, and even in school this has not formed part of the curriculum. However, it has now been acknowledged that exercise contributes to health and fitness, and I hope more women will be encouraged to take some exercise and that there will be designated facilities available for women to use. I was pleased to hear that the first women's sports centre in the Kingdom has recently opened in Al Khobar and that sport is now part of the curriculum in women's private schools.

At the 2012 Olympic Games all participating countries had women competing within their teams for the first time in history. Saudi Arabia was one of the countries for whom this had never happened previously and it is a huge step forward for women and equality. Saudi's Sarah Atlar ran the 800 metres and Wojdan Shehrerkani competed in judo. The two athletes come from differing backgrounds, Atlar having spent a great deal of time in the USA and currently a student there, and Shehrerkani, who has been coached at home in Saudi by her father. It would appear that whilst this historical event was covered by Western tabloids, the press in Saudi Arabia didn't go into print on the matter. Unfortunately within the online Saudi community there were many negative comments about the women who had taken part by those who take the more traditional stance that women should not take part in sport. It is clearly still a contentious issue in Saudi.

Football has always been and continues to be popular, although Saudi Arabia has been excluded from hosting international sporting events, including the world cup, as women are not allowed inside the stadiums. However, recently a proposal has been submitted to the authorities to lift this discriminatory ban in the larger city stadiums, providing implementation strategies of separate entrances for women and family areas which would minimise the potential for harassment. Research into how this could be implemented is underway, although no decision has yet been made. If this policy was passed it would mark yet another milestone for women in the country.

Women's university football teams have been formed in the last few years, and have played against each other in recent times. Due to perceptions of acceptable behaviour, however, most women who take part do so anonymously. There has been no comment that I am aware of to date from the authorities, on whether women could now be allowed to take part in competitive sporting activities under Sharia Law, although I am sure this matter has been the topic of hot debate which has not been widely publicised.

On a more positive note in April 2013 Saudi Arabia registered its first female trainee advocate which effectively means that Saudi women can now receive a permit to practice law. This in itself will result in a wave of changes across the Kingdom.

The King Abdulaziz City for Science and Technology was constructed in the 1980s in order to ensure the advancement of science and technology in the country and houses the electronics research institute, energy research, resource and development, petroleum and petrochemical research, astronomy and geophysics and space research. The organisation is an independent scientific research centre, on the King's authority.

King Abdullah Economic City is being built off the Red Sea to the north of Jeddah, as a catalyst to create investment, global trade, commerce and industry in order to create employment and opportunities for the Kingdom's young population, as around forty per-cent of the current population are under the age of fifteen. The economic city will house two million people, and will contain a sea port, an educational zone, a business district with commercial, mixed use and retail outlets, a finance island, an industrial area and a resort area. The city is one of five which is being built to stimulate foreign and domestic investment in the Kingdom.

Plans are currently underway for the creation of an atomic and renewable energy city in Riyadh. Population growth and migration into the cities in recent times has meant an immense surge in demand for electrical power. The King Abdullah City for Atomic and Renewable Energy will play a crucial part in ensuring the supply of drinking water and electricity for the population can be met, reducing the depletion of the country's hydrocarbon resources and prolonging them as an income source and rapidly expanding renewable energy opportunities. Understandably, reassurances have been given that nuclear energy would only be used for peaceful purposes in the future.

As I write this today the world has and continues to change. Many of the countries in the Middle East have come through the recent protests, and are moving towards democracy in some form or another. For Saudi Arabia there will be changes ahead which will be inevitable but how far they will go and what will happen along the way is impossible to predict. With a more educated population, more educated and working women, more information readily available through the internet and more Saudis returning home after having undertaken their studies in the West many of the restrictions placed on them are increasingly coming into question.

Some brave Saudi women continue to protest regarding their right to drive, and in June 2011 several dozen women drove cars in Riyadh to make their point. At the same time in Kiev, the Ukraine's feminist rights group drove round the Saudi Embassy topless for maximum publicity, wearing facial coverings to show their support for Saudi women on this issue. A video was made by a Saudi woman on YouTube suggesting women just take to the wheel but she was sent to prison for a week after its release. In October 2013 more than sixty women drove cars as part of an organised protest against the ban on women driving in the Kingdom. Two days after this protest, a Saudi comedian Hisham Fageeh posted a music video on YouTube, called 'No woman, no drive', a spoof on Bob Marley's 'No woman, no cry' which had been viewed more than had million times within a couple of days. When interviewed about his stance on the issue, he simply stated that the purpose of the short clip was to entertain, not to take sides. Some Saudi women who are against changes to permit women to drive in the Kingdom supported the video, but my personal interpretation of it was that it was very much tongue in cheek by merely stating the current situation and what many women are told there. Sadly five days after that, a Kuwaiti woman was arrested when she had driven over the border into Saudi in an attempt to drive her diabetic father to hospital. Many Saudi women have driving licences for other countries and it is clear protests on this matter will continue.

There is no doubt that with the social networking sites now available the world is a more accessible place and it is far easier to get hold of information and knowledge. Many Saudis and expats have posted their videos on YouTube for the world to see, whether young Saudis are showing off their car-skating skills, or women trying to get their point across or raise awareness on an issue, or perhaps an attempt to start a campaign or just to initiate dialogue, or filming some of the sights depicting life in the Kingdom. There are a number of good expat information sites, and bloggers who are recording their experiences for anyone who has an interest in reading them. Being able to access this type of information gives a personal view into life in Saudi first-hand.

There are now plans afoot for the creation of a new governmental agency to be set up to regulate video sharing sites in the Kingdom. There are currently more YouTube users per head than any other country in the world and this is causing the government concern due to the number of productions made that question or criticise the Kingdom's ways in a land where doing this is seen as incitement and recognised as a punishable offence. There has been a dramatic increase in the numbers of productions made which criticize the Kingdom's Royal Family, low salaries, corruption and unemployment together with personal opinions which do not reflect the image and views of the strictly traditional Saudi regime.

Countries in the area are unsurprisingly on edge regarding social and online media which played a part in the Arab Spring uprisings in 2011. An e-publishing law granted local news websites to be blocked if they did not apply for a licence. A Saudi who co-founded a blog site that discussed the role of religion within the Kingdom was sentenced to seven years in prison and 600 lashes in 2012 for violating cybercrime laws. A recent retrial led to an amendment of ten years, 1000 lashes together with a fine of one million Saudi Riyals, although the prosecution was calling for apostasy, the death penalty for insulting Islam. In January 2014 new laws were introduced to eradicate political and religious dissent in the Kingdom, one of which went so far as to define atheists as terrorists.

The United Nations formed an anti-terrorism group in September 2010, the United Nations Centre for Counter Terrorism, to tackle terrorism across the world which is chaired and led by Saudi Arabia. There have been numerous initiatives to tackle terrorism centred round education, inclusion and community involvement. At the time of writing this, the last Al Qaeda terrorist attack in Saudi in which innocent people were killed was in February 2006, when the oil refinery at Al Abqaiq was thwarted. The Kingdom's crackdown on terrorism has clearly been successful in dismantling Al Qaeda's organisation within Saudi to date and on-going progress is still being made. Initiatives and action taken to combat terrorism include tackling those responsible with the aids of training and technology, combatting financing terror by implementing financial, border controls and banking regulations and understanding and addressing the mindset behind those responsible in order to overcome extremism by public awareness campaigns, public and religious education, global faith dialogue and establishing counter radicalisation and rehabilitation programmes. In March 2009 British Airways resumed its flights to Saudi Arabia, six years after they ceased operating in the Kingdom, which demonstrates that the demand for the service was there and that the perceived level of risk had fallen.

In March 2011 a signed petition by leading academics, businessmen and activists called for a declaration of national reform, a gradual evolution towards a constitutional monarchy. Previous petitions had been submitted and in 2005 municipal councils were set up. Recently massive pay increases were implemented across all of the Saudi ministries and it has been announced that women will be allowed to stand as candidates and cast ballots in the municipal elections in 2015. In January 2013 King Abdullah appointed thirty women to advise on policy and legislation within the Shura Council, which is a massive step forwards with women making up twenty percent of the council. Clearly the Saudi government are taking measures in an attempt to keep its people content and avoid the kind of demonstrations and unrest that has been taking place in many of the nearby Middle Eastern countries in recent times.

In June 2011, the Specialised Criminal Court, which is a non-Sharia court set up in 2008 started to hear the cases of those charged with terrorist activity on behalf of Al Qaeda, such as possession of explosives, missiles, weapons, chemicals or smuggling items into Saudi for terrorism purposes. Charges also heard included links to or involvement in the Riyadh compound bombings in 2003. In September, thirty-eight Saudis and three others were brought to court charged with training in militant camps in Pakistan, fighting in Iraq and inciting militants to fight there, financing terrorism, transporting weapons, forging documents and harbouring suspected terrorists. Later in the year a woman was sentenced to fifteen years in prison after having been found guilty of sheltering people who were on wanted lists in the Kingdom, inciting terrorism, possessing firearms and financing terrorism together with sending money to Al Qaeda. She had denied the charges, claiming she had been kidnapped by two Al Qaeda activists whom she had previously been married to.

There are many debates which women have quietly raised for years in Saudi as to what is and is not acceptable - their place in society, in the family, in the workplace, their legal rights, their education, their dress code, their behaviour and their independence. In the last ten years, there has been a marked change in this area, with many more women now in the workplace than the five and a half per-cent when we went out, as a direct result of the education, growth and opportunities now available to women through government policies and initiatives. This isn't necessarily apparent, as many women are working in segregated workplaces, where they do not come into contact with or work beside men. There have been openings in female-only bank branches, lingerie and clothes shops, beauty and therapy salons and female only educational establishments. Many women are now choosing to run their own businesses or pursue artistic activities. Government initiatives have been launched and a ministry set up with the aim of advancing the education and career opportunities available for women in the Kingdom. The latest figures indicate that as many as twenty-one percent of Saudi women are now in the workplace, which is a considerable increase in such a short time. Women in the UK have the suffragettes to thank for giving them the right to vote. In Saudi at the moment, women do not yet have the right to vote, but in 2011 King Abdullah approved legislation to allow this to happen in 2015 and also to allow women to stand for election without the approval of their husband or guardian. In April 2013 Saudi registered its first female trainee advocate allowing Saudi women to practice law in the Kingdom with a permit. In January 2014 the first female Saudi lawyer set up a women only law firm in Jeddah to represent Saudi women and relate their cases in court. It is clear things have started to change considerably in some ways but not others.

I feel that an individual's beliefs should be respected and that every woman in Saudi should be able to make her own choices in terms of what is right for her and her family. It is the right to be able to make those choices that is important.

On 6 June 2011, King Abdullah issued a ruling that men were no longer to work in women's lingerie shops or departments. I am sure his decision on this matter made a lot of women within the Kingdom very happy and relieved that they would be able to purchase underwear in shops staffed by women.

In 2011 the Princess Nora Bint Abdul Rahman University was opened, with a capacity for fifty thousand students. It is the largest women's only University in the world, and has been designed to be car-free, paper-free and eco-friendly. Saudi Arabia also provides female students with one of the world's largest scholarship programmes for women. I have heard that the number of female schools have now outnumbered male schools, but there is a larger female population. Huge college-building initiatives have also been set up to educate women across the Kingdom. Education has been pivotal in Saudi policy and modernising the country. Numerous universities have been set up, and for the country's residents their education is available to them free, which is a wonderful legacy for the Kingdom's young population and their future. Young Saudis in the city in particular, must feel pulled simultaneously in two directions between traditional expectations and more Western or technological influences, which must cause inevitable conflict in their everyday lives, on so many levels, regardless of their stance or viewpoint.

Many of Saudi Arabia's Arab neighbours have changed their working week days, so that their weekends are Friday and Saturday, increasing the days which they are able to conduct business in the region and with Western businesses from three to four. The proposal to follow suit had been strongly rejected in 2007, but in June 2013, a Royal Decree was issued with immediate effect. Saturday 29 June was the first Saturday to fall within a weekend in Saudi and not the beginning of the working week.

Whilst we were in Saudi, visas were available for the masses of Muslim pilgrims attending and taking part in the Hajj or Umra, but visas were not generally granted to Westerners. To obtain a visitor's visa, you required to be sponsored by a Saudi individual or company, which in itself is a lengthy process with much paperwork. Transit visas were issued to travellers whose journeys necessitated a stop-over en-route before reaching their final destination. Most visitors to Saudi were doing so to fulfil their religious undertakings, and Saudi tourism centred round that. To work in Saudi you are required to have a work permit or business visa, which was sponsored by the company you worked for. If visiting on business, in addition you would be required to have a valid sponsor in the Kingdom from an acknowledged reputable Saudi business, together with an invitation letter certified by the Chamber of Commerce and Ministry of Foreign Affairs. I was interested to learn that quotas are set for work visas by the ministry of labour and if the number has been met, or a country blacklisted then your work visa would automatically be refused. This effectively meant that even after having secured and signed a job offer there was still a risk that the job could fall through.

When we were first out in Saudi, iquama holders who wished to travel outside their city of residence needed to obtain a travel letter from the authorities giving them permission to do so. As part of the push towards tourism this practice ceased in 2006.Things changed somewhat for a short while and a few expensive approved organised tours and visits became available to select groups of non-Muslims, taking in some of the sights and giving a glimpse of life in Saudi. This more recently has been curtailed and now visit visas are only issued on occasion to pre-selected groups on a limited basis. Well-heeled pilgrims are encouraged to stay on or extend their visit to the country and see the sights. Tours are available through the more upmarket hotels, once you are in the Kingdom. In Riyadh, the tours tend to include visiting the two tallest towers in Kingdom and the shopping centres there, a visit to the souqs and sightseeing tours of historical sites and museums.

Independent Saudi Tour Operators have also set up throughout the Kingdom and provide numerous excursions ranging from day trips to two week desert excursions. Sand surfing, being a passenger in a sand buggy or dune bashing, desert fossil hunts, desert diamond hunts (precious stones of topaz, amethyst and citrine can be found in some areas around Riyadh), falcon and saluki hunts, camping with the Bedouin, snorkelling or diving in the Red Sea and Arabian Gulf or exploring the coral reefs, or attending a camel or horse race could also be included on the itinerary. Whilst there is no doubt that a flavour of the country can be obtained from experiences such as these, it only reinforces to me how lucky I have been to spend the time I have had in Riyadh and to have had the relative freedom to see the sites I chose to see whilst I lived there.

A hotel management school was set up shortly after we went out to Kingdom, in line with the plans to rapidly expand the industry to cater for increasing business and tourism requirements. More hotels now cater for women to utilise their facilities within them. Previously, women could only stay at hotels if accompanied by a guardian, but it is my understanding that the rules have been relaxed somewhat to allow business-women to go about their business. However due to the culture, and the fact that Muslims are so protective of their women, most women will only stay in hotels if accompanied by their husband. Women can now travel alone providing they have a consent form from their male guardian or relative granting them permission to do so. SMS authorisation was implemented providing a woman with the necessary permission from a male relative or guardian to travel, even if it was just from one of Saudi Arabia's provinces to another or to travel outside the country. This has recently been suspended but it is thought that revised permissions will be implemented.

Any woman entering Saudi Arabia alone still requires to be met by her sponsor or male relatives, and she requires to have confirmed accountability of her accommodation for the duration of her stay on her person. Entry to the Kingdom may be refused to any visitor behaving indecently according to the fastidious local laws and customs, so it is advisable to ensure your behaviour, clothing or belongings will not hinder your entry into the country on arrival.

Saudi women also still require approval from their male relative or guardian for many aspects of daily life which we take for granted to be within our human rights in Western society. A woman's guardian has the power to grant her permission to travel, to study, to get a job, to travel, to open a bank account, to marry, to set up a business, or to have elective surgery, none of which can happen without his consent. Whilst many Saudi women clearly obtain the permission they require, undoubtedly others do not fare so well.

The Ministry of Culture and Information in Riyadh has been proactive in promoting Riyadh's culture and have set up numerous associations providing cultural advancement, education and information. There are now government websites providing up to date information on the country. Some of the reforms issued by the Saudi Ministry of Education have been unprecedented, as differing schools of theology are now being introduced to students for the first time in the curriculum's history, with the aim of encouraging tolerance through textbooks. Some of the previous textbooks which were widely used were critical of other religions, and it was considered that this may have contributed to the radicalisation of some young Muslims. This issue in a country where only Islam is officially practiced is a massive step forward, and I am convinced will have a massive impact on the younger generation.

There are no public cinemas in Saudi Arabia, as they are officially banned. A number of films have been made by Saudi directors either out of the country or unofficially, but in order to watch them Saudis have had to travel to neighbouring countries to watch them. Saudis are able to watch films privately through satellite channels on their televisions, or DVDs.

Over the past few years, a handful of films and documentaries have been shown officially at cultural centres, some of them to men only, and some screenings being held for men and children or women and children at differing times. There is a growing underground cinema movement within the country known as Red Wax, made up of Saudi film makers who meet to watch films tackling taboo, political or social issues and then discuss and reflect on the content of what they have seen at the end. Some Saudis have requested that public cinemas should be built, and recently Prince Abdul Aziz Bin Ayaff, the mayor of Riyadh has supported this view on the condition that control of the facility would be given to the ministry of culture and information. However, there is much opposition to this by the Islamic police in particular, who feel that Islamic values would be under threat. It is a big thing that this previously taboo subject is now even being raised openly, and I am certain that all Saudis will be eager to see how this matter develops.

Historically there were some cinemas in the Kingdom, mainly in Jeddah and Mecca showing mainly Turkish and Egyptian films during the 1970s, but they were all shut down in the 1980s due to the perceived perception that the movie industry was sinful and that it was not Islamic to support public places which could enable different genders to meet in the dark. I also learned that Jeddah hosted a film festival (without films being shown) for the region in 2006 and 2007, but an hour before the 2008 opening ceremony it was cancelled due to last minute hitches. However it is rumoured that this was on the direct orders of the Ministry of the Interior.

I was astounded to establish recently that a film shot entirely in Riyadh with an entirely Saudi cast was released in July 2013 in the UK. Haiifaa Al Mausour's extraordinary tale of a ten-year-old Saudi girl who dreams of owning a bicycle doesn't sound out of the ordinary to a Westerner. The fact that the film was made despite death threats, and that the director spent most of the time locked in a van directing the filming via walkie-talkies and telephone due to the fact that she couldn't be seen mixing with the male actors is incredible, but even more so, is that as a result of the film, the law has been relaxed to allow Saudi females to ride bicycles (albeit that they have to have their male guardian's or relative's permission to do so, they must be wearing the full *abaya* and that it can only be in a recreational area where this behaviour is allowed).

In 2012 a new Chief of Commission for the PVPV was appointed, who appears to be far more liberal in his approach than his predecessors. Within two weeks of taking up his appointment, he banned volunteers from taking up positions, which is a move he is implementing to attempt to curb the group's most outrageous violators, who have given them a bad name in the past. He has also confirmed that he has plans to set up a nationwide call-centre, where complaints relating to inappropriate behaviour can be investigated. Previously, anonymous callers could report inappropriate social behaviour, which could lead to false allegations being made. This should make a massive difference, but it will be interesting to see how far things will move forward.

It was great to learn that women as well as men were permitted to attend the Riyadh Book Fair in March 2013 and that the PVPV did not confiscate any of the books on display.

I read many articles in the press that never failed to amaze me while I was in Riyadh but there appeared to be a greater willingness within the press to criticize authority than there used to be until 2011. Articles condemning wrongful arrest were written in cases such as the arrest of a Saudi who kissed his seventy year old mother's hand when he was released from hospital, the arrest of a young woman whose uncle was escorting her to a job interview and the arrest of a man for driving his elderly female neighbour to hospital to name a few. Raising awareness by highlighting the plight of these individuals leads to awareness, discussion and debate on issues such as these and hopefully will help those who find themselves in such situations.

Throughout the time we spent in Riyadh, private worship was allowed in your own home, but no formal religious services of any other religion was permitted in the country. We did hear of a select few religious gatherings which had taken place in the desert, but it was always after the event. Towards the end of the time we spent in Saudi, rules were relaxed and bibles were permitted to be brought into the country for an individual's private use, which was yet another major turning point. However bringing in more than one bible is not a good idea, as you could find yourself accused of trying to convert others and end up being sent back home. Although the official rules have been relaxed on this issue and the Kingdom desires to be seen to be more tolerant, it will depend on the customs officer as to what, or whether an item is confiscated.

The fact that we used to live in Saudi Arabia crept into the conversation when I was with a group of older boys who know my oldest son recently, and I was somewhat taken aback at some of their questions. One of them asked if I thought most Saudis were terrorists or supported terrorism and another asked if I felt threatened when we lived out there. Personally, I feel the press and media have a lot to answer for, and I hope I set them straight and gave them something to think about with my replies. I have to admit that before spending time in Saudi Arabia, I, like them, knew more about the news stories centred round terrorism by a tiny, tiny minority, than I did about the country itself, its religion, its people and its family-friendly way of life. Unfortunately it is down to the fact that the publicised terrorist activities of a small minority can so easily give out an entirely different impression than the reality of the country as a whole, where the vast majority of its population are law abiding, religious, family centred and peaceful citizens. Yes, there are terrorists and undesirable factions within Saudi society, as there are within every society across the world, but the Saudi government have and continue to make great efforts to tackle this ongoing issue head on. On 6 May 2014 sixty-two members of an alleged Al Qaeda group were arrested in Saudi following evidence of a plot to assassinate government officials as well as foreign targets.

All Saudis that we met and spent any time with, both men and women, were embarrassed about 9/11 and most of them raised the subject the first time we met and apologised for their fellow countrymen, who had not been acting in accordance with true Islam. They all couldn't emphasise enough that Saudi Arabia and its people did not support behaviour of that kind.

Through my Western eyes, Saudi Arabia is still very much a country of contradictions, in a country whose top cleric recently openly condemned the recent kidnapping of schoolgirls in Nigeria by Boko Haram, but whose King has been keeping four of his daughters confined to two rooms within his palace for the last thirteen years and has forbidden any man to seek their hand in marriage. Princess Sahar, now aged forty-two, and her three sisters have been punished for their outspoken beliefs that women in Saudi should be free. Recently she has been active on Twitter and has a video which is calling for rebellion against the ruling regime, which she is all too aware could land her the death penalty. With the poor living conditions and treatment she and her sisters have endured she has clearly had enough. With other sad stories of Saudi princesses over the years, not to mention ordinary Saudi women, human rights in Saudi generally and the rights of women have a long way to go in a country whose human rights are based on Islamic religious law under the rule of the Royal Family. Change is inevitable, but what it will take and how it will come about is another matter.

I consider myself and my family to have been fortunate to experience life in Riyadh and believe that as a direct result our lives have all been culturally enriched. I hope that some of my shared experiences have given a few laughs, but that some have also been thought provoking, and have given an insight into the expat lifestyle and Saudi culture through my eyes. I make no apologies for the fact that my insight is a narrow one, from a Western woman who was a trailing spouse, living on a Western compound with a young family when security was paramount. That is the extent of my experience at the time, which emphasises how the times we were living in impacted on our everyday activities, where we decided to go and when, and what we decided to do and not to do. Clearly there is an element of risk to everything that we do in our lives, but while we were in Riyadh, the perceived threat was very real, even though statistically it had been proven that we would have been far more likely to have been involved in a car crash than a terrorist incident.

For anyone who is considering taking up an opportunity such as the one I did, each individual's experiences will be unique. Your life is whatever you make of it, and it is up to you to make the most of it. I am very glad I did.

Saudi Arabia is a rapidly developing country whose growth is unparalleled. It will be interesting to watch the Kingdom's on-going evolution unfold, which I am convinced will be on its own contrasting terms, finding its unique way forward in the modern world, whilst maintaining its conservative cultural and religious identity, a delicate balance of contradictions between old and new, tradition and change.

16680922R00118

Printed in Great Britain
by Amazon